THE SPIRITUAL JOURNEY OF A VERY IMPERFECT MAN

PART 2

UNDERSTANDING THE BIGGER PICTURE

Graham L Martin

Kingdom Publishers

The Spiritual Journey of a Very Imperfect Man
Part 2 *Understanding the Bigger Picture*
Copyright© Graham L. Martin

All rights reserved. No part of this book may be reproduced in any form by photocopying or any electronic or mechanical means, including information storage or retrieval systems, without permission in writing from both the copyright owner and the publisher of the book. The right of Graham L. Martin to be identified as the author of this work has been asserted by him in accordance with the Copyright, Designs and Patents Act 1988 and any subsequent amendments thereto. A catalogue record for this book is available from the British Library.

All Scripture Quotations have been taken from the New International Version Study Bible, The Message Bible, The New Living Bible, English Standard Version Bible and The Defenders Study Bible.

ISBN: 978-1-911697-42-8

1st Edition by Kingdom Publishers
Kingdom Publishers
London, UK.

You can purchase copies of this book from any leading bookstore or email **contact@kingdompublishers.co.uk**

To the lovely Audrie; my wife, sweetheart and best friend

ACKNOWLEDGMENTS

I have been 'best man' at six weddings, and, during my speech at the last one, remarked, "this time I'm determined to get it right." I have no idea how many times the text to this book has been re-written, but the fact that it is now probably about as 'right' as I can make it, is down to all the great guys who reviewed it for me.

So my thanks to Kevan Sutton, Rob Glenister, Mike Graveney, John Coe, David Slater, Ian Stackhouse, Val Lee, Paul Ratcliffe, and my old mucker, BC.

Many thanks also to my son, Kevin, daughter, Rachel, son-in-law, Kamran, and my great friend, John Coe. Although you guys may be largely unaware, your contributions during some very 'lively' discussions have given me greater, and much needed, insight into certain topics – cheers!

Most importantly, I really must emphasise how amazing my wife, Audrie (Aud), has been throughout all the extreme difficulties of recent years. Without her extraordinary love, commitment and strength, I doubt that I would today be at large in society, let alone capable of writing a book of this nature. She is, and always will be, my one and only soul mate – "friends forever!"

FOREWORD
BY IAN STACKHOUSE

Giving a reason for the hope that we have - otherwise known as apologetics – is an ancient Christian practice and one that has exercised the finest theological minds. Whether it has the power to actually convert anyone to the claims of Christ is an interesting question; I tend towards the view that faith is more existential than it is rational. But even so, apologetics is an important discipline (1 Peter 3:15), and one that demonstrates that faith is not 'a leap in the dark' but a profoundly logical step to take. And I truly believe that this is what Graham has sought to achieve in *The Spiritual Journey of a Very Imperfect Man*. Part 2 is his attempt, and a very good one at that, to reconcile the Christian gospel to the way things are in the world, and to the rigours of human reasoning.

What makes Graham's work fascinating, however, if not unique, is his decision to preface his apologetic with something of a personal testimony in which logic and reason give way to crisis and grace. In other words, even Graham has come to see that for all his questioning (which you become aware of after only a few minutes of meeting Graham), in the end it is love that holds and keeps us – the love of God in Christ Jesus our Lord. Like many people, he has discovered this wonderful truth in the second half of life, so the fact that this testimony is part one of a two-part book maybe is slightly the wrong way round. But either way, I admire Graham for his courage in telling the story and his honesty in opening up on what was an incredibly intense period of his life. It confirms to me something that I alluded to earlier, which is that most people come to faith, or deepen their faith, not as a result of logic but of crisis; although now that Graham has this experience, I suspect his reasoning with people about the Christian faith will simply become even more compelling. It will have that essential warmth and compassion which ought to accompany every communication of the gospel – even apologetics. Whether Graham will possess the same winsomeness when it comes to telling others about his beloved Torquay United, I very much doubt. It is the hope that is the most painful aspect of supporting such a team. But joking aside, I commend this book to you, not out of any sentimental loyalty to Graham, but because I truly believe in theology written from the grass roots.

Rev Dr Ian Stackhouse
Senior Pastor, Guildford Baptist Church (Millmead)
August 2021

PREFACE

The second part of my spiritual journey describes and explains a selection of objective evidence, supplemented by relevant background knowledge I have gained along the way. In particular, the varied discussions corroborate and build upon the subjective experiences of the first part, with the resultant worldview being compared to several others, including science. The writing commences at a position 'lower down the mountain' than that already reached in part 1, which is assumed to have been read first, meaning that some pressing of the rewind button is initially required.

As with part 1, every effort has been made to ensure that the writing is user-friendly and informal, albeit that the more detailed chapters seven and eight plus the appendix, which also cover certain commonly asked questions, require a bit more reader input. Much of the writing accordingly contains illustrations from a variety of sources, particularly my professional career as a chartered civil engineer (geotechnical) and my much more important sports career! involving pole-vaulting, weightlifting, football etc. In an era where success in sport is sometimes measured by total earnings, I think mine related solely to the reimbursement of expenses for one pole vault competition.

This second part makes many references to the writings of C.S. Lewis (1898-1963), Irish-born literature professor, literary critic, and novelist. These are included because this man has probably helped me the most in understanding what I believe. There are also many allusions to the letters of the Apostle Paul (1st century AD), whose conversion is outlined in chapter four.

The single term 'Church' (capital 'C') corresponds to the entirety of all legitimate Christian denominations and groups, with the one reference to the 'established Church' (chapter three) relating to the Church of England and/or the Roman Catholic Church.

Unless stated otherwise, all biblical citations relate to The New International (NIV) Study Bible: 2000 Edition. Although this version, when speaking of human beings, commonly refers to 'son' or 'sons', these titles can often be viewed as 'child' or 'children' respectively. The adoption of capital letters at the start of all personal pronouns (He, Him, Himself, His) in relation to God/Christ has been preferred throughout, a variation in line with certain modern translations (e.g., the New King James Version - NKJV), albeit that the NIV does not employ this practice.

All websites and URLs cited are correct as of March 2021.

All names, apart from those of close family and friends, have been changed.

CONTENTS

ACKNOWLEDGMENTS	7
FOREWORD	9
PREFACE	11
INTRODUCTION	15
CHAPTER ONE	19
Setting the Scene	19
CHAPTER TWO	31
The Likelihood of Ultimate Reality/God and the Possibility of a Relationship with Plebs Like Us	31
CHAPTER THREE	42
The Influences of UK Society 2020: Do We Really Know Our Own Minds?	42
CHAPTER FOUR	80
The Bible and Jesus Christ: Can the Record be Trusted? (the truth criterion)	80
CHAPTER FIVE	133
We Are All Sinners and Need a Saviour (the relevance criterion) "You cannot be Serious Man, You cannot be SERIOUS!" (John McEnroe, Wimbledon, 1981)	133
CHAPTER SIX	168
Jesus Christ – A Unique Being with a Unique Mission	168

CHAPTER SEVEN — **208**

    Science and Related Philosophy — 208

CHAPTER EIGHT — **246**

    Eastern Spirituality, Islam, Judaism - Reflections, Comparisons & Questions — 246

APPENDIX — **315**

    Accuracy of the Biblical Record – Further Appraisal — 315

INTRODUCTION

Going back a couple of generations or so, many kids were forced to go to Sunday School; seemingly for most to subsequently conclude that they had outgrown any imparted knowledge, and couldn't quite see how songs like *Jesus Wants Me For A Sunbeam* might benefit them in their approaching adult lives. In today's UK, it appears that this attitude of having outgrown Christianity, when it is thought about at all, extends across the major part of society itself – we are now more mature and better informed, so all that narrow-minded religious stuff is, at best, of only nostalgic value.

There is accordingly a strong movement today, in both the UK and other Western societies, to be increasingly open-minded; a generally positive development and something for which I have definite empathy. The generation before my own often appeared to do things in a certain way simply because that was the way they had always been done. There was also the phrase *a place for everything and everything has its place* (I'm getting wound up merely writing this stuff down!). Finally, the classic, *When are they going to settle down*? Well hopefully never.

Despite this greater openness, most people still fall short of being fully open-minded, Western society typically being closed to a specific line of reasoning that has particular relevance to religions and worldviews in general. This is the proposition that although some, or perhaps even many, of these views may well contain truth within them, a record of consistently accurate truth and the presentation of the complete picture can be found in only one (Christianity). This viewpoint is totally *un-PC* and probably unthinkable, if not offensive, to the majority of citizens making up UK 2020. So to stop people switching off (assuming they've made it this far), it is necessary to provide a brief explanatory heads-up. In particular, with so many beliefs on the market, why should Christians be correct in theirs and accordingly consider themselves to have *more* truth than anyone else? Isn't that just arrogance resulting from a lack of humility?

When asked to describe Christianity in ten words or less, the late Southern Baptist preacher, Will Campbell, is known to have said, *"We're all bastards, but God loves us anyway."* [1] That totally-*in-your-face* sentiment lies at the heart of the Christian gospel, which also declares that, unlike human beings, with our numerous varied and often serious imperfections, God is perfect. So if all of this is correct, and it certainly appears to turn up in various forms in other worldviews, there must be a chasm between ourselves and God - that is some kind of universal bridge is required. The Christian claim, unlike the multitude of (seemingly) man-made religions and worldviews which we might reasonably take to represent humankind's attempt to build this bridge from our side, is that God Himself has done all the necessary building work from His side.

Christians accordingly believe, based on what they consider to be extensive objective evidence and related subjective experiences, that the universal bridge is Jesus Christ; who, rather than being some religious teacher or guru reaching out for divine enlightenment, actually represents God Himself reaching in with voluntary and deliberate self-disclosure and revelation. That, of course, is a very bold and indeed unique claim; but, if true, would inevitably be a total game-changer and place this worldview in a completely different category to all the rest. But is it true, and how can we find out?

Many people, and I certainly used to be one of them, consider that *blind faith*, which is obviously never a good thing, suitably sums up the mindset of today's UK Christians and *religious people* in general. Yeah, ok, sometimes this opinion may well be correct, but what about the proposition that blind faith is actually of greater relevance to the general public as a whole? I'm talking here about life-after-death issues, which are so important that, at the very least, we should be as certain of what

---

[1] Will D. Campbell, *Brother to a Dragonfly*. Seabury Press, 1977, pp. 220-24.

we do not believe in, as what we do. I know this is a bit heavy-duty considering that I haven't yet made it out of the Introduction, but the truth is we are all under a death sentence – we just don't know how and when.

So from where do we get our opinions on these matters? From time to time, I hear various people confidently assert things like, "You only live once" or "You're a long time dead." Maybe; but I'm pretty sure that they have never met anyone who has actually returned from the grave to reliably confirm that they were correct in their view that this physical life is all you get. Thus, assuming that these statements represent the sum-total of their *evidence* (and maybe they don't), then this outlook does indeed appear to be a case of blind faith. Conversely, Christians can at least claim to obtain their information from the person of Jesus Christ, the only being to have an apparently credible *resurrection CV*. It is, therefore, necessary to check out this seemingly unique individual and His alleged power over physical and eternal life and death.

Christianity, as for other areas of life, undoubtedly has room for a range of opinions concerning what might be deemed noncrucial aspects, with certain individuals and denominations attaching greater importance to particular teachings than their counterparts. Fair enough; there has to be flexibility, and dogmatism is always a very unattractive trait. However, when it comes to the central features of the Christian message; specifically, where we are considering Jesus Christ and His extraordinary either/or claims, including those relating to deity and our future existences beyond the grave, we discover that, ultimately, it's simply not possible to avoid a definitive conclusion, one way or the other.

Thus, while a non-committal approach to spiritual matters might be my natural preference, I find that the core Christian gospel will not allow me this option. This is because its message is so strong and uniquely defined that it has to represent either the greatest-ever news for planet Earth or the only other possible alternative of complete fabrication, and thus the *grand-daddy* of all conspiracy theories, past, present and, no doubt, future.

This book and in particular chapter six, which I like to think of as my *pièce de résistance*, hopefully throws further light on the above. It is based on the four gospel records and a classic book called *The Day Christ Died* by Jim Bishop,[2] a 20th century American author; and is specifically included to demonstrate the immense difference between the carefully recorded trial, crucifixion and bodily resurrection of Jesus Christ and the legendary genre of tales relating to the alleged resurrections to the status of gods by, for instance, dead Greek and Roman human leaders. This view is endorsed at the start of the chapter by C.S. Lewis. Certainly, for anyone who wants to go straight to the 'heart' of the Christian message, the associated total word count of about 15,000 has got to represent an easier task than initially grappling with the whole Bible which comes in at about 800,000.

My own core beliefs, which I have held for over forty years, are consistent with mainline global Christianity; so their truthfulness does not depend upon me (thank God!), but rather the big world stage where they are either universally correct or universally incorrect.

It is recognised, in relation to the above, that the existence of *absolutes* (sometimes referred to as *grand narratives*) is often viewed with scepticism and cynicism in today's Western societies and that words such as 'correct' or 'incorrect' may, therefore, be deemed as meaningless. This view is accordingly considered within this work.

I am also aware that the term, *New Age*, is not popular with many of those holding related views, who would probably prefer something like, *Mind, Body, Spirit* or perhaps no title at all. In the interest of clarity, however, I am pretty much forced to refer to *New Age* throughout, and describe its adherents as *New Ageists.*

Similarly, I'd like to use a rather more positive word than *non-believers* in connection with people who are not Christians but have been unable to come up with anything more appropriate. Anyhow, no offence intended.

---

[2] Jim Bishop, *The Day Christ Died*. Greenwich House, 1984.

CHAPTER ONE

Setting the Scene

The first part of my spiritual journey, *A Roller Coaster Life*, is based almost entirely on subjective experience, which is of course entirely valid evidence. However, when dealing with matters as crucially important as religions and worldviews, including life after death issues, it is surely highly desirable to endorse and anchor these utilising related, but independent, objective evidence. But can this actually be done, and is the attempt even relevant and worthwhile given the plurality and multi-ethnicity of modern Western society? My belief is obviously that it can; although, for a work of this kind, necessarily subject to certain limitations concerning purist Eastern spiritual convictions, teachings and practices. Specifically, because the natures of these are typically foreign to the thinking of most Westerners, subsequent discussions are mainly concerned with how they impact Western New Age beliefs and minds initially grounded in Western culture. The term *Eastern spirituality*, as adopted in this book and discussed in chapter eight, thus relates predominantly to the teachings and worldviews most influential in the West, namely *Pantheistic Monism*, as per some schools of Hindu philosophy, and Zen Buddhism.

One of the main reasons for the above restriction is that intellectually-based evidence ordinarily has little relevance to Eastern spirituality. The more mystical and experience-based related approach is often largely ontological – that is concerned with being, existence, becoming and, hopefully, achieving 'oneness' with discerned reality, whatever this might be. There are also focuses on gaining enlightenment, with language regularly being almost redundant in most forms of Eastern spirituality. In contrast, Western thought, including the apologetics often associated with Christianity, is primarily epistemological (if I want to say this word in public, I have to practice first). Apologetics is typically defined as a reasoned defence and explanation of the various teachings and beliefs put forward, with the *broader* epistemology including topics such as logic, reason, rationalism, ideology, systematic belief approaches and the like – in other words, about how we process knowledge. Little surprise then that my conversations, usually as epistemological *Adrenalin Man*, with those holding predominantly Eastern views, have generally ended in frustration on both sides – we were coming from totally different perspectives.

That is not to say that Christianity can be thought of as irrelevant for Buddhists, Hindus and Sikhs etc. – far from it. It's rather that Westernised logical thought, which occurs frequently in this second part, is unlikely to play a prominent role in at least the earlier parts of Eastern spiritual journeys.

There are undoubtedly many ways of describing religions and worldviews, and how the two categories differ from one another. This is not, however, an appropriate forum for an in-depth discussion, with attention being drawn instead to the fact that every religion is ultimately a worldview and that many address the same basic questions. What is the supreme reality – the really real?, Who or what am I?, What is my purpose or indeed that of the whole human race?, What happens when I die? and How should I be best thinking about and living my daily life in the here and now? It is therefore deemed sufficient to simply provide a few brief and hopefully relevant thoughts.

Commencing with religion, the origins of today's major faiths generally date back thousands of years (only 500 years or so for Sikhism) and are accordingly indelibly intertwined with national and individual culture. Indeed, to change faith from one religion to another often represents a rejection of culture and heritage, a painful divorce resulting in opposition ranging from enforced estrangement to physical harm and even death. Running in tandem with this, and it's appreciated that this is the broadest of 'broad-brush' statements, current major religions relate primarily to cultural/ethnic backdrops and associated family loyalties, with adherents perhaps taking on the various beliefs and customs of their parents and older relatives without too much questioning.

In terms of development, some see an evolutionary process whereby religion is slowly journeying upwards from primitive origins (everything, including inanimate objects, having souls) to the divine, whereas others consider that some kind of historic breakdown between humanity and a sovereign being has resulted in spiritual degeneration, with religion representing the efforts of mankind (conscious or unconscious) to effect a reconciliation. For future clarity, it is important to emphasise that true Christianity as opposed to *Cultural Christianity*, both of which are subsequently discussed, is not a religion in any conventional sense of this word.

Modern worldviews and their societal effects are inevitably far more transient than ancient religions, with related ideologies typically arising from certain thoughts, philosophies (spiritual or otherwise), and customs etc. broadly acceptable to specific contemporary people groups. In particular, studies show how adherents generally view *reality* using certain basic assumptions and images which, although seemingly rational and consistent, may or may not be accurate. It also seems that those with specific worldviews typically base their respective affiliations on matters of preference and choice, which appear to come down to present lifestyle and life after death issues, balances between the two depending largely on the person's character and age. An approach of, say, "what is the most enjoyable and best fit for me?" often at least partly related to the praiseworthy aims of personal improvement and greater self-knowledge, may well dominate in the earlier years, many dating sites also reflecting the importance of applicants' spiritual beliefs being compatible, with life after death issues possibly prevailing in older individuals.

However, maybe I'm over-thinking all of this, as the following internet quotation suggests, *"It only depends on what you think; philosophy is the question of life and its meaning... Religion is just a bunch of people that think they know the answer and make judgments based on irrelevant stories and misunderstood ideas."* - CharismaticSadist, 9 years ago.

Well said sir or madam….Quality and profundity combined!

So why are the chief features of preference and choice for worldviews within Western society now apparently taking precedence over the more traditional chief features of truth and relevance? To at least partially answer this question, it's necessary to again emphasise that the existence of absolutes is commonly viewed with scepticism and cynicism in the West, due mainly to the comparatively recent dominance of secular thought patterns. This has resulted in words such as *right* and *wrong*, *correct* and *incorrect*, and even *good* and *evil* quite often having very little relevance in modern Western psychology. What on earth will happen if the planned gender-neutral *ze* replaces *he* or *she*? Conversations will be so complicated and tiring!

In view of their importance to some of the following discussions, it is probably useful to try and determine what is meant by *absolutes*, with the various worldviews and disciplines offering up varied definitions. The following short list hopefully provides some assistance:

The Absolute – *Ultimate Reality is something that is the supreme, final, and fundamental power in all reality* (Wikipedia).
The Absolute (or Absolute Truth) – *Ultimate Reality; God* (Bing Dictionary).

Absolutes   – *Values or principles which are regarded as universally valid or which may be viewed without relation to other things* (Bing Dictionary).

These descriptions, or combinations thereof, are thus assumed throughout, albeit that the title, *Grand Designer*, is sometimes substituted for God in science-related discussions to maintain the consistency of this genre.

Whether modern day science as a body actually believes in absolutes is a moot point. The official party line is undoubtedly to deny absolute or universal truths, although the overall impression gained from relevant literature and, particularly, television documentaries and news stories, appears to indicate the complete opposite. Perhaps most significantly, science's relentless pursuit of a single theory that will unlock the major puzzles of the universe (the *Theory of Everything* [ToE]) looks very much like the chasing after an absolute.

Science is almost always portrayed as atheistic by TV companies, even though an appreciable number of UK scientists are Christians. We also, as a nation, seem to have largely forgotten that many of the founding fathers of modern science ($16^{th}/17^{th}$ centuries) were Christians, whose faith in God and a consequently ordered universe gave them the confidence to persevere and succeed. Finding relevant and balanced approaches to this topic is, nevertheless, still possible on the radio, although the internet seems the best option. Typing into a search engine the names of one or more of the following renowned Christian thinkers is a good starting point:

- John Lennox - British Professor Emeritus of Mathematics at Oxford University and philosopher of science.
- Alister McGrath - British Professor of Science and Religion at Oxford University.
- John Polkinghorne – World-leading British theoretical physicist and theologian, knighted by the Queen.
- Francis Collins - American physician-geneticist, noted for his landmark discoveries of disease genes, and his visionary leadership of the Human Genome Project (HGP).
- Os Guinness – English author and social critic.

Most people in the UK are unlikely to have heard of the four scientists in the above list, with, as previously intimated, virtually all the science that seems to get through to the average person informing them that they are basically accidents, implying that they have no real value. However, it hardly needs to be said that so many news stories more or less scream out the precious nature and overriding importance of human life – surely a very odd contradiction when you think it through (which maybe most of us don't).

Returning briefly to part 1, which deals with many aspects of life, from the humorous to the tragic, what would seem to be the most important feature overall? Difficult to answer; but probably that there are two persons, Audrie and me, who have had powerful spiritual experiences leading onto changed and improved lives due to claimed encounters with the risen Jesus Christ. But what's so special about that? Many other people have also been affected by life-changing events, which they put down to eclectic spiritual and all manner of different experiences. These must surely have at least equal validity, why the need to bring Jesus Christ into the equation? Isn't it all subjective anyway?

Indeed, my discussions of the Christian faith with very many people having different or seemingly no beliefs during the forty or so post-conversion years, have most frequently resulted in responses something along the lines of, "Well, it's great if Christianity helps you, Graham, but quite frankly, it's simply not for us." These individuals therefore again perceived the whole thing to be entirely subjective; and, as time has gone on, it has become increasingly clear, as stated before, that the *new kids* in town, *preference* and *choice*, have largely replaced the more traditional categories of *truth* and *relevance*. This change of attitude is demonstrated by the fact that in pre-Christian days I would say things like, "Everyone knows the Bible is full of contradictions" (not that I knew any), thereby unintentionally appealing to a *universal* absolute truth, whereas many individuals in current Western societies knowingly or unknowingly tend to throw out this category altogether.

It, therefore, follows that any person or group claiming to have some sort of monopoly on what they consider to be Ultimate Reality/Absolute Truth are often viewed in current Western and certainly UK society, as narrow-minded, bigoted and intolerant. The related, often indignant, contrary arguments normally go something like,

"What right has anybody to impose their belief system upon others? We see the world in one way and others see it in another – so what.

If our beliefs work for us, and their beliefs work for them, then great.

Why the need to judge?

But if we can take something that we like from their system and add it to our own, then even better. It may even be possible to combine the various and best spiritual insights and produce an inclusive synthesis (a process known as syncretism, or, less charitably, *pick and mix spirituality*) so that everybody is happy.

Working towards this scenario is surely far more open-minded and reasonable than arrogantly and dogmatically insisting that one set of beliefs is correct and all the others are wrong, either wholly or in part.

Besides, there are so many permutations and unknowns that trying to sort it all out makes the recent Brexit negotiations look like peanuts.

It's simply a waste of energy.

We are all equal at the end of the day, and no-one can know anything for certain – each to their own."

Continuing this line of thought, might it be reasonable to conclude that Islam works best for Muslims, Hinduism works best for Hindus, Judaism works best for Jews, Christianity works best for Christians, New Ageism works best for New Ageists etc? It all comes down to cultural background and differing individual tastes. And even here, there are similarities - at least among the major religions of the world.

In particular, they all have their sacred writings (Quran, Vedas, Tanakh/Bible and so on); they all meet in specific standalone buildings (mosques, temples, synagogues, chapels and so on); they all have separate denominations or similar; and they all have their leaders of, exclusively or predominantly, male gender (although it seems that this position is now being challenged in many areas). Most worldviews additionally seem to insist that there is more to life than our five senses might tell us and that in some strange way, which may not even be consciously recognised and identified, we are all found to be wanting and consequently coming up short; with some unknown entity – most commonly viewed as a judgement-dependent afterlife - lurking just over the physical death horizon.

This type of thinking often leads on to the commonly held belief that to fully engage with or appease whatever might lie beyond, there is a need to align and harmonise our minds and souls with some kind of something; albeit that there is no consensus concerning what this may involve. Is there Ultimate Reality? And if the answer appears to be *yes*, is conscious personality involved? Or, more expansively, are we dealing with He, She, They, It, Some of them, All of them, or Nothing? And how can we find out? Would it help if we could tap into something loosely called *higher knowledge*? Some related discussions are later included under both New Age and Eastern spirituality.

It is also easy to feel that life is difficult enough without having to grapple with worldviews and potential personal implications, such as meaning and purpose. In the first-ever episode of The *Fall and Rise of Reginald Perrin* [3], Reggie has come home late and his wife, Elizabeth, complains that his supper is all dried up. Reggie replies something like, *"Darling, if you represented the time the world has existed by the height of this room, mankind wouldn't even reach the top of the carpet underfelt; in the circumstances, it, therefore, doesn't seem that important that my supper's all dried up."* We don't want to think like this too much – it sort of does our heads in.

---

[3] BBC Television Sitcom, 1977-1979, based on novels by David Nobbs.

So perhaps the only realistic conclusion to all of the above is to simply acknowledge that we may not have the ability to discover or even perceive an entity such as Ultimate Reality which, in any event, may not even exist. So why bother? Why indeed, when there are quotations like this in the public domain, *"In fact, it has been said that the chance of human beings, unaided, being able to find Ultimate Reality is approximately the same as an ant discovering the planet Saturn"* (author unknown).

I would love to see the associated statistical analysis, and wonder whether there might be more chance of the ant discovering, say, Mars. The main point here seems to be that the discovery of any Ultimate Reality might well involve getting to grips with the whole nature of infinity, and our brilliant but inevitably little and limited brains of only about 3lbs in weight are simply not equipped with the *infinity gene*. The subject of infinity is briefly considered, in conjunction with several other scientific topics, in chapter seven.

This quotation from Albert Einstein, one of the greatest scientists of all time, also apparently agrees with the fact that an infinity gene is needed to make sense of everything. This is his answer to the question of whether or not God exists, *"Your question is the most difficult in the world. It is not a question I can answer simply with yes or no. I am not an Atheist.......The problem involved is too vast for our limited minds. May I not reply with a parable? The human mind, no matter how highly trained, cannot grasp the universe. We are in the position of a little child, entering a huge library whose walls are covered to the ceiling with books in many different tongues. The child knows that someone must have written those books. It does not know who or how. It does not understand the languages in which they are written. The child notes a definite plan in the arrangement of the books, a mysterious order, which it does not comprehend, but only dimly suspects. That, it seems to me, is the attitude of the human mind, even the greatest and most cultured, toward God. We see a universe marvelously arranged, obeying certain laws, but we understand the laws only dimly. Our limited minds cannot grasp the mysterious force that sways the constellations."* [4]

Thus, if scientific and philosophical reasoning is perhaps going to have a really tough time discovering Ultimate Reality, what about religion? The academics Holmes and Rook in a passage based on the thinking of a young Karl Barth, later considered by many to be the greatest Christian theologian of the 20th century, state that, *"God is utterly, radically, incomprehensively above and beyond and before anything we human beings can even dream of. Theologians and churches had been satisfied with imagining a god they could grasp and understand, but this was just an idol; the one true God was forever infinitely beyond our grasp, beyond our understanding."* [5]

Barth is here recognising that Ultimate Reality is *wholly other* compared to everything else, and beyond working out for finite men and women with their shortcomings and limitations. This viewpoint is also shared to a large extent by Eastern religions, with Jiddu Krishnamurti, a very profound and thought-provoking Indian philosopher, believing that the state of *not knowing* typically results in a disordered mind, and that order and freedom are only attained when this *unknowability* can be accepted as a normal part of being human. To quote him directly, *"When such a mind says, 'I do not know', then it is totally free. It has denied the disorder and because it is free, it has found order."* [6]

Something that goes hand in hand with the above reasoning is the way that the word *tolerance* is often perceived in contemporary UK culture. Most people rightly understand that this should mean acceptance and respect for the worldviews of others, including listening and maybe learning from their inputs into relevant conversions. However, unlike the 'more certain' past, it all seems to go a bit woolly beyond this, with

---

[4] G. S. Viereck, *Glimpses of the Great*. Macauley, New York, 1930, pp.372-373.
[5] Stephen Holmes and Russell Rook, *What are we waiting for?* Paternoster, 2008, p.4.
[6] Jiddu Krishnamurti. *The Awakening of Intelligence*. HarperCollins Publishers, 1987, p.313.

many individuals and people groups now apparently concluding that putting forward reasons for favouring a specific viewpoint shows not only arrogance but also intolerance towards, and the rejection of, those holding different beliefs. And if these differences extend to life after physical death issues, some might ask, "Who are you to take on the role of heavenly ticket-master?" "What sort of humility is this?" I think this reaction represents a step too far and that, provided different opinions are presented with modesty and concern for others, a watering down of seemingly legitimate facts simply to avoid possible disagreements constitutes an unnecessary devaluing of what is in someone's heart and may even deprive their listeners. And as a final thought, tolerance must have limitations – for instance, how can we be tolerant of intolerance?

Maybe not surprisingly then, it seems that many people in the Western world, when they think of Ultimate Reality/God at all, assume that they can believe in whatever 'reasonable' image they choose - that is as long as it 'works' for them and doesn't impinge upon any other person's 'reasonable' god. No comparison is justified, because who are we to say our opinion about any possible Ultimate Reality is better than anyone else's? It accordingly follows that we could already be well on the way to the existence of billions of individual *gods* whereby "Oh My God" (OMG) might, in reality, represent the *god* each person has within their own head – perhaps based entirely on subjective thoughts and experiences. Thus, to reiterate, those of us referring to Christianity as, *The Truth*, are often deemed to be narrow-minded, bigoted, intolerant or, possibly, even fanatical. And certainly, all of this seems perfectly reasonable and correct as long as two basic conditions apply. The first is that Ultimate Reality does not exist and the second, which follows on, is that even if this entity does exist, He/She/They/It/Some of Them/All of Them/Nothing has not or have not revealed this fact to us earthlings in a form that we can understand.

If, however, the contrary is true on both counts, we are no more permitted to have our own ideas about the associated nature and possible character than for any person we have not yet met. For instance, someone who has never met me might think I'm a seven-foot-tall Jamaican limbo dancer, but if I actually show up, then GAME OVER. And however much that person might still believe I'm something else, it will make absolutely no difference to my actual identity, with no ultimate change of heart on their behalf presumably preventing any kind of meaningful relationship. Thus, for this scenario, we have no authority to redefine the nature of Ultimate Reality, nor dictate how we might relate to or align with such an entity, even if all of this doesn't fit neatly into our specific preconceptions.

To summarise, although there seems to be little evidence to suggest that finite human beings can reach out to discover Ultimate Reality for themselves, this does not necessarily mean that we cannot understand and form relationships with any such entity should there be a related reaching into our world and a communicative responsibility. Indeed, the latter process finds a (lesser) counterpart in the early parts of all our lives, whereby it is only the passing of knowledge from the higher (parents or equivalent) to the lower (ourselves as babies or infants) that enables us to grow up satisfactorily. Imagine having the pressure at two years old to work the world out and your place in it without outside help. The possibility of the existence and recognition of Ultimate Reality/God plus the potential for meaningful relationships are considered in the next chapter.

CHAPTER TWO

The Likelihood of Ultimate Reality/God and the Possibility of a Relationship with Plebs Like Us

Is there any evidence for the existence of Ultimate Reality/God and, if so, is there the possibility that we can recognise and even form relationships with any such entity that might be reaching in? My opinion is that the short answer to both of these questions is, *yes*, with the following bullet points providing some of the main reasons.

- ❖ Very many worldviews search for Ultimate Reality. Although most, or maybe even all, of these could be largely, or wholly, in error, the fact that so many apparent counterfeits exist is undoubtedly a strong indication of the genuine. We know, for example, that criminals don't go to the considerable efforts of counterfeiting money, famous paintings, priceless jewels etc. unless the genuine exists.

- ❖ C.S. Lewis once said that there is provision for our every desire – for instance, we get hungry and there's food, we get thirsty and there's water, we have sexual appetites and there's love-making and so on and so on. Lewis specifically cites an *"unquenchable desire that tells us we are made for heaven"* [7] and there is undoubtedly a massive spiritual hunger right across the globe which has existed for thousands and thousands of years. Prayer and meditation are thus vitally important for countless people around the world, with even those having no declared spiritual beliefs often unconsciously acknowledging the existence of God

---

[7] Philip Zaleski & Carol Zaleski, *The Fellowship: The Literary Lives of the Inklings.* Farrar, Strauss and Giroux, 2016, p.310.

– see Chuck Colson example below. This universal quest for the spiritual, whether recognised or not, is well summarised in a 1994 Daily Telegraph article by the journalist, Mary Kenny. She writes, *"In all cultures and at all times, human beings have conceived of a spiritual life beyond the body."* [8]

- ❖ Almost 3,000 years ago, Solomon, the King of Israel at the time, wrote these words, *He (God) has made everything beautiful in its time. He has also set eternity in the human heart;* (Ecclesiastes 3:11), something affirmed by the rock guitarist Eric Clapton's song, *Tears in Heaven*. Written after the tragic death of his four-year-old son, Conor, this song includes the line, *"Would you know my name if I see you in heaven?"* [9] *This is* from the West Ham website on 24th February 2016, *"On this day 23 years ago. Remembering our Captain of WEST HAM & ENGLAND (Bobby Moore) & now HEAVEN ELEVEN, who sadly passed away, GOD BLESS YA, SIR XXX."*

Again, the poet *and singer songwriter, Leonard Cohen, when his* soul-mate *and former lover, Marianne, was dying (July 2016),* wrote, *"Well, Marianne it's come to this time when we are really so old and our bodies are falling apart and I think I will follow you very soon. Know that I am so close behind you that if you stretch out your hand, I think you can reach mine."* [10]

There is simply so much stuff like this concerning the famous and loved who have died, whom we often perceive as *looking down at us.* It is also very significant that there is a fairly common hope for future conscious individual recognition. When it comes down to it, people the world over, even the *non-absolutists,* are often desperate to know what has happened to their departed loved

---

[8] Mary Kenny, *The Daily Telegraph*, London.
[9] Eric Clapton, *Rush (soundtrack)*, Duck/Reprise, 1992.
[10] https://www.yahoo.com/entertainment/leonard-cohen-penned-letter-long-130710635.html

ones and whether they will be able to meet up with them again.

A final and slightly different example concerns a guy called Chuck Colson who, during the late 1960's and early 1970s, held one of the most powerful jobs in the USA - Special Counsel to President Richard Nixon. Colson admits to having been a very nasty person at this time, being known as Nixon's *Hatchet Man* – the title he got for doing all his dirty work. He later converted to Christ, but this next incident occurred well before all of that.

Colson recalls that one day he was out on a lake with his ten-year-old son, who he was teaching to sail. At one point he hands the tiller to his son who, as he begins to sail the boat by himself, becomes full of pure joy and elation. Colson then says, *"I found myself in that one unforgettable moment quietly talking to God. I could even recall the precise words: 'Thank You, God, for giving me this son, for giving us this one wonderful moment. Just looking now into this boy's eyes fulfils my life. Whatever happens in the future, even if I die tomorrow, my life is complete and full. Thank You'. Afterwards, I had been startled when I realised that I had spoken to God, since my mind did not assent to His existence as a Person."* [11]

So what are all these examples telling us? Well, it would appear that we all possess a divine spark or 'spiritual DNA', which can be ignited by certain life events and plays out in the form of expectations beyond the grave following the deaths of those we love and admire. Furthermore, it doesn't seem that big a step to believe that this universal inborn spiritual DNA might well have been imparted by Ultimate Reality, enabling human recognition and consequent reciprocal relationships.

❖ This is a fairly well-known quotation from Albert Einstein, *"The most incomprehensible thing about the universe is that it is*

---

[11] Charles W. Colson, *Born Again*. Hodder & Stoughton, 1995, p.132.

comprehensible." [12] In other words, if the whole of creation was a freak and, overall, random occurrence which eventually produced *human-being accidents*, why on earth would these accidents be able to make sense of the universe? Both the mathematical/physical universe and our logical minds, which can at least partially understand the related governing laws, thus appear likely to originate from the same source and be compatible with that source.

John Polkinghorne puts it like this, *"We are so familiar with the fact that we can understand the world that most of the time we take it for granted. It is what makes science possible. Yet it could have been otherwise. The universe might have been a disorderly chaos rather than an ordered cosmos. Or it might have had a rationality which was inaccessible to us…..There is a congruence* (compatibility) *between our minds and the universe, between the rationality experienced within and the rationality observed without."* [13] The reasoning, rationality and logic that our minds utilise thus appears to be a second human attribute pointing to spiritual recognition and potential relationships with Ultimate Reality.

- ❖ Starting with the rationality experienced within, as seemingly evidenced by the *Universal Moral Law*. The very robust reasoning behind this proposal was originally put forward by C.S. Lewis in *The Poison of Subjectivism,* an essay confronting the view that as the various cultures have such widely different norms for behaviour, any conclusion about a shared moral law is unfounded. Lewis, learned in many cultures, calls this, *"a lie - a good, solid, resounding lie."* He continues, *"If a man will go into a library and spend a few days with the 'Encyclopedia of Religion and Ethics', he will soon discover the massive uniformity of the practical reason in man. From the Babylonian Hymn to Samos,*

---

[12] Sonja Bargmann, *Ideas and Opinions.* New York: Bonanza, 1954, p. 292.
[13] John Polkinghorne, *Science and Creation: The Search for Understanding.* London: SPCK, 1988, p.20.

from the laws of Manu, the Book of the Dead, the Analects, the Stoics, the Platonists, from Australian aborigines and Redskins, he will collect the same triumphantly monotonous denunciations of oppression, murder, treachery and falsehood; the same injunctions of kindness to the aged, the young, and the weak, of almsgiving (charity to the less well off) and impartiality and honesty." [14]

This apparent universality seemingly causes all human beings to frequently (and instinctively) appeal to an absolute external moral standard. At its simplest, this might be referred to as the concept of *right and wrong* or as an unwritten law placed within all of us, often spoken of as our *conscience*. Francis Collins takes the argument on a little further, *"What we have here is very peculiar: the concept of right and wrong appears to be universal among all members of the human species (though its application may result in wildly different outcomes). It thus seems to be a phenomenon approaching that of a law, like the law of gravitation or special relativity. Yet in this instance, it is a law that, if we are honest with ourselves, is broken with astounding regularity."* [15]

And again, from Einstein, *"You are right in speaking of the moral foundations of science, but you cannot turn round and speak of the scientific foundations of morality."* [16]

Going back into antiquity, the 1st/2nd century Greek Stoic philosopher, Epictetus, considered that everyone is born with an innate understanding of the meaning of words such as good and bad, right and wrong, appropriate and inappropriate, happiness, duty and obligation.

---

[14] C. S. Lewis, *Christian Reflections*. Fount Paperbacks, 1985, p.104.
[15] Francis S. Collins, *The Language of God*. Free Press, Simon and Schuster, Inc., 2006, p.23.
[16] Albert Einstein, *Advice to a Young Scientist*. London, Harper and Row, 1979, p.31.

Much of the foregoing appears to be borne out by modern life with many people, when in *crunch* situations, expecting life to be *fair* and saying things like, "I'm a good person" and, "this should or ought to be the case." Some also appeal to their version of fate-related justice – what goes around comes around etc. Secular psychology, unsurprisingly, usually frowns on reflections of this kind, presumably because they point towards some kind of external moral standard. But to attribute the origin of words like *good*, *should*, *ought* and *fate* to solely naturalistic evolution surely places too much responsibility on such an impersonal and substantially random process.

By the same token, people never seem to say, "I don't agree with your personal moral standards" when accused of, say, lying or being selfish ("it's all about you" etc.), but automatically respond out of their inborn moral law by either refuting or, more rarely, agreeing with the allegation. Furthermore, if we really could create our own moral code then this would inevitably spell the end of legitimate guilt. We'd simply forgive ourselves for breaking our own rules etc., and just get on with life.

Considered from another angle, it seems that the moral law will actually ask us to save a drowning person even if they are an enemy. And it further appears most unlikely that this feature of human nature can be attributed to a naturally evolved empathy. This is because if one holds to an *earthbound* atheistic view of evolution, as above, then the clearly *selfish* process of natural selection utilising the survival of the fittest mechanism must surely neutralise any empathetic tendency. It thus seems reasonable to assume that the moral law has been independently imparted to the human race and that its very presence is evidence for the existence of a related law-giver – quite possibly some kind of superior life-form with personality and intelligence (Ultimate Reality/God?).

As a final contribution to this particular discussion, a theory commonly known as *cultural Darwinism* bucks the above opinions by proposing that the morals and values we see today are the result of a cultural process analogous to biological evolution. In this model, the self-replicating DNA/gene is replaced by a cultural self-replicator, coined 'meme' in 1976 by the eminent British evolutionary biologist and neo (new)-atheist, Richard Dawkins. The related study of 'memetics' has, however, become less plausible as time has gone on, and is now regarded as a failed paradigm by most researchers. The main reasons for this are very substantial, and include factors such as the inability to test for scientific/observational evidence together with the questionable applicability of the biological analogue and the actual nature of the meme, assuming it even exists in the first place! Alister McGrath is particularly helpful here, expanding these major shortcomings in a concise and readily understandable format.[17] Although there are alternative naturalistic theories concerning how ideas and beliefs may spread within a culture, none apparently provide specific insights into whether these are right or wrong, good or bad.

- ❖ Again, reflecting upon the *rationality experienced within*, why is it that so many of us seem to believe we are really important when we're actually so small and very finite in all dimensions? I remember, a few days before my 50th birthday, thinking something like, I've only been around for fifty years and in the same time again I'll probably be dead (or virtually dead). I haven't even been to the other side of the very small planet that I live on, which is itself inconsequential compared to our own Milky Way galaxy let alone the whole universe - and yet I think I am so important. I think about myself so much, and my opinions must be heard by all and sundry. WHY?

---

[17] Alister McGrath, *Dawkins' God, Genes, Memes, And The Meaning Of Life.* Blackwell Publishing, 2007, pp. 119-138.

And how can we blithely talk about billions of years, when we can't even imagine a million years. Even one million days represents about 2,700 years. I very much doubt whether this question concerning our evident worth can be satisfactorily answered by science, philosophy or any other earthbound system of thought. It is, however, within the realm of theology and Judeo–Christian[18] thinking, where, almost at the start of the Bible, there is the statement, *"Then God said, 'Let us make man in our own* (spiritual) *image, in our likeness...'."* (Genesis 1:26a)

On this basis then, it's at least feasible to believe we're important, and even special and loved, because Ultimate Reality tells us (inwardly) that we are. In other words, similar to when kids achieve almost all of their full potentials simply because their parents also told them that they were important and especially loved. So if this is correct, Ultimate Reality/God, as posited above, might well turn out to be a *superior life-form with personality and intelligence*. Furthermore, the claimed spiritual likeness (to God) of created human beings is undoubtedly consistent with the possibility of meaningful intercommunication. Another similarity to parenthood, with parents, although far more knowledgeable and developed, still being able to teach their children to speak.

Ironically, taking the opposite view to people's worth and value seems only to confirm the above. As an example, Friedrich Nietzsche, a 19th century existentialist philosopher[19], upon

---

[18] Judeo-Christian is used here as an abbreviated term for describing the combined effect, under certain circumstances, of Judaism and Christianity.

[19] Existentialism considers there to be no inherent meaning or purpose in life, although individuals can generate meaning for themselves. This meaning must, however, remain private and personal, and unconnected to any sort of Ultimate Reality. Nobody can specify meaning for anyone else. This philosophy became increasingly popular in the UK and Western society as a whole during the 20th century. Although having religious roots (Kierkegaard, 1813-1855), existentialism is now generally considered to be atheistic, as assumed in this book.

hearing about a natural disaster that had destroyed Java in 1883, wrote to a friend, *"Two hundred thousand wiped out at a stroke – how magnificent!"* [20] Nietzsche was in effect saying that if there is no Ultimate Reality – that is no God, then all value judgments are arbitrary. Justice has to come down instead to our culture and individual temperaments. Would most sane people today feel comfortable about making that sort of statement when they heard of any similar disaster – say the fire at Grenfell Tower in West London in the summer of 2017, where (only!!) seventy two people lost their lives?

❖ This next consideration is from the *rationality observed without* and specifically concerns the incredible fine-tuning of the universal mathematical/physical laws, a phenomenon, although not necessarily its interpretation, accepted across the whole scientific community and often summarised by means of *fundamental constants.* Although scientific opinions vary concerning their total number, there seems to be little dissent from the view that these constants are ultimately responsible for the size and expansion of the universe plus its consequent ordered behaviour – in particular, overall long-term stability with properties conducive to biological life arising on the Earth. To pick just one example of what is cumulatively known as the *strong anthropic principle*, the scientific genius, Stephen Hawking, in his iconic book, *A Brief History of Time*, makes this statement, *"If the rate of expansion one second after the big bang* (see chapter seven) *had been smaller by even one part in a hundred thousand million million, it* (the universe) *would have recollapsed* (his word) *before it reached its present size. On the other hand, if it had been greater by a part in a million, the universe would have expanded too rapidly for stars and planets to form."* [21]

---

[20] Friedrich Nietzsche, cited by Tim Keller, *Walking With God Through Pain & Suffering.* Hodder & Stoughton, 2015, p.107.
[21] Stephen Hawking, *A Brief History of Time.* Bantam Books, 1996, p.126.

Taken at face value, the above account appears to be highly indicative of a grand designer, although scientists of an atheistic disposition commonly prefer alternative explanations, such as those associated with quantum mechanics, a multiverse, and what is known as the *weak anthropic principle*. The subject is again taken up in chapter seven.

- ❖ What do we really think when we look at an essentially unpolluted night sky where numerous stars are visible? – as per the time I was in India with Kev. I reckon that during those moments when we are simply awed by the sheer majesty of what is on display, it's quite easy for us to go along with the opening line of the OT Psalm 19 - *The heavens declare the glory of God.*

    Furthermore, Brian Cox, a professor at the cutting edge of particle physics and a well-known TV presenter, is quoted as saying, *"The world is beautiful to look at, but even more beautiful to understand."*[22] and Brian Greene, a leading theoretical physicist from the USA, has written an excellent book discussing some of the various (currently known) mathematical/physical laws governing the cosmos titled, *The Elegant Universe*.[23] To my knowledge, both are currently atheists or agnostics. Going back to the 17th century, Johannes Kepler, the German mathematician and astronomer, said, *"The chief aim of all investigations of the external world should be to discover the rational order and harmony which has been imposed on it by God and which He revealed to us in the language of mathematics."* [24]

---

[22] Brian Cox, *The Forces of Nature*. BBC Television series of four episodes, 2016.
[23] Brian Greene, *The Elegant Universe*. Vintage, 2000.
[24] Johannes Kepler, Collected Quotes – Quotable Mathematics.
https://quotablemath.blogspot.com/2019/11/johannes-Kepler-collected-quotes.html.

Finally, the specific location of our planet, enabling us to *see the heavens* is apparently at odds with most other parts of the Milky Way, where little of the universe is visible. – From an article in the October 2009 *Trumpet* Print Edition titled, *The Perfect Seat for Viewing the Universe*.

In summary, it seems perfectly reasonable to deduce the following: Firstly, the existence of Ultimate Reality/God appears to be the best explanation of the cumulative effect of the foregoing eight points and, secondly, that relationships with such an entity could well be possible. So maybe not that far away from this quotation by James Sire, a renowned specialist author on worldviews, *"Human beings can know both the world around them and God Himself because God has built into them the capacity to do so and because He takes an active role in communicating with them."* [25]

However, even given this, how much of our ability to recognise and form relationships with any such transcendent entity is hampered by the influences of UK society in 2020? This is the subject we turn to now.

---

[25] James Sire, *The Universe Next Door.* InterVarsity Press, U.S.A., 2004, p.34.

CHAPTER THREE

The Influences of UK Society 2020:
Do We Really Know Our Own Minds?

The society we live in is pluralistic and multicultural, with so many opinions and so many *voices*. It is therefore difficult to determine which ones are correct and most relevant to our own lives, and which ones are not. Furthermore, as previously intimated, there are some voices out there that claim all such comparisons belong to old-fashioned methods of thinking and have no place in our current *enlightened* Western culture. On top of this, we have to recognise that UK society is altering all the time (e.g., the 2016 Brexit decision and its future consequences) and that its views may, therefore, be no more permanent or reliable than changes in fashion. So whether we realise it or not, our short little lives inevitably relate to a *snapshot* of history, where the popular attitudes and beliefs of the time may or may not be correct and reliable. Thus, although most of us probably think of ourselves as independent people who know our own minds, we cannot help but be affected by our worldview, in turn largely dependent upon the pervasive and encompassing changing cultural patterns and norms of society.

So what is today's UK society all about? What's going on? Or, to quote no lesser personage than my maternal grandmother in the 1960's, "The world's gone mad." I'm not quite sure what she would think and say if she returned now, but it's clear that the incredibly complex and frequently confusing nature of our society means that breaking it down into manageable chunks is not an easy task. As a former civil engineer, looking at many variables is something I have been fairly used to; however, the sheer number in UK society has almost done my head in. When it comes to the deeper issues of life, everything is simply so hard to label and categorise. Nevertheless, it still seems possible to at least consider and briefly discuss what appear to be the main influences that have shaped and are shaping overall UK culture; specific sub-cultures, such as *Millennials* and *Generation Z*, necessarily being excluded.

The chosen approach is, firstly, to describe some of the advantages of present-day society compared to previous generations and, secondly, due principally to its integral role in the moulding of our country's history, to consider both the past and present influences of Christianity. The discussion then moves on to expounding the natures and impacts on our thinking of what appear to be the three current main players, namely Postmodernism, New Age, and Political Correctness (PC). All of these have been on the rise in the UK and Western society (including the USA) for six or seven decades and encouraged, to greater or lesser degrees, grass-roots secular characteristics such as humanism, naturalism, individualism, hedonism, consumerism and materialism.[26]

Modern Britain has various *advantages over previous generations*, with the National Health Service (NHS) probably representing the pick of the bunch; supremely demonstrated by its incredible response to the current Covid 19 pandemic. It's certainly extremely hard for most of us present-day citizens to imagine how we would cope in its absence.

Then there are the advantages due to the markedly reduced influence of the aristocracy and class system; in particular, greater equality plus less hypocrisy and *judgmentalism*. Looking back to the 19th century, the incredible importance placed on class and position was downright disgusting. And going hand in hand with this are the much improved rights of today's workers compared to past centuries. We also now have a greater handle on the dire situations affecting various nations across the globe, and many associated charities are well supported. Part of this understanding has come from the benefits of increased travel, most people in this country never venturing further than ten miles from their

---

[26] One of the consequences of our largely secular society appears to be an increased fear of, and reluctance to talk about, death, with euphemisms such as 'passed away' or simply 'passed' becoming ever more common. Very different to Victorian times, when the dead were often laid out in the 'parlour' for people to pay their last respects.

birthplace before the advent of the train. Those with learning difficulties and mental health issues are additionally better understood and far less marginalised than in the past. Indeed, many sufferers were hidden and treated as outcasts, including the 'forgotten Prince John' (1905-1919), the youngest child of King George V, who had epilepsy and autism.

Before the recent major shift in attitudes, people, and particularly the men, often got through the tougher times in their lives by simply gritting their teeth and somehow just keeping on going – that is modern Stoicism or, less charitably, emotional illiteracy. It's interesting that top male tennis players of the modern era, such as Federer, Djokovic and Murray, can sometimes publicly break down and cry, win or lose, whereas this would never have been the case in the days of Borg, McEnroe and Connors.

Today's UK society is also addressing past inequalities concerning women and the black population (e.g., the *Black Lives Matter* movement), albeit that much work, hopefully avoiding *positive discrimination,* still appears to be necessary. Sport has also become less elitist with more opportunities for the *average Joe*. There is a story that when Roger Bannister broke the four-minute mile in 1954, a trade union leader called Jimmy Reid held up some running spikes and asked the thousands of workers at the meeting whether they had a pair of their own. Virtually no hands went up. While on this topic, those engaged in para-sports are now generally treated in like manner to able-bodied athletes, with Prince Harry's *Invictus Games* giving similar opportunities to injured armed services personnel.

In addition to the above, more effort now appears to be put into finding people jobs that are right for them and that they might even enjoy. That is not to say that there still aren't many exceptions to this but in my much younger days we did hear an awful lot of, "We fought a war (or two) for you, you long-haired louts (sometimes I still miss my hair), so you should be grateful to have any job at all." That was what was said, although these guys were undoubtedly absolute heroes in defending our country. And unlike in my day, many young men in current UK society seem able to cook, and we are all now, with our many showers, definitely cleaner as a nation – whatever happened to *Sunday night is bath night*?

Finally, isn't it absolutely stunning that we now have remote controls for virtually all of our various gadgets? Young people today have no idea of the sheer effort involved in making it all the way to the TV set to change channels or using keys to open car doors! And I'm not bitter.

Although there is no doubt that *true Christianity* has always been an overwhelming force for good, the fact that this knowledge is somehow generally kept below radar has resulted in most of us in the West having no idea of its amazing universal impact. The numerous related advantages are well documented by Paul Backholer in his excellent book, *How Christianity Made The Modern World* [27]; sourced for much of the following.

Most of us living in today's UK probably take for granted our democracy and related benefits, such as free speech, religious freedom, belief that all are created equal, political accountability, and right against illegal imprisonment (*Habeas Corpus*). We may also be largely unaware that these, and many other, privileges have been the result of prolonged and hard-fought sacrificial struggles, of which Christians have often been at the forefront. Examples of such include,

- the authoring of the *Magna Carta* in 1215, a significant first step towards peoples' liberty, by Stephen Langton, the then Archbishop of Canterbury;
- the Peasant's Revolt of 1381, a new precedent for mass demonstrations and a warning to unjust governments, led by the Rev. John Ball;
- the achievements of Oliver Cromwell (1599-1658), a puritan Christian who, although of very mixed reputation, managed to permanently limit the power of the Monarchy and sow the seeds of

---

[27] Paul Backholer, *How Christianity Made The Modern World*. Faith Media, 2009.

modern democracy;
- the passing of the English Bill of Rights in 1689, which shaped the infancy of modern democracy;
- the reformers of the 19th and early 20th centuries, many of whom were Christians, who increased the rights to vote (suffrage) of the adult population from 2% in 1832 to almost 100% in 1928. The 2018 film, *Peterloo*, accurately portrays the story of the 1819 Peterloo Massacre where British forces attacked a peaceful pro-democracy rally in Manchester, and clearly conveys the message that the working people of that time had virtually no voice or representation of any kind.

Today's British people owe a tremendous debt to their, often Christian, forebears, and although UK democracy is still far from perfect (hardly a reasonable expectation for any system of administration), it remains the envy of those living under the many oppressive and cruel regimes so evident in other parts of the world. To quote Sir John Mortimer, CBE, QC, (1923-2009), playwright and atheist, *"Our whole history and culture in Europe is based on Christianity, whether you believe it or not. Our culture is Christian; Shakespeare, Mozart – all that makes life worth living is part of the Christian tradition."* [28]

Because of the vast array of Christian-related benefits (Backholer considers 37 in distinct brief chapters), it's easy to end up with a rather lengthy discussion. So, to keep it nice and simple and thereby avoid a prolonged history lesson (not nearly as sexy as geotechnics), the following descriptions relate to just four categories - The Legal System and Morality, Workers' Rights and Social Care, Education, and Healthcare.

The British author, Stephen C. Perks, particularly known for his books concerning interrelations between Christianity and Sociology (including the publication, *'Christianity and Law'*) says this, *"Our legal system was formed and developed over centuries under the dominating influence of*

---

[28] John Mortimore, *The Daily Telegraph*. London, 28th April 1999.

the Christian religion" and *"Our very concepts of justice, due process and the rule of law are Christian ideals that we should never have known had the Christian faith not taken root in this land and transformed the nation from a pagan into a civilised society."* [29]

Lord Denning, one of the leading lawyers in England and Wales during the 1960s/70s, spoke plainly about the link between judges who had been influenced by Christianity and the shaping of common law; a view shared by George Polson QC, who said, *"The true basis of English common law is Christianity."* [30] This basis has been exported to many countries, including the USA. Former president, Barack Obama, is on record as saying, *"Our law is by definition a codification of morality, much of it grounded in the Judeo-Christian tradition."* [31]

Even the BBC, hardly big on the Bible, has written, *"In the Ten Commandments, Moses outlined a basis for morality which has lasted over 3,000 years and been embraced by two-thirds of the world's population."* [32] Finally, Daily Mail journalist, Melanie Philips affirmed that, in the UK, *"The Bible is the moral code that underpins our civilisation..."* [33]

The British Industrial Revolution (approximately mid 18th to mid 19th centuries) dramatically changed living conditions, when an economy founded on manual labour was replaced by one based on industry and manufacturing. The mass production of textiles and iron, plus the development of steam power and the rise of the factory system characterised this period, with an associated massive increase in the demand for coal. However, although this resulted in Great Britain becoming very prosperous, the working people - men, women and

---

[29] Stephen C. Perks, *Christianity and Law: An Enquiry into the influence of Christianity on the Development of English Common Law.* Avant Books, 1993, 2003.
[30] George Polson. *Speech on The Christian Content of the Rule of Law and its Contribution to Human Rights.* 19th February 1969.
[31] Barack Obama, *The Audacity of Hope.* Random House Audio Publishing Group, 2006, pp.216 - 219.
[32] *Religion and Ethics,* BBB - Religions - Judaism: Moses
[33] Philips. *The Daily Mail,* London, 7th September 2006.

children - were treated appallingly. Some cotton mills were operating 24/7, and children were labouring up to 18 hours a day. Even kids as young as five were forced to work down the mines in absolutely abysmal conditions.

All of this was taking place in *Christian* Britain (see below), and there was accordingly a tremendous need to take the message of Christ out of the churches and into the streets and industrial areas. Someone had to make a stand against the ever-increasing poverty amid abounding wealth. Of those who did, many seem to have been evangelical Christians - such as Charlotte Elizabeth Tonna, whose discerning and emotive writing revealed the terrible plight of working-class women and woke the consciences of the middle and upper classes. Others include Lord Shaftesbury, whose work led to *The Factory Act* of 1847 and other legislation that dramatically improved the working conditions for women and children; and George Muller and Thomas John Barnardo, who opened orphanages, and between them, rescued, and rehabilitated more than 160,000 children, significant numbers of whom had been enduring shocking working conditions.

The founder of the Salvation Army, William Booth (1829-1912), is another who not only preached the Christian gospel, but also reached out to the many homeless people by providing, amongst other things, lodgings, meals, and work opportunities. According to Backholer, between its formation on the streets of East London in 1865 and an audit in 1899, the *Army* had lodged approximately 11 million homeless people, served 27 million meals, found work for 9,000 people, and even traced 18,000 missing individuals. Booth's book, *In Darkest England And The Way Out,* controversial when published in 1890, was used as a blueprint for today's welfare system (including the creation of the NHS in 1948), the progress towards which had been greatly advanced in a 1942 report by William Beveridge, British economist and Christian reformer.

Over the centuries and millennia, education has typically been the province of the favoured few – the rich and powerful, who have often used their knowledge to rule over and control the masses. Indeed, the main and perhaps only, authentic opposition to this state of affairs has come from the Church, with Christianity being the foundation upon which most Western education has been built. To quote Backholer, *"From medieval times, the Church provided education to all classes of society, in monasteries, at public schools, orphanages, charity schools, grammar schools, church foundations, or by the chaplains to private households …. From 1833 onward in Britain, the state began to follow the Church's example and invest in education. Twenty years before state education began in 1870, a government commission found that about 2 $^1/_2$ million children in England attended day school. Almost all of these were run by churches, chapels and Christian charities."* [34]

The Sunday school movement, which roughly paralleled and interconnected with this more general education, officially commenced in 1780 and by 1903, six million children across England were in regular attendance. Finally, the translation of the Bible into English from the 16th century onwards, which gave every citizen the incentive to learn how to read, is considered to have made a very positive contribution towards greater levels of literacy.

For over a thousand years Christianity was the main provider of healthcare in the West, with Christians often being the driving force behind many of the related services, including the building of hospitals. And in more recent times, Edward Chad Varah, a British Anglican priest, established the Samaritans (1953) as the world's first telephone crisis hotline for those contemplating suicide, and Dame Cicely Saunders, a committed British Christian, founded the hospice movement (1967).

Florence Nightingale (1820 -1910) is generally recognised as the principal pioneer when it comes to modern healthcare, particularly nursing, in the UK and many other parts of the world. Florence was born into an upper-class wealthy family, who expected her to follow the usual route of *marrying well* and becoming an obedient wife. However, she considered that God was calling her to something else and, against all

---

[34] Paul Backholer, *How Christianity Made The Modern World.* Faith Media, 2009, p.54.

the odds, made it to the front line of the Crimean War (1853-1856) as head of a team of nurses. She discovered appalling conditions, with overcrowded hospital wards containing sewage discharge and rotting dead animals, patients covered by rags smeared with dried blood and excrement, contaminated water supply and inedible food supplies. Florence immediately set about putting radical remedial procedures in place, including sanitising the wards, bathing and clothing the patients, and enabling the provision of satisfactory food and water. Within six months, the hospital case-fatality rate had dropped from 32% to 2%. She returned to England a hero, and despite continual ill-health, reformed nursing practice and had a major effect on public health.

Strange as it may sound today, the link between the transfer of disease and unwashed hands was not officially recognised, at least in the West, before Florence Nightingale's reforms. Indeed, Ignaz Semmelweis, an enlightened young physician working in Vienna in the 1840s, was ridiculed and ostracised when he insisted on thorough and repeated hand washing for all medical procedures. However, about 3,200 years earlier, Moses specified detailed instructions concerning public health, which, although inevitably somewhat crude by today's standards, were still well advanced of those existing before Florence Nightingale. These, and many other insightful and effective medical exhortations recorded throughout the Bible, are highlighted in an excellent book, *None Of These Diseases* by S. I. McMillen, a 20th century American doctor.[35]

Although the reasons for this country's extensive Christian heritage are many and varied, there is one episode which probably takes precedence over all the others. This is known as the *British Great Awakening* or the *Evangelical Revival*, which commenced in 1739 (in England) and had a hugely significant effect, directly or indirectly, over perhaps the following 150 to 200 years. Immediately before this, Britain had been experiencing one of the most morally debased periods in its history. There were burglars in the cities, highwaymen in the countryside, cock-fighting, bull-baiting, bear-baiting, almost universal alcoholism, and

---

[35] S.I. McMillen, *None Of These Diseases*. Marshall, Morgan & Scott, 1984.

weak and often corrupt churches. Mobs and rioting were also commonplace. This heaven-sent revival, (humanly) led by clergymen John Wesley and George Whitefield, resulted in meetings where tens of thousands of people were converted to Christ, sometimes with accompanying miraculous healings (as per the New Testament [NT], and particularly great news at a time of pretty basic medical treatments). There are also accounts of small chapels being inundated by thousands of people, and prayer meetings going on for six or seven hours – something that may sound very odd and boring to those of us today, but, as I have experienced on a smaller scale, not when there is the awesome presence of God in the house.

This is how Backholer describes the effects upon society of the British Great Awakening, *"Unfaithful husbands became moral, thieves went honest, alcoholics spent their money on the family, addicts were freed and all the problems associated with it went into remission. The streets were safer, the poor found jobs, the problems of others became the burdens of the Church.......faith in the churches soon impacted every area of the lives of the citizens; workers' rights were protected, fair wages called for, better living conditions demanded, healthcare required, education facilitated and representation commanded. As prudence grew, the new Christians could give of their time and money to support charities and missions abroad"* [36] (the Protestant work ethic + *moral capitalism*).

Many historians also believe that this more compassionate and moral climate prevented a bloody revolution in Britain, as occurred in France close to the end of the 18th century. We so much need something like this today in our often directionless and morally lost UK society.

If I was an atheist or sceptic reading this, I would in all likelihood have got pretty uptight by now. This is unbalanced! What about the violent and infamous crusades during the medieval period, and the Catholic/Protestant persecutions in the 16th and 17th centuries? Where

---

[36] Paul Backholer, *How Christianity Made The Modern World*. Faith Media, 2009, p.105.

was the supposed love of God when many priests and nuns inflicted emotional and/or physical and/or sexual abuse on the little children entrusted to them? And why do we never seem to hear of any loving accounts concerning how these nuns dealt with the young unmarried mothers put under their care? The thing is that atrocious acts of these natures represent the complete opposite of the life and teachings of Jesus Christ, who considered that the greatest of all, rather than lording it over those around them, should be the servant of all (as He unfailingly lived out). We also need to understand that the established Church has sometimes not only greatly hindered the message and purpose of true Christianity but, on occasions, by denying the love and transforming power of the Christian gospel, actually become its persecutor.

When the love and transforming power of the Christian gospel are denied and rejected, the almost inevitable result is *Cultural Christianity*, *Churchianity*, or (the Christian) *religion*; the latter being a word which conjures up, in many peoples' minds, thoughts of a crutch to support the weak on an individual basis and the mass-manipulation of humanity at a corporate level. The term, *church-goer,* again evokes generally dismissive thoughts (tea and biscuits may come to mind), because it is often associated with this Cultural Christianity, whereby someone says they are a Christian because they were born in a historically Christian country, were christened as a baby, and attend church (often only occasionally, but even sometimes regularly, year in year out). The 20th century American evangelist, Billy Graham, once said that *the physical act of going into a church building no more makes someone a Christian than going into a garage makes them a car.*

Cultural Christianity is predominantly man-made and its effect might be a bit like an inoculation, giving a person just enough to stop them from getting the real thing. It is perhaps best identified by asking the question, If God were to completely withdraw from a particular church today, would virtually everything go on as though nothing had happened? This is very sobering, and all churches and every individual believer should ask themselves this question every now and then. Just to be completely clear, unlike the adherents of many religions, it is not possible to become a true Christian simply by being born into a particular nation or culture or undergoing certain rituals.

So leading on from these brief insights into Christianity's historic role within British society, how do we gauge its present contribution and influence? The best method of doing this is probably to consider the Christian faith under two separate categories. The first concerns the actual message and its effectiveness in transforming peoples' lives, and the second, which should follow on (as it did in the British Great Awakening), relates to the *social gospel*, whereby practical contributions are made to society as a whole.

Dealing with this second question first, the answer can be viewed as pretty positive. Christian-based charities and communities still make an enormous and vital input, both financial and action-based, into the nation's welfare. Indeed, the greatest contribution to free childcare comes from churches and para-groups, with members of the Church of England alone estimated to contribute about 22 million hours of voluntary service per month. As a further example, Christians Against Poverty (CAP), an organisation only founded in 1996, now helps some 21,500 families every year.

Things are not, however, so positive when it comes to the message of Christ's gospel, and its influence on the thoughts and attitudes undergirding today's UK society. My general impression is that, while there are still people who refer to Britain as a Christian country (incidentally, not necessarily believers), the most realistic description is that it is now largely, although not entirely, *post-Christian*. In other words, although there are still many good Christian churches and passionate individual believers in today's UK, apparently including the present Archbishop of Canterbury, Justin Welby, there seems to be insufficient overall strength to create more than generally localised impacts with the country as a whole being essentially unmoved. There may indeed be lots of bright *Christian dots*, but they are not really that joined up. This tends to be confirmed by recent research undertaken in connection with *Alpha*, a very successful evangelical project that has been ongoing for several decades, which revealed a general lack of understanding by Britain's young people concerning the nature of Jesus Christ and His ministry.

It must, therefore, be concluded that while this country owes a past and continuing social debt to Christianity and is still at least partially underpinned by a related morality (whether or not people recognise the connection), the associated beliefs now have only a peripheral influence on the UK's spiritual climate. The main reasons for this current situation are twofold – firstly, the continual internal weakening of corporate Christianity itself, as for too long much of the Church has been operating in its own natural strength and ability, and secondly, the aforementioned external subversive influences, such as Postmodernism and Political Correctness (facilitated by a typically *Christian-hostile* traditional media), as overall society has become increasingly secular. To put it another way, a Church which can easily be affected more by society than vice-versa. Finally, the thought processes relating to general Western culture have been attacked and weakened by a *no plausibility structure* status quo (see below), whereby few boundaries exist and pretty much anything appears possible.

The above factors have resulted in a UK society containing many individual and corporate voids, which, as has been proved in the past, always require filling. These have been, and are being, filled by various atheistic and spiritual beliefs (particularly New Age) and, looking a bit further into the future, quite possibly Islam. However, this conceivable scenario takes no account of the fact that seemingly increasing numbers of people believe that the Christian Church is currently being pruned and made ready for a great move of God; no doubt different to but maybe having a similar or even greater national impact than the 18th century British Great Awakening. Revivals of this nature are certainly happening in other countries worldwide, where there is huge Christian growth; particularly China, sub-Saharan Africa, Latin-America and parts of the Middle East. Indeed, Iran is currently experiencing very large numbers of Muslims converting to Christ and China is on course to become home to more Christians than any other country in the world by 2035.

Although many people in UK society today probably take on certain views relating to *Postmodernism* as a matter of course, comparatively few, which included me before some research, appear to understand what it entails. Postmodernism represents many of the changes, in art, architecture, literature, philosophy and similar areas, which have taken place in Western society and culture from the 1950s/60s onwards. It seems to have started as a reaction against *modernism*, which adherents of the new order believed to have failed in its mission to utilise principally human reason to improve the world and better mankind's lot (as particularly demonstrated by two World Wars and the intervening Great Depression).

Modernism, which can be traced back to the 18th century *Enlightenment* and even the *Renaissance* (late 15th to early 17th century in Britain), was accordingly optimistic about life and society, believing that humankind was basically on the way up. It also believed in the existence of absolutes, which could be discovered by using human reason and rationality in conjunction with science, although it placed virtually no importance on religious knowledge.

Postmodernism deeply distrusts the whole premise of absolutes, emphasising instead the relative and subjective for virtually everything, including science and, of course, religion. The view that what might be *true* for me may not be (and almost certainly isn't) *true* for you plus the reduced importance (or even demise in certain circles) of *right/good* and *wrong/evil* concepts, negations central to Postmodernism, have accordingly foreshadowed and heralded in a new era of *freedom*, where *anything goes* and *if it feels good, do it.* Not surprisingly, a postmodernist outlook does not allow for the possibility of miracles and therefore has no alternative but to utilise naturalistic constructs in any related discussions, debates, or writings.

Postmodernism may also be viewed as a development of existentialism. In particular, whereas existentialism considers that a person can only draw conclusions based on their own circumstances and experiences (sometimes termed *pre-existing horizons*) and is thus in no position to determine objective truth, Postmodernism extends this to society as a whole, which it considers cannot reach out beyond its own self-constructed values and supposed truths.

This all adds up to uncertainty and unrest within UK and Western society as each *power-group* vies to promote its own *normalities* and self-interests. Unlike the vast majority of current and previous cultures, there appears to be no universally acknowledged plausibility structure; the acceptance of which is taken as read, and deviation from which is regarded as inadmissible. According to Lesslie Newbigin, a 20th century British theologian and missionary, *"A 'plausibility structure' is a social structure of ideas and practices which creates the conditions which determine whether a belief is plausible."* [37]

This present state of affairs in the West is confirmed by the Roman Catholic writer Richard Rohr, who says, *"I cannot think of a culture in human history, before the present postmodern era, that did not value law, tradition, custom, authority, boundaries, and morality of some clear sort. These containers give us the necessary security, continuity, predictability, impulse control and ego structure that we need, before the chaos of real life shows up."* [38]

And from Mark Bair, a Cincinnati pastor and writer, in a 1995 paper titled *'The Postmodern Phenomena of New Age Spirituality...'*, *"If any one statement expresses my observation it is: 'if nothing is true, then everything is true. In other words, if nothing is true in the objective sense, then anything is possible in the subjective sense. Anything can be true for me."* [39]

Finally, G.K. Chesterton (1874-1936), another gifted Roman Catholic writer, once wrote, *"When men choose not to believe in God, they do not*

---

[37] Lesslie Newbigin, *Can the West be Converted?* International Bulletin of Missionary Research, 1987, p.2.

[38] Richard Rohr, *Falling Upward*. John Wiley & Sons, Inc., 2012, p.25.

[39] Mark Bair, *The Postmodern Phenomena of New Age Spirituality: Examples in Popular Literature.* Ashland Theological Journal 27, 1995, p.56.

thereafter believe in nothing, they then become capable of believing in anything!" [40]

So how does all this work out in actual life experience? To start with, it is evident that the relativist and subjective approach, as per Postmodernism, is certainly relevant within an artistic environment, such as the appreciation of paintings or sculptures, and is, furthermore, probably the best way of comparing or contrasting most things in our society. For example, one person's favourite colour might be red, whereas someone else may prefer blue; another person might like cats, whereas someone else may prefer dogs; I might think that sports programmes are more enjoyable than period dramas whereas Aud, no doubt, thinks the exact opposite – and so on ad infinitum. These types of individual differences are simply not important. Moreover, I might feel as much excitement and happiness from Torquay United being promoted back to the football league (sad though this may be for any human being to have as a goal in life) as a Manchester City supporter may feel upon winning the Premiership – it's all relative, whatever works for you etc.

There are, however, areas where the relativistic/subjective viewpoint is simply not going to cut it. For instance, if a friend of mine believes gravity acts sideways and I believe it acts upwards, and we then go to the top of a ten-storey building and both leap off, I can categorically guarantee that what is *true* for me, will also be *true* for him. Again, there are many types of known cancer (about 200, I understand); so let's imagine the possible future scenario whereby our medical expertise has improved to the point where every cancer can be completely eradicated by simply taking a single pill every day for a certain period – easy-*peasy*. But obviously, each pill would only be effective for a specific cancer. I think people would think I was completely insane if I insisted on taking a pill for lung cancer even though I actually had pancreatic cancer. They would certainly want to know why I had decided to do this, and would

---

[40] G.K. Chesterton, *Goodreads*. https://www.goodreads.com/quotes/44015-when-men-choose-not-to-believe

no doubt be puzzled and confused if I said something like, "Look, there are many different kinds of cancer pill, and it would be so narrow-minded of me if I insisted that it had to be a specific type – I'm a bigger man than that."

Looking at this from a slightly different perspective, some people insist that, "It doesn't matter what you believe as long as you're sincere." Although this general approach might sometimes be OK, there are obvious exceptions. For instance, imagine running across a motorway at rush hour without looking and just sincerely believing the road to be clear– I think *splat* covers it.

It is, therefore, clearly evident that, on occasions, there is absolutely nothing wrong in insisting on a single *correct* answer to a question or particular situation (it could save your life – physical and/or spiritual). Feelings, intuition, instinct and the like are not always sufficient on their own to avoid personal tragedy; some factual knowledge may well be imperative.

Another perhaps more obvious objection to Postmodernism's distrust or even complete dismissal of absolutes, is to point out that the latter is of itself an *absolute statement*, a general approach that can be adapted to other viewpoints. For instance, to say that the world is *meaningless* only has relevance if this term can be contrasted with *meaning*. Similarly, *bad* only gets its identity from the distortion of *good*. Indeed, although people may undertake an unpleasant and personally costly task because it seemed *the right and good thing to do*, I have yet to come across anyone who has done something they considered to be ghastly and off-putting simply because it seemed *the wrong and bad thing to do.*

Nevertheless, despite the above inconsistencies and limitations, it appears that the UK is increasingly moving into relativistic *postmodernity*, in which each of us determines for ourselves what is or isn't reality and what is or isn't truth. If there really is no Ultimate Reality then, as noted previously, everything within the spiritual arena becomes a matter of personal interpretation. We, therefore, have no way of determining meaningful distinctions between different worldviews, and can only conclude that all beliefs must be considered equally valid; an ideology known as *philosophical pluralism*. No worldview accordingly has the right to pronounce itself true and all others false, or even inferior. But what do we then do with all the obvious contradictions? Well, perhaps as long as we adhere to a no plausibility structure whereby anything and everything is possible, we can jettison reason and rationality and make all our decisions based solely on feelings, intuition, instinct etc. Again – if it feels good and works for us (at least in the immediate or temporary), then do it.

So how postmodern are we in today's UK and Western society? The answer, in my opinion, is, very, and we are certainly paying for it. Returning to Friedrich Nietzsche, perhaps his most famous quotation, in 1882, is, *"God is dead."* He then goes on to say, *"God remains dead. And we have killed him."*[41] What most philosophers understand by this is not that Nietzsche necessarily believed in the death of a literal God, but rather that the Western world's reliance on religion as a moral standard/compass and source of meaning was now at an end. Because of this implicit absence, Nietzsche made two specific predictions: Firstly, that the 20th century would be the bloodiest of them all – there were accordingly more killings in this century than the sum of all those relating to the previous nineteen, and secondly that the 20th century would be one of madness – this also appears to have been proved true, and things have seemingly become even worse in this early part of the 21st century.

As a themed variation on Nietzsche, the Nobel-Prize winning Russian writer and dissident, Aleksandr Solzhenitsyn (1918-2008) said this, *"Over a half-century ago, while I was still a child, I recall hearing a number of old people offer the following explanation for the great disasters that had befallen Russia, 'Men have forgotten God; that's why all this has happened.' Since then I have spent well-nigh 50 years working on the*

---

[41] Friedrich Nietzsche, *The Gay Science*. 1882. Current Publisher, Cambridge University Press.

history of our revolution; in the process, I have read hundreds of books, collected hundreds of personal testimonies, and have already contributed eight volumes of my own toward the effort of clearing away the rubble left by that upheaval. But if I were asked today to formulate as concisely as possible the main cause of the ruinous revolution that swallowed up some 60 million of our people, I could not put it more accurately than to repeat, "Men have forgotten God; that's why all this has happened."* [42]

In 1968, Andy Warhol, an American artist, director and producer, famously said, "*In the future, everybody will be famous for fifteen minutes*"; a prediction that has been at least partially fulfilled by the recent rise in celebrity culture, largely facilitated by social media and so-called Reality TV. However, at some cost, because what is clearly on offer most of the time is *the Celebration of Mediocrity*.

Some of the *madness* relating to PC is cited a bit later on but, for the time being, I shall content myself with a couple of examples from *Reality TV*. The UK and many other nations are undoubtedly hooked on these types of programmes, some of which are clearly better than others - for instance, the 2017 series of *Astronauts, do you have what it takes?* is awesome. However, there is some pretty weird stuff out there, such as when Scottish Politician, George Galloway, infamously role-played a doting cat next to *owner,* actress Rula Lenska, in a 2006 episode of *Celebrity Big Brother*. I know it was attempted in a light-hearted manner, but surely this degrading behaviour and complete loss of human dignity was unacceptable for (even) a politician. Yet somehow, he remained an MP until 2015.

I don't know quite how to describe this second programme, other than to say I've watched it only once, and this by accident (that's my story and I'm sticking to it). It's called 'Naked Attraction', and is similar to Cilla Black's 'Blind Date' (1985-2003), except for the fairly crucial difference

---

[42] Aleksandr Solzhenitsyn,*1983 Templeton Address.*
https://www.nationalreview.com/2018/12/aleksadr-solzhenitsyn-men-have-forgotten-god-speech/

that individual contestants select their partners from a total of six candidates by looking solely at their genitals (everything else is hidden)! In the episode I watched one of those doing the selecting was bisexual and so, to the cheers of the audience, the choice was broadened to cover both male and female genitalia.

What has happened? Will all of this, and more, become so normal and acceptable that people holding my views end up as being seen as prudes and killjoys (if we're not already)? Is there *any* limit to how *open-minded* and *cool* that we, as individuals, or UK society as a whole, can become? Is a no plausibility structure society really plausible in the long-term?

Because there are no real guidelines relating to Postmodernism, many people, as mentioned above, set their own reality/truth and decide what *works best* for them. Sometimes this involves intuition, which may result in a certain degree of success. And, as would be expected, some are more proficient at this than others. I particularly have my son in mind here, who seems to be very savvy in this area. So there is no doubt that intuition can work and indeed work well, especially when used in conjunction with the closely related instinct and insight plus experience. It can, however, still be a *fickle friend*, particularly when extended to decisions associated with global matters. For example, one might reasonably assume that at least some of the people caught up in the 2007/2008 financial crash (due to the collapse of the US subprime borrowing market) based certain decisions on intuition, and accordingly felt good about their prospects going forward. In the end, however, it was not their individual realities, but actual hard and universal financial realities that brought it all tumbling down. One final point: these comments are directed towards the effectiveness of human intuition within everyday life, becoming progressively less relevant as one moves into the spiritual arena. This is considered below in conjunction with New Age.

In addition to the claimed absence of absolutes, there are now even signs of a developing *post-truth* culture within Western society. This may be the main reason why more people in the public eye, particularly politicians, seem to be getting away with initially saying one thing and then, very shortly afterwards, saying the complete opposite; sometimes insisting that both versions are simply *alternative truths*. Nevertheless, it appears unlikely that this type of behaviour will ever become the norm, as this would almost certainly lead to most peoples' lives becoming increasingly chaotic and dysfunctional. In particular, virtually all of us require honesty in so many areas, such as relationships (family, friends, business associates), medical and financial advice, buying a house or car and on and on. How often do we read the newspaper headline, *The Real Truth about...?* Even Donald Trump's pithy term, *Fake News* appeals to the existence of *True News*. Finally, upping the stakes, all of us would surely want the real and complete truth to come out if loved ones had died in mysterious circumstances or if we had been wrongly accused of a serious crime. We would also want justice in both cases.

New *Age* thinking bucks the overriding atheistic trend and perspective of modern Western society; many people, and perhaps particularly the young, having rightly concluded that human beings comprise not only bodily matter but also spirit/soul. In what sometimes feels like an overwhelmingly materialistic and consumerist modern Britain, this recognition and insight is to be applauded. New Age ideology is difficult to define, and there are differences of opinion concerning whether or not it represents a religion. Broadly speaking, its aims are understood to include evolution and transformation at both individual and societal levels, greater reverence for the natural world, and a linking up with the more unusual scientific theories (such as quantum mechanics – briefly discussed under chapter seven).

New Ageists are to be commended for the great emphasis they normally place on their spiritual journeys, and some Western Christians could certainly learn from this. The contrast, where it exists, is probably primarily due to the strong and continual attention that most New Ageists give to individual improvement and greater self-knowledge, whereas Christians can sometimes become rather slack in their spiritual journeys, maybe faltering due to mistakenly thinking that they have somehow *arrived*. When searching ceases, both into God and our own selves, there will almost certainly be resultant stagnation and little growth in profundity and self-awareness. This is a very apt confession from Tim Keller, a New York pastor, *"Our faith is largely abstract and intellectual and not very heartfelt."* [43]

Ultimately though, while in no way minimising the significance and necessity of individual improvement and greater self-knowledge, it is very important to keep in mind whether or not these goals represent the main and highest purpose for human beings.

It is additionally important that the current focus on open-mindedness in Western society is recognised by Christians and fully taken on board when explaining their own beliefs. It's no good automatically dismissing various New Age teachings and experiences as *wild and wacky*, without first realising that similar views may exist for New Ageists and others when considering the claims of the Christian gospel. This message is, after all, based on the (not entirely obvious) premise that Ultimate Reality/God entered into our world through a virgin birth to an unmarried teenage Jewish girl.

So how to describe New Age? According to Wikipedia, this is a generic term covering a range of spiritual or religious beliefs and practices that developed in Western nations during the 1960s/70s; even though much of their substance dates back to the 18th and 19th centuries. New Age may also be known as *The Bride to Postmodernism*, which provided and still provides fertile soil for it to thrive and prosper. A particularly pithy definition of the overall ideology comes from an article in Time Magazine (December 1987), where it is stated to be *"a shifting kaleidoscope of beliefs, fads, and rituals."*

Russell Chandler, an American writer and award-winning journalist, provides a third and more comprehensive description, *"By and large, New Age is a modem revival of ancient religious traditions, along with a potpourri of influences: Eastern mysticism, modem philosophy and*

---

[43] Timothy Keller, *Walking With God Through Pain & Suffering.* Hodder & Stoughton, 2015, p.228.

psychology, science and science fiction, and the counterculture of the '50s and '60s... Also contributing to the New Age way of thinking is Chinese Taoism, which believes that there is a single principle underlying everything (the 'Tao'). *Ancient Gnosticism and its doctrine of enlightenment is also an influence, as well as strands of Neoplatonism, medieval witchcraft, Greek mythology, and Native American thought."*[44] In summary then: *syncretism on steroids*, although it should be emphasised that all of these influences, from the mundane to the very unusual, are most unlikely to be believed by a single person or even a specific people group.

There is so much that could be said about such an eclectic set of beliefs, and this without even including the apparently weird, complex, and, some might say, supportive world of quantum mechanics. However, at this stage, three main points come to mind. The first is that Eastern spirituality, particularly Pantheistic Monism (see chapter eight), appears to feature in much New Age thought and, second, that the Chinese *Tao* seems to be very similar to the *Logos,* central to Greek Stoicism. Third and finally, Alister McGrath considers New Age to relate to Christianity in like manner to the Gnosticism of the 2nd to 4th centuries; the superficial similarities (to the Christian faith) of both diverse, esoteric, and mystical movements arising from forced and heretical Scriptural interpretations. [45]

The obvious corollary is that few, if any, of the views relating to either Gnosticism or New Age are consistent with those of the apostles (the sent-out ones), or the early church fathers (certain Christian leaders, often academics, coming along for the next three hundred years or so), or indeed the great majority of modern scholars. Both ideologies are additionally loose enough to include Jesus; the Gnostics believing that His descent from heaven to Earth was only spiritual and not bodily, and New Age sometimes adding in Jesus Christ as one of the enlightened

---

[44] Russell Chandler, *Understanding the New Age.* Grand Rapids: Zondervan, 1991 & 1993, pp.43 & 45.
[45] Alister McGrath, *Christian Theology – An Introduction.* John Wiley & Sons Ltd, 2017, p.13.

masters, but certainly not as the unequivocal Son of God.

When it comes to living out their personal beliefs, New Ageists commonly rely on characteristics or *giftings* such as intuition, insight, instinct, feelings, emotions, imagination (not imaginary), signs, premonitions, visions and dreams. These are then usually checked by subsequent experiences and feelings (good or bad energy) and maybe more signs, with meditation often playing a prominent role. All of these features have positive aspects and thus a potential place in guiding us through this often difficult and problematic world.

So how do we judge between the offerings, particularly the more exotic, of New Age and the gospel of Jesus Christ – which one, if either, represents higher knowledge or *cosmic consciousness* (see below)? Are we solely dependent upon our backgrounds, opinions, preferences, and indeed pride and prejudices? (could be a book in there for someone). I think not. Following on from the aspiration at the start of chapter one, it seems essential when assessing the authenticity of an individual's apparent spiritual encounters, experiences, received messages etc., to check if these can be supported by independent objective evidence.

The latter appears to be absent in the above list of characteristics relevant to New Age beliefs, all of which fall within the subjective realm. It is, therefore, very difficult to ascertain the reliability of associated personal guidance and experience – do they originate from encounters with Ultimate Reality or from within the human mind or indeed from a more sinister source? It must be emphasised at this point that solely subjective experiences may well be entirely genuine, as per Kev's vision for me when I was in the psychiatric unit, and some of his subsequent dreams and premonitions. Nevertheless, while we remain entirely within the subjective, we will inevitably be vulnerable to deception. Additionally, in a largely existentialist and postmodern society, where each person determines their own truth and reality and what is true for one is generally not true for the other, how is it possible for anyone to reliably interpret and decide upon the credibility of another's spiritual insights and experiences?

To put it another way, it doesn't seem possible to validate New Age experiences and/or guidance, no matter how dramatic – everything has to remain inside the head, and judged accordingly. This is sometimes known as *fideism*, a system which is *justified* entirely by its own internal standards, with no confirmation from external sources, including other human beings, being relevant. Conversely, checking by means of both objective evidence and sharing/discussing with others are available to the Christian, the word given to me in November 2014 being particularly helpful in the latter respect. This is dealt with in detail at the end of part 1.

To further demonstrate the importance of having authentic and *reality-consistent* objective evidence, I cite James Sire's appraisal of a book called, The Aquarian Conspiracy (1980) by New Ageist, Marilyn Ferguson. Sire summarises the overall message as follows, *"What a glorious New Age is dawning: a new world peopled by healthy, well-adjusted, perfectly happy, absolutely blissed-out beings – no disease, no war, no famine, no pollution, just transcendent joy. What more could one want?"* He then responds to this by saying, *"Critics of this utopian euphoria want <u>one thing</u>: some reasonable, <u>objective</u> assurance that such a vision is more than an opium pipe dream. But during the moments the self is immersed in subjective certainty, no reasons are necessary, no objectivity is required."* [46]

Some of the teachings and practices of New Age, such as Russell Chandler's earlier reference to *medieval witchcraft*, are clearly occultic, and James Sire picks up on a further relevant concept/belief known as *animism*. His full description is abbreviated by Mark Bair, who writes, *"Animism is the orientation of the so-called 'primal' or pagan religions, which see the universe as inhabited by countless spiritual beings. These spirits range from vicious to kind. To get by, people have to placate the*

---

[46] James Sire, *The Universe Next Door.* InterVarsity *Press,* U.S.A., 2004, p.181.

evil spirits and woo the good spirits. To our aid come the witch doctors and shamans who attempt to control the spirit world." [47] Sire also states the following, *"ultimately there is a unity to all of life – that is, the cosmos is a continuum of spirit and matter; 'animals may be ancestors of men, people may change into animals, trees and stones may possess souls."* [48]

Although I have no direct experience of shamanism or similar, I do know what it's like, due to attempted suicides and an initial lack of repentance, to end up on Satan's turf – it is real, it is horrible, and it is terrifying! I therefore consider myself sufficiently qualified to at least make a few related comments. As a very broad overview, shamans attempt to communicate with, and influence, the spirit world, from whence they acquire *hidden* knowledge supposedly concerning those who have died and/or predictions relating to the futures of those still in the land of the living (divination). This knowledge may be received either as external messages or involve changes in consciousness, typically by means of a trance, when the shamans become temporary mouthpieces for demons who speak through them (the *umbrella* term for both types is *channelling*). The revealed information, even on occasions in a language unfamiliar to the shaman and sometimes apparently proceeding from the pit of the stomach, can be very detailed and intimate, and may also occur in conjunction with some kind of healing; thus indicating to those present that everything is genuine and absolutely *pucker*.

Only it isn't! People have been taken in by Satan, the master liar and deceiver, who masquerades as an *angel of light*. (2 Corinthians 11:14) And human intuition, instinct and insight on their own, no matter how good, will give absolutely no help at all in this dark and most dangerous spiritual arena.

---

[47] Mark Bair, *The Postmodern Phenomena of New Age Spirituality: Examples in Popular Literature.* Ashland Theological Journal 27, 1995, p.60.
[48] James Sire, *The Universe Next Door.* InterVarsity Press, U.S.A., 2004, p.177.

One of the keys to a greater understanding of New Age thinking is to appreciate why and how the movement began. This can seemingly be traced back to the fact that many young and disillusioned people in the West, possibly influenced in part by the Beatles' encounters with the Indian guru, Maharishi Mahesh Yogi (originator of transcendental meditation), were looking to the East for new ways of thinking and living in the 1960s/70s but found Eastern spirituality simply too foreign and difficult to be fully taken on board. They were accordingly searching for a new consciousness along more Western lines, something that would hopefully be less demanding and counterintuitive. Thus while Eastern spirituality appears to be the main ingredient of New Age for many adherents, its specific brand has undoubtedly been compromised by Western influences.

New Age thought accordingly corresponds fairly closely with the East in its orientation towards mystical experience, which typically rejects reason as an acceptable guide for spiritual matters; but unlike prevailing Eastern teachings where much, including the physical universe and human personality, is considered to be *maya* (illusory - deceptive), places great importance and value on the individual.

The self is, therefore, considered to be the prime reality, with the visible universe also having physical substance. It is not illusory, and is accordingly subject to the laws of nature and thus *cause and effect*. This visible and known universe corresponds to our five senses and what we might term our *ordinary* consciousness. However, say the New Ageists, there is a second invisible universe that can be accessed via *doors of perception* such as transcendental meditation, trance, drugs, ritualised dance, certain types of music and so on. This second universe is not familiar to most of us earthlings, relating, as it does, to an abnormal state of consciousness where many things of a seemingly impossible nature, such as two bodies occupying the same space at the same time, are allowed to exist. This is known as *cosmic consciousness*, with proponents of this concept/experience including philosophers Carl Jung and Abraham Maslow, and the novelist Aldous Huxley.

The term cosmic consciousness was introduced in 1901 by a Canadian psychiatrist, R M Bucke, and defined in a classic study by William James as follows; *"The prime characteristic of cosmic consciousness is a consciousness of the cosmos, that is, of the life and order of the universe. Along with consciousness of the cosmos there occurs an intellectual enlightenment which alone would place the individual on a new plane of existence – would make him a member of a new species... With these come what may be called a sense of immortality, a consciousness of eternal life, not a conviction that he shall have this but the consciousness that he has it already."* [49]

Cosmic consciousness, alternatively known as *self-realisation*, is considered to be the core experience of the New Age Movement or the *New Consciousness*; wherein traditional categories of time, space and morality tend to vanish and a person, or perhaps more accurately their *Higher Self*, becomes one with the whole cosmos. Indeed, even beyond this state, as there is an eventual recognition that the self creates all reality and is, so to speak, both the cosmos and the cosmos-maker. For instance, the American actress Shirley MacLaine says, *"Know that you are God; know that you are the universe."* [50]

David Spangler, a leader of a Spiritual Dynamic Experiment known as Findhorn (in Scotland), goes even further than MacLaine, *"I AM now the Life of a new heaven and a new earth. Others must draw upon Me and unite with Me to build its forms.... There is always only what I AM, but I have revealed Myself in new Life and new Light and new Truth...It is My function through this centre* (Findhorn) *to demonstrate what I AM through the medium of group evolution."* [51] Much as I am tempted, I refuse to comment directly on these claims and simply suggest that comparison be made with the subsequent selected *I AM* statements of Jesus Christ.

---

[49] William James, *Varieties of Religious Experience*. P.306. (Based on Gifford Lectures delivered in Edinburgh, 1901/1902).

[50] Shirley MacLaine, *Dancing In The Light*. Bantam Doubleday Dell Publishing, 1987, p.350.

[51] David Spangler, *Revelation: The Birth of a New Age*. San Francisco: Rainbow Bridge, 1976, pp.110 & 121.

There are various kindred reports of profound spiritual, psychological, and physical experiences, quite often in conjunction with mind-altering drugs such as LSD, Mescaline and Ayahuasca. Some of these relate to certain people, such as MacLaine and Spangler, perceiving the self as a *god* in *control of creation*, with descriptions of how they have seen themselves in maybe thousands of previous incarnations. Many proponents of New Age additionally consider that the universe represents a closed system, whereby nothing can get in and nothing can get out (an opinion often shared by atheistic scientists). It, therefore, follows that there can be no outside involvement but rather that everything is controlled by the self operating from the inside.

The general consistency of the above is confirmed by *The World's Religions, A Lion Handbook* which summarily states, *"The message of the New Age is fundamentally that we are more than we imagine. If only we can understand our divinity, and our oneness with all creation, we can bring peace to ourselves and contribute to the evolution of our planet."*[52]

It's perhaps not surprising that adherents are often convinced that if they really believe in themselves, they can, given time and effort, achieve absolutely anything. Not that it isn't a really good thing to have a positive approach; indeed, it is probable that most of us can improve in many areas of our lives, perhaps massively more than we think. Nevertheless, however hard I trained, I know that I could never have broken 10 seconds for the 100 metres (this wasn't achieved by a white man until 2010) and could not have been an academic of the standing of C.S. Lewis, even if I studied for centuries.

There have been many different and colourful New Age experiences, and I choose just one example, which I find particularly interesting. It is described in a book called, *Embraced by the Light*, by Betty Jean Eadie and encapsulated in Mark Bair's 1995 paper. Unlike Shirley MacLaine and David Spangler, whose views are probably towards the periphery of New Age thinking, Eadie is generally considered to represent the middle

---

[52] *The World's Religions, A Lion Handbook*. Lion Publishing plc, 1994, p.405.

ground of this ideology. The following most informative dialectic is quoted, in a slightly abbreviated form, from Bair's paper:

Bair - *"As I read the book, it became obvious why this book is so popular. It affirms virtually everything the average American would want to hear while having not a shred of material that would offend. If ever there was a book that could be the spiritual undergirding for political correctness, this is it. What is the basis of its legitimacy? The experience of being temporarily dead, of course. Eadie claims to have had an encounter with angels and Jesus Himself while her physical body lay dead in a hospital room. She describes her experience in vivid imagery."*

Eadie - *"I felt a surge of energy ... and my spirit was suddenly drawn out through my chest and pulled upward, as if by a giant magnet... I was above the bed, hovering near the ceiling ... My new body was weightless and extremely mobile ... Before I could move, three men suddenly appeared at my side ... A kind of glow emanated from them.... I sensed in them great spirituality, knowledge, and wisdom... I began to think of them as monks-mostly because of the robes—and I knew I could trust them ... They had been with me for 'eternities', they said... The fact of pre-Earth life crystallized in my mind."*

Bair – *"Notice that Eadie perceived things non-cognitively. Like others we have seen, she places a premium on this 'higher mode' of understanding. The implication is that if something is really important or true it will have to come to you by bypassing your mind. Notice also her basis for trusting the spirit beings. She 'sensed' it. It was not by evaluating the content of their claims. .....The beauty of their being tells us nothing about whether they are benevolent or malevolent spirits. Eadie's Mormon leanings stand out as well with her claim to have an eternal spirit that had known these beings from before her entrance into her mortal body ('pre-Earth existence'). She goes on to describe some more non-verbal intuitive communication."*

Eadie – *"They somehow communicated a feeling of peace and told me not to worry, that everything would be all right. As this feeling came in me, I sensed their deep love and concern. These feelings and other thoughts were communicated to me from spirit to spirit – from intelligence to intelligence. At first, I thought they were using their mouths, but this was because I was used to people 'speaking'. They communicated much more rapidly and completely, in a manner they referred to as 'pure knowledge'. The closest word we have in English to define it is telepathy, but even that does not describe the full process. I felt their emotions and intents. I felt their love. I experienced their feelings."*

Bair – *"Eadie displays the frightening faith in the authority of feelings that has so engulfed our culture. If you feel love, how could it be questioned? Like Deepak Chopra (a modern 'alternative healing guru', who considers that our perception of reality is the key to life), Eadie also has her own version of creating your own reality. She believes that 'Simply by thinking positive thoughts and speaking positive words we attract positive energy ... We can create our own surroundings by the thoughts we think..' Then, in an incredible example of reality turned on its head she says: 'I understood that life is lived most fully in the imagination--that, ironically, imagination is the key to reality"...." One may wonder, was her near-death experience imagination or reality? Eadie says she feels no need to give evidence for the tale* (and others in her book). *The authority is in the experience."*

Bair concludes, *"The popularity of Eadie's book is a chilling example of the epistemological relativism discussed earlier. If nothing is true, then everything is true."* [53] - as per the earlier Chesterton quote.

This summary and final quotation is again from James Sire, *"The danger of self-deception – theists and naturalists alike would add the 'certainty' of self-deception - is the great weakness of the new consciousness at this point. No theist or naturalist, no one at all, can deny the 'experience' of perceiving oneself to be a god, a spirit, a devil or a cockroach. Too many people give such reports. But so long as self alone is king, so long as imagination is presupposed to be reality, so long as seeing is being, the*

---

[53] Mark Bair, *The Postmodern Phenomena of New Age Spirituality: Examples in Popular Literature*. Ashland Theological Journal 27, 1995, pp.74-76.

imagining, seeing self remains securely locked in its private universe - the only one there is. So long as the self likes what it imagines and is truly in control of what it imagines, others on the 'outside' have nothing to offer." [54] - fideism.

Amidst all that has been discussed thus far, it is interesting to recall that New Age considers us to be the prime reality and even *gods*, atheistic science considers us to be *accidents*, and true Christianity and Judaism consider us to be *unique beings made in the (spiritual) image of God* who tells us (inwardly) that we are important, precious and loved.

Before starting to research *Political Correctness (PC)*, I simply thought, presumably like many others, that it was a fairly recent ideology which, although originally necessary and beginning well, had now become a bit of a joke or *madness*. These views are indeed backed up by a Wikipedia definition and a couple of ridiculous examples from the internet: Wikipedia – *"Since the late 1980s, the term has come to refer to avoiding language or behaviour that can be seen as excluding, marginalising, or insulting groups of people considered disadvantaged or discriminated against, especially groups defined by sex or race."*[55] That is a much-needed emphasis on acceptance and inclusivity, and thus very positive.

The first internet example concerns a UK recruiter's job advert for *reliable* and *hard-working* applicants being rejected by the jobcentre as it could be offensive to unreliable and lazy people, with the second relating to a UK Council banning the term *brainstorming* and replacing it with *thought showers*, because local lawmakers thought the term may offend epileptics. There are also many other absurd examples out and about in society which, if allowed to prevail, could end up with the loss of the great British sense of humour and our ability to laugh at ourselves.

---

[54] James Sire, *The Universe Next Door.* InterVarsity Press, U.S.A., 2004, p.183.
[55] Wikipedia

However, it turns out that there is a lot more to it than that, although a book of this nature can inevitably give only a broad outline. The roots of PC are understood to go back to the 1st World War, although it only became a formalised political ideology in 1923; emerging from a think tank called the *Frankfurt School* (subsequently, *The Institute of Social Research*) in Germany. Its main purpose was to determine why Russian Communism was not spreading into Western civilisation as a whole, and recommendations were then put in place to remedy this situation. These are typically referred to as, *The Frankfurt School 11 Point Plan*, and comprise the following:

1. The creation of racism offences.
2. Continual change to create confusion.
3. The teaching of sex and homosexuality to children.
4. The undermining of schools and teachers' authority.
5. Huge immigration to destroy national identity.
6. The promotion of excessive drinking.
7. Emptying the churches.
8. An unreliable legal system with bias against the victim of crime.
9. Dependency on the state or state benefits.
10. Control and *dumbing down* of media.
11. Encouraging the breakdown of the family.

Sound familiar in UK Society 2020?

It is generally held that the 1923 ideology is best described as transforming the beliefs and theories of original (economic) Marxism into *Cultural Marxism*, although the term *Political Correctness* was soon employed to disguise its left-wing roots and beliefs. Quoting from a paper titled, *The Origins of Political Correctness,* by American author and speaker, Bill Lind, "*Economic Marxism says that all of history is determined by ownership of means of production. Cultural Marxism, or Political Correctness, says that all history is determined by power, by which groups defined in terms of race, sex, etc., have power over which other groups. Nothing else matters. All literature, indeed, is about that. Everything in the past is about that one thing."* [56]

Lind also refers to the Italian Marxist theorist, Antonio Gramsci, who considered that the workers would never see their true class interests, as defined by Marxism, until they were freed from Western culture, the capitalist order, and particularly the Christian Religion.

Rather than producing any viable alternative, PC proponents simply called for the most destructive and universal criticism possible, which they considered to be the best method of bringing down the current order. They then endeavoured to achieve this objective primarily by altering peoples' speech and thought patterns, directing that any vocalising of personal beliefs was disrespectful to others and had to be avoided to make up for past prejudice and injustices. There were also further tweaks to ensure the suppression of any discussions that might reveal the lack of common sense within PC ideology, which used fear as its main weapon of enforcement - in Western democracies, the subtle fear of saying the wrong thing and for totalitarian regimes, such as fascism and communism, the fear of vicious reprisals.

It is clear that the above undertaking has had a significant influence on the shaping of today's UK society with many of the beliefs and traits emerging from *The Frankfurt School 11 Point Plan* being evident. One of the associated results, as touched on previously, is the powerful resistance to Christianity from traditional UK media, particularly television companies, meaning that the many excellent scientists who happen to be Christians are not given relevant platforms to air their views. Although the BBC has gone on record denying any anti-Christian stance, the radio show host Simon Mayo, in an interview with the Daily Telegraph as far back as January 2010, stated that, *"The BBC is driving religion to the margins"* and *"...is at the forefront of the new atheism."* [57]

---

[56] Bill Lind, *The Origins of Political Correctness*. Speech delivered on 5th February 2000. https://www.academia.org/the-origins-of-political-correctness/

[57] Simon Mayo, *The Daily Telegraph*, London, January 2010

The BBC has also played a leading role in an initiative, now essentially complete, to get rid of BC (Before Christ) and AD (Anno Domini – *in the year of our Lord*), and replace them by BCE (Before Common Era) and CE (Common Era). Boris Johnson, then a journalist, reacted strongly against this in a Daily Telegraph article published in September 2011. This was titled, *'BC or BCE? The BBC's edict on how we date events is AD (absolute drivel)',* and included the statement, *"Objecting to the use of Christ's birth to mark each year is puerile political correctness."* [58] Yep, that's Boris for you.

In any event, this *achievement*, which did not affect the related Gregorian calendar, the most used civil calendar in the world today (including China), is hardly protecting the rights of disadvantaged groups, as per the earlier Wikipedia definition - unless of course, we include the BBC in this bracket.

Again, in an episode of the ITV series *Britain's Got Talent*, aired 14th April 2018, a gospel choir gave a very competent rendition of the *Negro-spiritual* song, *Oh Happy Day*, but managed to leave out all references to Jesus. It certainly seemed rather unfinished when, instead of singing the line, *when Jesus washed my sins away*, the choir repeatedly sang the phrase, *Oh Happy Day* with ever-increasing intensity right up until the end of the song. Anyway, the judges and audience loved it; PC? – certainly looks like it to me. I say more about this later, but for the time being it does seem rather strange that, although this choir apparently could not sing the name of Jesus in connection with a worship song, phrases such as *for Christ's sake* or *Jesus Christ* are frequently used as curses in many TV programmes.

And then, as touched on previously, there are now plans to bring in gender-neutral pronouns such as *ze* or *they* instead of *he* or *she*, with some universities even proposing that they will mark students down if they persist in adopting the traditional method. Can this enterprise, if widely adopted, actually result in anything but confusion? It obviously

---

[58] Boris Johnson, *The Daily Telegraph*, London, September 2011

doesn't conform to *utilitarianism*, which promotes the view that the correct and best courses of action are those that provide the most benefit for the most people. While clearly not appropriate for all life circumstances, this approach can be effective in curbing the disproportionate demands of certain minority lobbyists, which may well infringe the rights of others.

It's very easy to go on. For instance, what about the celebration of Christmas? This is now so commercialised and generally removed from the spiritual arena that some people feel obliged to take out expensive loans (check out some of the truly immoral APRs) simply to cope with this event. And while I'm on it: Oh Lord, please save us from '*Crimbo*' – a truly dreadful word.

Enough ranting, and a minor degree of redress. The BBC 2 programme titled, *The Debt Saviours* relating to the work of CAP, aired 5th October 2018, was excellent, and BBC 1's *Songs of Praise* is now decidedly better than in the past.

Moving away from the Christian aspect, and on to some of the many other areas where PC exerts very significant influences. This is a direct quote from an article by Zoie O'Brien for the 12th August 2017 edition of the Daily Express, *"Asian rape gangs who target white teenagers are not handed longer jail sentences because of political correctness and fear among the judiciary, the Government's senior legal advisor has said."* [59]

Another result of PC is that some doctors today are reluctant to even gently and compassionately use words such as *fat* or *obese*, even though no change in eating habits may well result in a patient's death. And why is it that some male scientists are now having to fear *knee-jerk* condemnation and suspension for expressing views such as women have made lesser contributions to science than men? It seems to me that they are simply stating the broad truth, although it must equally be

---

[59] Zoie O'Brien, The Daily Express, London, August 2017

emphasised that discriminatory male dominance plus traditional lifestyle roles have radically restricted the scientific opportunities available to women.

In any event, why this fixation that we must all be the same? Can't women generally be better than men in some areas and vice-versa? All people are equal in worth, but it is clearly not possible, or indeed desirable, for them to be equal in capability and function. Some are brighter than others and some are stronger etc. The object then must not be to make all people the same, but rather to give everyone equal opportunities. Make no mistake: in Western democracies that pride themselves on their freedom of speech, PC is the No.1 enemy.

So that represents a brief commentary on UK society 2020, insofar as it reflects some of the deeper issues of life. In summary, there are clearly certain advantages over previous generations, whose Christian legacy is still evident in the form of the *social gospel* and, to a lesser degree, moral standards. The associated beliefs, however, while still impacting and transforming lives at individual and localised levels, have only a peripheral influence on the UK's overarching spiritual climate. This has resulted in a UK culture containing many individual and corporate voids, which are being filled by various atheistic entities resulting from the effects of Postmodernism (no absolutes) and Political Correctness (eroding freedom of speech and thought) plus New Age (general rejection of reason and rationality). When we add in the fact that science is usually portrayed as atheistic by traditional media and that many young people are in the grip of the superficialities common to much social media, then a no plausibility structure society is surely a very fitting overall description.

The answer to the question posed at the end of the previous chapter thus appears to be self-evident. Today's primarily secular, complicated, and often morally directionless UK society is ill-equipped to seriously contemplate the possibility of relationships with any transcendent Ultimate Reality/God that might be reaching into our nation.

As noted previously, the preferred and surely most reliable method of appraising worldviews is to utilise relevant objective evidence backed up by consistent personal subjective experience(s) or vice-versa. Indeed, I can cite my conversion as one example of this, becoming *born-again* before I could properly comprehend its meaning and implications; completely unaware, that similar experiences had already transformed the lives of hundreds of millions of others and were known about and explained in many parts of the NT. Having recounted this personal experience in part 1, the next chapter accordingly moves on to the objective.

CHAPTER FOUR

The Bible and Jesus Christ:
Can the Record be Trusted? (the truth criterion)

This chapter hardly needs any introduction beyond its title. Consistent with the current slogan for a leading garden wood treatment, *It does exactly what it says on the tin*, the purpose here is to examine the truthfulness and reliability of both named entities - that is the Bible and, most particularly, Jesus Christ.

Strong indications for the existence of Ultimate Reality have already been discussed. Of these, attention is particularly drawn to the *rationality observed without*, such as the compatibility of the cosmos' elegant mathematical/physical laws with human minds, and the *rationality experienced within*, such as the moral law; both of which appear universal to the human race. Although these features give no definitive insights into the nature of Ultimate Reality, they nevertheless point in the general direction of some kind of superior life-form with personality and intelligence.

When we move on to Jesus Christ's claims to Ultimate Reality/God and the core message of the Christian gospel, there is no avoiding a stark either/or decision. Does this gospel represent the greatest-ever news for planet Earth or the only other possible alternative of complete fabrication and hence the greatest hoax ever perpetrated on the human race?

There is certainly no doubt that the apostles and the early church fathers believed the former to be the case, and also considered this whole matter to be of crucial importance. For example, the Apostle Paul, in his first letter to the Corinthians, says this, *If only for this* (present) *life we* (the believers) *have hope in Christ, we are to be pitied more than all men.* (1 Corinthians 15:19) And, *If the dead are not raised, 'Let us eat and drink, for tomorrow we die.'* (1 Corinthians 15:32b) In other words, if there is no life after physical death, then everything, apart from making the enjoyment of every single moment of this present life our absolute priority, is a pointless waste; because who knows how much time we have left before total and utter oblivion. Live only for today, as per hedonism.

As a bit of background, the Apostle Paul, who wrote about 30% of the NT, experienced an amazing conversion on the road to Damascus. Formerly known as Saul (of Tarsus), he was an extremely strict Jew and had made it his chief priority to imprison, and potentially murder, followers of Jesus, whom he considered to represent a dangerous sect and threat to Judaism. The NT book of Acts records that he was poleaxed and temporarily blinded by a stupendous encounter with the risen Christ, subsequently resulting in a radically changed life and mission. The 'Corinthians' were the believers in the newly formed Church at Corinth.

It may also be helpful, having already considered some of the general similarities between various major religions, to keep in mind three key concepts. These concern the possible essence of Ultimate Reality, the conditions for and subsequent nature of any potential relationships with ourselves, and the likelihood of this entity actually giving us some help in this direction. Reflections of this type are more likely to throw up differences than similarities, and one would like to think that they form at least some part of our schools' Comparative Religion studies – I have my doubts though.

Family Bibles are great things. Typically large and heavy and dating back 100+ years, they can be used for so many different purposes. For instance, they can be displayed in a bookcase, along with Shakespeare and Dickens, to indicate that we are well-read; or they can be stood upon immediately before a family photograph to increase our apparent height by several inches; or, best of all, they can be used to smash up a ganglion cyst should we ever have one (this latter application has been experienced by the manager at my gym – I have no details!). In any event, everyone is cool when the Bible is talked about in this way. However, this coolness immediately vanishes for some people if the Bible is ever referred to as the *Word of God*. On the occasions when I have attempted to promote this view, those listening have sometimes responded by pointing out that the sacred scriptures of many religions make similar claims, and who am I to pronounce such a judgement. They may even have added something like, "If you'd been born in another country, your whole method of thinking and belief system would be very different – you need to get out more."

However, given that my experience of church and the Bible (albeit rather limited) seem to have been entirely negative growing up, I had, unsurprisingly, first come to the conclusion that, *in the very unlikely event of me ever adopting a religion, it certainly wouldn't be Christianity*. I, therefore, consistently maintained that the Bible was complete rubbish and, unlike the religious *weirdos* who believed that stuff, the thought of basing my life on a single book (and man-made at that) would have been far too restrictive for a free spirit like me. As I have said before, this opinion continued right up to the time when I read the Bible for myself.

Similar attitudes to this still exist today, with the Bible being rubbished by individuals and groups who have hardly read it. And Christians, who may well be the only *Bible* that people do get to read, are not always the best advert for an incredible gospel (the word means *good news*). The reasons for this no doubt vary but, going forward, it is hoped that Christians are not always perceived as being against everything, but rather as people who have something very positive to offer society. As part of this, it is paramount that believers cease to get hung up over issues that are simply not that important, and definitely shouldn't belong with their core beliefs. All of this can result in non-believers, listening to an explanation of Christianity or some related topic, judging the messenger rather than the message. That was certainly my reaction back in the day, based almost entirely on the energy coming across (was the particular religious *weirdo* getting worked up and beginning to gabble?), rather than considering that *ze* (I think it works here) could possibly be conveying actual truth.

However, what if the Bible is indeed the Word of God, and what if the principal player, Jesus Christ, doesn't represent man-made religion (including Cultural Christianity) reaching out, but rather Ultimate Reality/God reaching in? What then?

But I'm getting ahead of myself. Having banged on so much about the need to substantiate spiritual words and experiences by relevant objective evidence, I must now engage in a bit of *expectation management*. In particular, the concepts of *faith* and *certainty*, and how these should be viewed when considering spiritual issues and connected matters. As it happens, I have not as yet met anyone who doubts that they exist or genuinely believes they are part of another person's dream or similar; and certainly, to my knowledge, I have always taken the fact of my existence for granted. However, amongst others, the 17th century French philosopher and mathematician, René Descartes, struggled with the whole question of his existence, before coming up with the phrase for which he is best known, *I think* (or reflect), *therefore I am*. Not being a philosopher myself, I have to assume that this phrase does the business, and René and his mates certainly seemed happy enough with it.

In current times, Roger Forster and fellow academic, Paul Marston, have co-authored a book called *Reason, Science and Faith*, which contains a comprehensive chapter devoted to this topic. They conclude, *"Current thinking, then, makes it very difficult to ignore or 'reduce away' the existence of the self-conscious 'self'."* [60] This statement and our natural instincts are therefore appealing to an extremely high level of certainty, and it seems to me self-evident that even the strongest and most robust *spiritual* faith cannot go beyond this.

So what is faith? According to Richard Dawkins, in a YouTube recorded debate with John Lennox, *"Faith is what you have when you don't have*

---

[60] Roger Forster, Paul Marston, *Reason, Science and Faith*. Monarch Books,1999, p.99.

any evidence." [61] This rather seems to me that Dawkins is thinking of blind faith, which is, of course, more or less worthless. Anyhow, Lennox responds by asking Dawkins whether he has faith in his wife, and, if he does, whether he has any supporting evidence. There then follows a slightly embarrassed pause on Dawkins' behalf until he says *"Let's generalise it, never mind about my wife!"* [62]

The real truth is that all people use (reasoned) faith much of the time. For instance, as I sit here typing in our first-floor study, I automatically assume by faith that the chair and the floor supporting me won't collapse, the ceiling will not fall in on me, and the computer monitor is not going to explode in my face. And that's without even worrying about where my next heartbeat is coming from, something for which I have only past evidence.

However, some people (and I think I used to be one of them) tend to believe, again probably unconsciously, that the whole essence of *faith*, as played out in the context of everyday life, becomes appreciably devalued when used in connection with anything *spiritual*. This is simply not true; both usages represent the same animal. Although only one of many, my particular definition of faith is, *something that goes beyond*. For example, take the case of a mathematician who cannot yet swim, but is determined to add this to his skill set. What can he do? In the first instance, he can undertake buoyancy calculations to show that human bodies can float in water (objective evidence), and then he can go to the local swimming pool where he can observe this happening (subjective experience). But at some point he has to go beyond this by faith and actually jump into the pool himself, resulting in the experience of swimming also becoming true for him (I know he could have met with failure, but it's always wise not to press the analogy too far).

This objective evidence + subjective experience + reasoned jump of faith seems to closely mirror the way C.S. Lewis became a Christian (told

---

[61] Richard Dawkins, John Lennox, *Part of 'God Delusion' debate.* 3rd October 2007. https://www.youtube.com /watch?v=3zPO-JUpf8U.
[62] Ibid.

later). Other peoples' conversions (including mine) no doubt differ significantly and perhaps cannot be summarised in such an analytical format, but all of the above three elements are likely to be present in some form and at some stage. Incidentally, atheism is a worldview and requires faith.

When it comes to the reliability of current main versions of the Bible and associated interpretation, the following discussion may be seen as a summary *heads up* concerning some of the main points, as considered in more detail in the appendix.

Perhaps the first thing to grasp is the incredible abundance of manuscripts upon which present-day Bibles, particularly the NT, are based. Indeed, the amount of relevant documentation is far more than that relating to ancient classical authors, such as Homer, Plato, Herodotus, Seneca and those involved in recording the lives of Julius Caesar, Alexander the Great and other leaders.

For example, if all the NT manuscripts could be stacked up on top of each other, their total height would be approximately one mile, compared with an average four feet high stack for ancient classical authors - whose writings are considered to be essentially trustworthy by most historians. Is all this amazing amount of material completely faultless and *golden*? Probably not; but there is so much quality information that the current estimation of NT accuracy is of the order of 99 to 99.5%. This is far too high for any doubts to exist concerning the reliability of any recorded events or main teachings. Or, to put it another way, while most scholars accept there to be a number of minor (copying) discrepancies and apparent ambiguities, these are invariably of little consequence and may even reduce as ongoing archaeological finds provide further clarification.

The Bible (*Byblos* in the Greek and Biblia in the Latin - both meaning *books*) is a document with its own unique style/format and quite remarkable history. It is a collection of 66 books (39 OT + 27 NT), written in three different languages over a period of almost 1500 years by a total of 40 separate authors from every walk of life - kings, fishermen, tax collectors, shepherds, prophets and a physician etc. Yet, as I have seen for myself, there is an amazing level of consistency throughout, highly indicative of some kind of *chief editor* who actually held the post for the required period of nearly $1^1/_2$ millennia. There is accordingly continuity between the Old Testament (OT) and New Testament (NT), or, as the $4^{th}/5^{th}$ century theologian, Augustine of Hippo put it, *"The New Testament lies hidden in the Old, and the Old Testament is unveiled in the New."* [63] This prophetic nature of the Bible, particularly concerning Jesus Christ, is extremely impressive, and a characteristic that is expanded upon later in the chapter.

The NT writer, Luke, is, in particular, held to be a first-class historian with Scottish archaeologist and leading NT scholar, William Ramsay (1851-1939), concluding, after 30 years of study, *"Luke is a historian of the first rank; not merely are his statements of fact trustworthy... this author should be placed along with the very greatest of historians."* [64]

Indeed, in terms of trustworthiness, archaeological finds have revealed Luke to be error-free when naming a total of 32 countries, 54 cities and 9 Islands in his gospel and the Acts of the Apostles, which he is believed to have also written. He is accordingly considered to be an excellent source of information for 1st century Palestine and the governing Roman Empire. This is not to say that the other NT writings are any less reliable and/or uncorroborated by relevant archaeological discoveries, but rather that Luke seems to have deliberately set out to make the historical record a central feature. [65]

The Bible, with an estimated six billion copies having been printed since 1815, is the unchallenged best-selling book of all time and is often

---

[63] Augustine of Hippo, as cited by Alister McGrath, *Christian Theology – An Introduction, Sixth Edition.* John Wiley & Sons Ltd, 2017, p.116.

[64] William Ramsay, *The Bearing of Recent Discovery on the Trustworthiness of the New Testament*: London: Hodder and Stoughton, 1915, p. 222.

[65] As far as this book is concerned, it is deemed satisfactory to assume that Palestine, seemingly first named as such in about 450 BC by the Greek historian, Herodotus, equates to Israel – that is the Promised Land, originally known as Canaan.

excluded from book bestsellers' lists simply because it would always be top. The whole Bible and solely NT section have been translated into approximately 670 and 1,500 languages respectively, with more than 2,100 languages having a translation of at least one of its grand total of 66 books. By comparison, the Quran and the Hindu scriptures have both been translated into a little over 100 languages. Jesus prophesied that *"..this gospel of the kingdom will be preached in the whole world as a testimony to all nations..."*(Matthew 24:14) This is, therefore, now well advanced with current projections, based on the very significant advantages due to computing, indicating that Bible translation will have commenced in all untouched estimated 5,000 world languages by 2050.

When it comes to interpretation, perhaps the most frequent question asked of Christians, including by me in pre-conversion days, is, "You don't take the Bible literally do you?" I guess the correct answer to this question has to be, "yes, when the particular passage demands it", and "no, when it doesn't." This must surely be the right approach because there are simply so many included literary genres; some of which, such as poetry, songs, and wisdom sayings/proverbs, enable the expression and visualisation of beliefs and experiences etc. in a manner beyond that possible using only prose. And, most of the time, determining which genre is the correct one is not difficult. For instance, when the prophet Isaiah says, *"...the mountains and hills will burst into song before you, and all the trees of the field will clap their hands..."* (Isaiah 55:12), he is clearly talking about great joy, and to take this passage literally would accordingly be rather ridiculous. Conversely, when C.S. Lewis commented, while not yet a believer, that the gospels *"read more like reports than stories"* [66], he was recognising their factual nature and that a literal approach was, therefore, the most appropriate.

While the NT writers all agree on the fundamentals of Jesus' life and ministry (for example, there is total unison concerning His crucifixion and resurrection), they are often putting forward their own specific agendas as appropriate for Jewish, Greek, or Roman recipients (John

---

[66] C.S. Lewis, *Surprised by Joy.* Geoffrey Bles (UK), Harcourt Brace (US), 1955.

also provides a wider overall context than the other three gospel writers). It is, therefore, hardly surprising that a comparison of the different NT accounts reveals some variation concerning the importance of and the related need to record certain lesser events, and that some details, although not contradictory *per se*, are reported somewhat differently. This is actually indicative of honesty and integrity, giving no suggestion of collusion between the writers. *Undesigned coincidences*, where there seem to be unplanned connections between two or more accounts, give further support to this view.

It should additionally be recognised that all language has limitations, and especially so when considering God and related topics. These entities are always *like something*, as we have no direct comparisons here on Earth. That is why associated descriptions require word constructs such as analogy, symbolism, anthropomorphism [67] and the like. However, this does not mean that these convey no real meaning and are accordingly irrelevant – far from it. For instance, when I recalled, in part 1, how the thought of trying to get out of bed had often seemed like having to climb Mount Everest, the general meaning was abundantly clear. Nobody was going to say that I didn't have the right to use that analogy because I had no experience of mountaineering. All the above word constructs are thus entirely valid, informative and reliable when used appropriately, although it is very important to allow space for the whole question of mystery.

Mention should also be made of *accommodating language*. The Bible is intended to be relevant to all nations and all generations; and it would thus be utterly pointless for it to include teachings concerning superstring theory, quantum mechanics or Einstein's theories of

---

[67] Anthropomorphism is where there is an attempt to transfer the meaning of a word from one kingdom to another. For instance, where it talks in the Bible about the *Arm of God*, it is referring to the universal power and authority of God, rather than suggesting that He actually has arms. Similarly, when Richard Dawkins named one of his Books *The Selfish Gene*, he was using this phrase as a way of expressing the gene-centred view of evolution, as opposed to describing a stressed-out little gene sulking and fretting over its required role of coding for amino acids/protein.

relativity. Even today, very few people understand these subjects, and then only partially. So, to ensure that all might understand, the Bible *accommodates* our limitations as human beings by generally using straightforward and fairly simple language (assuming a modern translation is read), which should give us no particular problems.

For instance, when the Bible talks about the sun rising and travelling across the sky, it is simply using accommodating or everyday language still common to us today. Most current newspapers give daily times of sunrise and sunset, and do not talk instead about the Earth's spin on an axis of rotation tilted at an angle of 23.4 degrees from its orbital axis about the sun resulting in first and final visibilities of this medium-sized star at such and such hours/minutes.

Of the various criticisms levelled against the Bible during recent times, there are two that seem to crop up again and again and are, therefore, probably best considered earlier rather than later. The first of these is that the Bible was written by human beings and not Ultimate Reality/God/Jesus Christ. This was actually the norm for ancient literature with, for example, the lives of Alexander the Great and Julius Caesar plus the Quran and most other major religious teachings being recorded by various writers and historians, some known and others not. However, what about more recent parallels? Do they exist or not? Yes, I think there are loads.

Take my own business, for example. I must have designed thousands of reinforced concrete piles (these also hurt if you sit on them), and yet I never placed any concrete or fixed any steel and only very rarely got involved with on-site supervision as I generally had no responsibility for workmanship – *thank God*. But the nature of the design had its own style and particular assumptions, both of which commonly exhibited certain differences to those of other designers. So although the piles were 100% constructed by others, they had my *spirit* within them. This is the claim made for the Bible; although it was written down by human beings, the actual guiding force is professed to be God's Spirit within them.

The building of the present St Paul's Cathedral (1668-1711), attributed to Sir Christopher Wren, represents a second and more macro example of the human spirit behind a construction project. This is because, although, as architectural designer and overseer of the works, Wren was undoubtedly the vision and inspiration behind this great building, he himself took no active part in its construction.

The second common criticism is that people can make the Bible *say* whatever they want, simply by *cherry-picking* certain bits. The Bible is indeed vulnerable to this extreme misinterpretation, due principally to the fact that its format of separate books, subdivided into distinct chapters and numbered verses, results in very small chunks of text that can be easily identified. Most Christian-related cults and sects seem to start with their leaders coming to the Bible with an existing particular heresy, which they then *prove* by hopping around all over the place. This bogus activity would certainly be much more difficult and time-consuming to carry out in conjunction with normal literature. And therein lies the clue to responsible and reliable interpretation; the Bible should be read in the same way as any other book, with perhaps the only slight difference being that the majority of people find it easier to start at Part 2 – The New Testament. Seven short guides to biblical interpretation, most of which are also relevant to everyday reading, are provided at the end of the appendix.

Having said all that, it is certainly not my intention to convey the impression that everything in the Bible makes sense to me. Some things don't and others shock me; the importance of unresolved questions being taken up again at the end of this chapter. I also need to affirm that I make no claim to any *higher*, *special*, or *secret* knowledge but have instead endeavoured to provide an objective assessment of the Bible's reliability, particularly the legitimacy of the traditional understanding concerning the events and teachings attributed to Jesus Christ.

An Objective Spine of Evidence

This objective spine comprises ten points, some of which are of an explicitly factual nature with others relating to explanations of certain features unique to the Christian faith.

Firstly, the entire Bible declares itself to be the *Word of the living God*; as per phrases such as, *God said*, or, *Thus says the Lord*, which occur approximately 3,800 times (so quite a lot). Although this seems at first sight to be a rather circular argument, let's remember that the Bible was written in three different languages over a period of almost 1500 years by a total of 40 separate authors from every walk of life - kings, fishermen, tax collectors, shepherds, prophets and a physician etc. All of these writers would presumably have confirmed that they were not putting down their own thoughts (although the styles of writing often reflect their backgrounds), but were rather being driven along by the Spirit of God; a fact corroborated by the amazing consistency of the overall compilation. It is therefore evident that this accomplishment, not even remotely replicated by the essentially mystical movements of 2nd to 4th century Gnosticism and New Age, means that the above phrases concerning God's chosen communication with human beings should be taken at face value – that is literally.

This second point endorses and extends the first. For whatever reason, many people, including me in pre-conversion days, start from the premise that the biblical writers invented stories or, at the very least, grossly exaggerated their accounts. This view is not, however, supported by the Bible itself, the second letter of the Apostle Peter containing the following statement, *"We did not follow cleverly invented stories when we told you about the power and coming of our Lord Jesus Christ, but we were eyewitnesses of His majesty."* (2 Peter 1:16) Peter had also previously stipulated that the chosen apostle to replace Judas (in the event, a guy called Matthias) must be, as were the other eleven, a person who had witnessed the entirety of Jesus' ministry from initial baptism to ascension.

Getting to the heart of the matter, it is undoubtedly very indicative of truthfulness that the biblical record does not hold back on the limitations, flaws and wrongful actions of all the principal characters (apart from the perfect portrayal of Jesus Christ – discussed subsequently), but gives a clear overall picture of these spiritual *heroes - warts and all*. And some of these warts were pretty bad. For instance, referring firstly to the OT: Jacob, the father of the brothers who formed the twelve tribes of Israel, was essentially a pathological liar and deceiver; Moses had a pretty serious problem with losing his temper; Saul, the first king of Israel, was psychotic and experienced deep depression, paranoia, and manic outbursts of anger resulting in attempts to kill his eventual successor, David; and David himself, generally considered to be Israel's greatest ever king, concealed his adultery and a resulting pregnancy by arranging for the husband of the very beautiful Bathsheba (a poor guy called Uriah) to be killed. I could go on.

When it comes to the NT, it's pretty obvious that Jesus' twelve disciples generally didn't have much of a clue as to what was going on. This brief example involves yeast. Even I, with my very limited culinary skills, know that yeast is used to get bread to rise, and it was no different in Jesus' day. However, back then, the word *yeast* (or *leaven*) also had a metaphorical and generally negative meaning; so that when, during a voyage by boat across the Sea of Galilee, Jesus told His disciples to watch out for the yeast of the Pharisees (certain religious leaders) and Herod Antipas (son of King Herod the Great), He was talking about the pride and hypocrisy of the former and the deceitfulness and cunning of the latter. So the disciples got into a little huddle to try to work out what this phrase meant, and concluded that it related to the fact that they had only brought one loaf of bread – duhhh!

It's also abundantly clear that although Jesus repeatedly told His disciples about His overarching mission to be crucified and bodily resurrected, they simply could not get their heads round it. And thus, when Jesus was indeed crucified, none of them were expecting a resurrection (a fact of some significance). Incidentally, did any leader (of anything) ever choose such a motley crew as these disciples, trusting that they would finally get their act together? – as, with God's help, they undoubtedly did. Invariably, leaders and great teachers surround themselves with very capable and like-minded followers to whom they can *pass on the baton*. For example, the famous Greek philosopher, Socrates, was the teacher of the famous Greek philosopher, Plato, who was the teacher of the famous Greek philosopher, Aristotle (also the teacher of Alexander the Great).

And how about the marauding young NT Saul, later the Apostle Paul, and his mission to imprison or murder the early followers of Jesus? In a post-conversion and first letter to his 'convert' Timothy, probably written in the AD 50s, Paul says this, *"Here is a trustworthy saying that deserves full acceptance: Christ Jesus came into the world to save sinners (wrongdoers) — of whom I am the worst. But for that very reason I was shown mercy so that in me, the worst of sinners, Christ Jesus might display His unlimited patience as an example for those who would believe on Him* [68] *and receive eternal life."* (1 Timothy 1:15-16)

Who would write that if it wasn't true? It is the exact opposite of the bluster we hear from our politicians much of the time and it certainly does Paul no favours. It's like me saying, "Audrie is a brilliant wife and the most patient person in the world." And why? "Because she puts up with me!" I think that may once have been funny, but probably not now. Anyhow, this *ruthless truth* concerning the principal characters involved is decidedly indicative of the truthfulness of the entire Bible. Not only that, but people today still often use the phrases, *don't take this as gospel* and, *this is the gospel truth*; thus inadvertently signifying that the historical record is not only truthful but can even be used as a universal standard by which to judge other claims to truthfulness. Finally, how many *Bibles* are there - e.g., The *Bible* of Bodybuilding, The *Bible* of Fishing, The *Bible* of Quantum Physics, The *Bible* of Aardvark Wrestling, and so many more; doesn't this again point to accuracy, reliability and thoroughness?

---

[68] Paul's phrase *believe on Him* is particularly forceful, and implies *reliance upon* rather than a simply superficial belief in Christ.

It appears entirely reasonable, given the sheer numbers involved, to treat this next superficially subjective evidence (point 3) as objective. This is the fact that, over the past 2,000 years, hundreds of millions of people from all over the world have been converted to Christianity by claimed personal encounters with Jesus Christ. To re-emphasise: not *by becoming religious*, or *converting due to impending marriage requirements*, but by *personal encounters.* Surely we can't all be fruitcakes?

How many people could, for instance, point to radically improved lives due to encounters with Father Christmas or the Tooth Fairy, or even a real historical figure such as Napoleon? These experiences of Jesus are, unsurprisingly, not identical or stereotypical but, as when talking to someone about a claimed common acquaintance, it will soon become apparent during the conversation that you both do indeed know (or not) this third party. I remember reading a biography about the 18th century former slave trader, John Newton, and realising that "Hey, I know this Jesus you're talking about." There were simply so many characteristics that I recognised. And, having mentioned Napoleon, here is one of his quotations which, I presume, speaks for itself – *"I know men and I tell you that Jesus Christ is no mere man. Between Him and every other person in the world there is no possible term of comparison. Alexander, Caesar, Charlemagne, and I have founded empires. But on what did we rest the creation of our genius? Upon force. Jesus Christ founded His Empire upon love; and at this hour millions of men would die for Him."* [69]

So is there anything similar in other worldviews to the *born-again* experiences of individuals as they become Christians through declared personal encounters with Jesus Christ? I have had Muslim and Jewish friends, both professionally and as a student. In all cases, their participation in the specific religion, as noted in chapter one, seems to have been due primarily to culture and ethnicity plus the beliefs of parents and families etc. (perhaps some similarity to Cultural Christianity). Nevertheless, there is no doubt that some Westerners

---

[69] Napoleon Bonaparte. https://justjesus.typepad.com/blog/2009/11/napoleon-bonaparte-and-jesus-Christ.html.

have converted to Eastern religions and, say, Islam due to the seemingly ineffectual, and sometimes discriminatory, nature of the supposed Christianity on show.

One example of the latter concerns the then Cassius Clay being made to leave a *Whites Only* café in his *Bible-belt* home town of Louisville, Kentucky, shortly after entering wearing his recently won light-heavyweight boxing gold medal from the 1960 Rome Olympics. For the *crime* of being black - absolutely disgusting. Any wonder that he subsequently changed his name to Muhammad Ali and joined Islam, where he was accepted. Some individuals may also have converted to certain religions for societal advantages, or even to fight for or against a particular regime. However, returning to the original question, it is pretty clear that none of the above can be viewed as serious alternatives to the *born-again* experiences of true Christianity.

As an addendum to all of this, it is evident that the little phrase *born-again*, which originally had a unique spiritual meaning, has now become somewhat devalued. For instance, there are now *born-again* atheists and *born-again* secular humanists (Audrie became a *born-again* cat-lover in 1994). However, the NIV Study Bible notes that this phrase can equally be translated as *born-from-above*, which is probably less ambiguous and more appropriate for today's UK society. It also specifically conveys how proactive God is. Even a superficial reading of the Bible, principally concerned with God/humankind relationships, reveals that God always makes the first move (and often the 2nd and 3rd etc). Indeed, gaining an increased appreciation of the proactivity of God due to the writing of this book has been a quite startling experience - a secondary echo of being born again.

The above order of communication is, therefore, the exact opposite of very many religions and worldviews, which are primarily concerned with humankind reaching out in an attempt to discover any such Ultimate Reality that may exist. Just to avoid any possible misunderstanding whereby we might wait for God to slide down a sunbeam and shout, *ta-da*! I reaffirm my opinion that He is frequently speaking and even appealing to us through the visible creation and using our consciences to *hear* His distinctive inner voice as it penetrates right down into our souls – as per the earlier Chuck Colson example.

These *born-from-above* experiences, unlike a specific culture (certain missionaries and their organisations have made mistakes over this in the past), are great world travellers, transforming people from right across the globe. Indeed, Millmead has members from over thirty different countries. Conversion to Christianity in certain parts of the world also often results in consequent rejection from families and/or torture and/or death. So these Christians must be experiencing and envisioning something pretty special to put themselves on the line in this manner; because, unlike some religions, persecution (including martyrdom), although it may confirm genuine conversion to Christ, can never be its basis.

It is very difficult to select a single example from the innumerable global conversions to Christ, but I'm going to choose the story of Sundar Singh, born into a Sikh family in Northern India (now Pakistan). It is 1903 and the most important person in Sundar's life, his mother, has recently died. Grief-stricken and angry, the 14-year-old Sundar decides that, unless God appears to him, he will end his life the following morning by laying his head on the track in front of the five o'clock train to Lahore. He waits and waits in his bedroom during the night hours until, at about 4.30am, a glow appears, even though the window shutters are closed. This glow becomes brighter and brighter until it is a piercing light, with a figure of a man at its centre. Sundar had expected this to be Krishna or perhaps Buddha, but to his great shock, he now recognises the figure as Jesus Christ. He cannot believe his eyes, because he's convinced that Christ has been dead for centuries. Yet there He is, His piercing eyes burrowing into Sundar's heart. The figure then speaks to him in perfect Hindustani, *"How long will you persecute me? I have come to save you. You were praying to know the right way. Why do you not take it? I am the Way."* [70]

---

[70] Sundar Singh, *Footprints Over the Mountains*. YWAM Publishing, 2014, p. 31.

Sundar drops to his knees asking Christ to forgive him and change him. Then the figure slowly fades away, and he is filled with a feeling of incredible peace and joy. Amazingly, he realises that the *Jesus* the local missionaries talked about was alive and the true Son of God. Because of this incredible encounter, Sundar spent much of the rest of his life tramping across the Himalayan high passes of up to 20,000 feet, enduring snow blizzards and worse, with only a light shawl and blanket for cover and, as per the general custom, almost always barefoot. He did this to take the Christian gospel to the nation of Tibet, enduring incredible torture and persecution in the process. He died at only forty years of age, and was known as, *The Disciple Of The Bleeding Feet*. He is still remembered and a museum is dedicated to him.

Similar visions and dreams are still being regularly reported, and are undoubtedly one of the main reasons behind the many Muslims in the Middle East currently converting to Christ. Of the cases known to me, Christ's words have always been in the individual's mother tongue; rather impressive examples of cultural *pre-existing horizons* being overridden by the supernatural.

There is, however, another side to this coin, which I have touched on previously. This is the fact that it's hardly possible to go a day in the UK, and presumably overall Western society, without hearing the name of Jesus Christ on someone's lips. Why? – Why should this be the case? There is surely nothing about His apparent denouement (the final act) on this Earth, when He was flogged to a pulp and crucified, that remotely suggests He would leave any sort of legacy at all, good or bad. We have to realise that, as recorded by both Jewish and Roman historians as well as the NT, Jesus was crucified with criminals and as a criminal - what legacies did the other thousands upon thousands of poor unfortunates leave?

Almost all TV films and dramas transmitted after the 9pm watershed use the name of Jesus Christ as an expletive when the going gets tough. Go to any football match, even young lads, and you will hear the name of Jesus being repeatedly used; particularly when something dramatic, like missing a penalty, occurs. I was talking to a very friendly middle-aged guy at the gym recently. Whenever I said anything at all surprising or even interesting (I still can), it was, *Jesus Christ this* and, *Jesus Christ that*. What's going on? Well, my best, and indeed only, take on this is that, as well as Jesus, Satan is still alive. Although I would have laughed about the possibility of a real devil in my SHDC days, I think his existence (no horns or pitchfork of course) is not dismissed quite so easily in today's UK. Satan loathes Jesus Christ and loves to hear His name used as a curse by people who have no idea of what is coming out of their mouths (I used to be one of them - blasphemy was simply a normal part of my vocabulary). Satan wants the name of Jesus to be literally ground into the dust as many times and in front of as many people as possible. This, I believe, is the only answer that makes any sense at all, and it may also be useful to reflect on this in conjunction with reading 'One Solitary Life' (see below).

The next three points (4-6) are my *bankers*, and, if this were a certain type of gameshow, the first of these would undoubtedly be the *Joker*. This particular objective evidence is based on energy and, specifically, that success for human beings almost invariably leads to its production and increase, whereas failure leads to the opposite; something borne out when writing journals during my weightlifting and pole-vaulting days. These were easy enough to write-up after a successful competition - e.g., for pole-vaulting: which pole or poles I was using, where my top hand was gripping, the wind direction, what I'd had for breakfast, and on and on. However, if I'd had a really bad competition by, say, *bombing out* (failing my opening height three times), then I didn't want to write anything at all – maybe something like, *really bad day, no-heighted*. End of.

From another sporting echelon; one female athlete, having won the final Diamond League race of the year after an otherwise poor summer season, exuberantly told the interviewer that this would give her the necessary inspiration and impetus to keep going through yet another intensive training programme during the cold and long winter months. Again, success = energy.

Regarding the question of why the whole energy thing is relevant to Jesus Christ, it seems particularly fitting to start with a piece of writing known as, *One Solitary Life*,

He was born in an obscure village, the son of a peasant woman.

He grew up in another village, where He worked in a carpenter's shop until He was thirty. Then for three years, He became a wandering preacher.

He never wrote a book. He never held an office. He never had a family or owned a house. He didn't go to college. He never visited a big city. He never travelled two hundred miles from the place where He was born. He did none of those things one usually associates with greatness.

He had no credentials but Himself.

He was only thirty-three when the tide of public opinion turned against Him. His friends ran away. He was turned over to His enemies and went through a mockery of a trial. He was executed by the state. While He was dying, His executioners gambled for His clothing, the only property He had on Earth. When He was dead He was laid in a borrowed grave through the pity of a friend.

Twenty centuries have come and gone, and today He is the central figure of the human race and the leader of mankind's progress. All the armies that ever marched, all the navies that ever sailed, all the parliaments that ever sat, all the kings that ever reigned, put together, have not affected the life of man on this Earth as much as that One Solitary Life.[71]

It is clearly evident that there is no realistic connection whatsoever between the last paragraph and the main part of the writing above the dotted line. Indeed, this represents a massive non-sequitur, defined in the dictionary as a *conclusion or statement that does not logically follow from the previous argument or statement*. What on earth took place? Why have we even heard of the name *Jesus Christ*, when, according to

---

[71] One Solitary Life. https://spreadjesus.org/1221-one-solitary-life-jesus-christ.html.

the Jewish historian, Josephus, the Romans crucified thousands upon thousands of Jews, including 3,000 in AD 7 alone? Who were the others? And, as intimated above, can anyone name any? I don't think so – apart from the thieves crucified on either side of Jesus, who are acknowledged simply for that fact.

One key aspect, the significance of which simply cannot be over-emphasised, is that Jesus Christ is not inscribed in history due to Him being a great martyr. This is discussed further in chapter six but, at this stage, it seems sufficient to concentrate on the fact that death by crucifixion was considered to represent absolute defeat and humiliation in both Roman and Jewish cultures. The Romans even considered that this punishment was so bad that it could not be carried out on those with Roman citizenship, no matter what their crime. This is a quote from Cicero (106 – 43 BC), one of Rome's most influential philosophers, *"It is a crime to put a Roman citizen in chains, it is an enormity to flog one, sheer murder to slay one; what, then, shall I say of crucifixion? It is impossible to find the word for such an abomination."* [72] The Jews viewed those crucified as proof of them being rejected and cursed by God - unimaginable shame. Absolutely nothing could be worse in their culture. The indisputable message concerning a person hanging on a cross, naked and exposed to all as a warning (nudity particularly offensive to the Jews), was accordingly writ large – THEY HAVE LOST AND THEIR CAUSE (if relevant) HAS COME TO NOTHING.

It is hardly surprising that the disciples completely bottled it at the time of Jesus' arrest, simply running away in case they too might be killed, or, at the very least, fleeing due to the total embarrassment and shame of wasting three years following an imposter. This account has a massive ring of truth and authenticity about it, with its very inclusion thus again reinforcing the Bible's reputation for *telling it as it is*. Why on earth would these followers make up a story that presented them in such a negative light? And it's also of relevance that non-biblical sources (listed

---

[72] Marcus Tullius Cicero.
https://www.quotemaster.org/qfcc2d8c34aa96fcc27704cbf071fc092.

by various NT scholars, particularly the American Gary Habermas) such as Josephus and the Roman historian, Tacitus, refer to the life of Jesus and His crucifixion, and additionally record that the *mad* Emperor Nero, when accused of starting the fire that destroyed Rome in AD 64, blamed the Christians and had a large number killed.

So there is a situation here that within a generation of Jesus' life on Earth, many believers had already made it as far as Rome (and some a lot further – the Apostle Thomas, for example, is thought to have taken the gospel as far as India). In actuality, thousands of people became followers of Jesus from very early on with, as referred to previously, numerous manuscripts (handwritten – no printing presses before the 15th century) being produced to record all the amazing happenings, including ongoing miracles, before the apostles and other eyewitnesses died out. All of this would have required incredible energy and a veritable explosion of power. Furthermore, there is the undisputed and astonishing fact that *died in the wool* parochial Jews, although not denying their roots, which related not only to very strongly held spiritual beliefs but also to individual and cultural identities, moved significantly beyond them to establish the Christian faith internationally. This is something, achieved in the face of massive opposition, which has never been satisfactorily explained by sceptics. The apostles had, therefore, by then moved on monumentally from their discipleship *duhhh-moment* concerning the yeast, managing to get into their heads what Jesus' teaching, the *kingdom of God* [73] (not religion), was really all about.

So what happened to turn it all around in such a massive way? Where did all this energy and power come from? It is certainly no secret. The NT declares that Jesus Christ was raised from the dead and then appeared on a number of occasions to His, at the time, broken followers. These included a crowd of about five hundred - a group of people who weren't even expecting a resurrection, could hardly have all experienced hallucinations at the same time and numbered far too many for any theory based on the comparatively recent *Chinese*

---

[73] The *kingdom of God* is wherever the reign of God is both paramount and in evidence.

Whispers game to have any possible credibility. Moreover, unlike this game, where there are no external checks as the communication is passed along, the message of Christ's resurrection almost immediately went public by being proclaimed out on the streets of Jerusalem.

The religious leaders who had opposed Christ were fully aware of and greatly disturbed by this, and would have loved to recover His body from the tomb to shut up all the various eyewitnesses – but of course, they couldn't.The NT also describes how the apostles and many other new believers were enlightened and empowered at this time due to dynamic spiritual fillings (or baptisms) by the Holy Spirit; Peter and John when confronted by the religious leaders, this time not running away, but instead replying, "For we cannot help speaking about what we have seen and heard." (Acts 4:20) Surely the appearances of the risen Christ and these supernatural experiences can be the only plausible explanation for their confidence and the related extraordinary birth and growth of the Christian faith. If it didn't happen this way, there is absolutely no reason to suppose that even one word would ever have been written, let alone an abundance of manuscripts. And we would certainly never have heard of the name, Jesus Christ.

If any further confirmation is still needed, there is good evidence from the writings of the early church fathers that most, if not all, of the apostles, except John, were killed for their faith, Peter apparently insisting on being crucified upside down as a mark of respect to Jesus (as above, he had certainly moved on from the denials following his leader's arrest). You simply do not get these sacrificial deaths if people know the cause (in this case Jesus Christ and His resurrection etc.) to be fraudulent. As a recent example, President Nixon's hatchet man, Chuck Colson, was enveloped in possibly the biggest scandal of 20th century US politics known as the *Watergate Affair*.

This resulted from a break-in (for various illegal operations, such as *bugging*) to the rival Democratic Party's offices under the authority of members of Richard Nixon's Republican administration during the presidential campaign of 1972. It is thought that Nixon himself only found out about this event a considerable time after it took place, but that he then, together with his closest advisors, decided to hush the whole thing up. However, after only a few weeks, one of these guys accepted a plea-bargaining option so that he would not have to go to jail. Colson records that these men, probably forming the most powerful group in the world at that time, *could not contain this lie for more than a few weeks;* and they weren't even being threatened by death, unlike the apostles.

It is, therefore, crystal clear that if there had been any doubt at all about whether Jesus Christ had been resurrected, one, or most probably all, of the disciples would have *fessed-up* very early on and the whole gospel message would have fallen flat on its face before it even got going.

This next argument for the deity of Jesus Christ (point 5) is again very powerful but often overlooked. It is the fact that Jesus is the only person who has ever realistically been considered to represent the *perfect man* or human being. This certainly seems to be the opinion of the vast majority of people worldwide who are familiar with His life, and, if not, who would be a universally acceptable replacement? This viewpoint is endorsed by various atheists and sceptics, such as Ralph Waldo Emerson, a 19th century writer, poet, and lecturer, who, quoting from Josh McDowell's 1972 version of *Evidence That Demands A Verdict*, said, *"Jesus is the most perfect of all men that have yet appeared."* [74] And even one of that century's most vitriolic opponents of the Christian faith, the writer David Strauss, was forced to confess, towards the end of his life, that in Jesus there was moral perfection. The Islamic scriptures also accept Jesus' pure, faultless, and blameless life. This portrayal of the perfect man is an amazing and, apparently, unique literary accomplishment.

So how was it done? John Stuart Mill, another 19th century philosopher, sceptic, and antagonist of Christianity, asks, *"But who among His*

---

[74] Ralph Waldo Emerson, as cited by Josh McDowell, *Evidence That Demands A Verdict*. Campus Crusade for Christ, Inc., 1972, p.127.

disciples or among their proselytes (converts from, almost certainly, Judaism) *was capable of inventing the sayings ascribed to Jesus, or imagining the life and character revealed in the gospels?"* [75] From my own experience as a consultant civil engineer, there appears to be little doubt that the writers would have required the perfect man (Jesus) with them and in front of them. That is in like manner to checking other professionals' reports and calculations, whereby having something in front of you to look at is so much easier than starting from scratch with a blank sheet of paper.

This is a fairly lengthy but very relevant quotation from the start of the Apostle John's first letter, *"That which was from the beginning, which we have heard, which we have seen with our eyes, which we have looked at and our hands have touched - this we proclaim concerning the Word of life. The life appeared; we have seen it and testify to it, and we proclaim to you the eternal life, which was with the Father and has appeared to us. We proclaim to you what we have seen and heard, so that you also may have fellowship with us." And our fellowship is with the Father and with His Son, Jesus Christ.* (1 John 1:1-3)

This quotation is very strong stuff, with its appeal to the senses, of itself very indicative of truth, surely being the only way that the portrayal of the perfect life could ever be achieved. And, far more significant than my own professional experience, how would the great portrait painters have fared if they hadn't had people to *sit* for them - for example, the *Mona Lisa* by Leonardo da Vinci? Or how would the great landscape artist, Constable, have been successful if he had stayed at home?

Furthermore, from consideration of the sayings and deeds of Jesus it can be seen that this is a being way beyond any other, either living now or in the past. Jesus even challenged the religious leaders of the time, who were pretty freaked out and threatened by Him, to prove that He had ever been guilty of any type of wrongdoing (fair enough, if indeed the perfect man), and elsewhere stated that He also had the authority to

---

[75] John Stuart Mill, Ibid.

forgive all human wrongdoings, something the Jews attributed solely to God. Have any of us ever heard of a person (who we respected) making claims of this nature and magnitude? Then, in Matthew's gospel, there is the statement, *"heaven and earth will pass away, but my words will never pass away."* (Matthew 24:35) Well, they are still here after two thousand years. As mentioned earlier, the production figures of the Bible far outweigh those of any other publication, and it has also been read by more people and translated into more languages than any other book in history.

So many of Jesus' sayings are simply staggering, and unlike founders of religions (for instance, Muhammad or Buddha), they can often be linked with specific miracles. There are, I believe, seven types of *I am* sayings/miracles. I list five:

- *"I am the vine; you are the branches....apart from me you can do nothing."* (John 15:5) He turned water into wine.

- *"I am the resurrection and the life"* (John 11:25) and *"No one takes it* (my life) *from me, but I lay it down of my own accord. I have authority to lay it down and authority to take it up again."* (John 10:18) He raised others back to life and was Himself resurrected.

- *"I am the way and the truth and the life. No-one comes to the Father* (God/heaven) *except through me."* (John 14:6) Luke records, as a historical event, Jesus visibly ascending from the Earth some seven weeks after His resurrection. This was in front of His disciples, gathered at Bethany on the Mount of Olives a few miles to the east of the ancient walled city of Jerusalem. (Luke 24: 50-51)

- *"I am the light of the World. Whoever follows me will never walk in darkness, but will have the light of life."* (John 8:12) He gave sight to the blind, including those with congenital blindness.

- *"I am the bread of life."* (John 6:35a) i.e., its true source and sustenance. He used only five loaves plus two small fish to feed 5,000 people, and seven loaves and a few small fish to feed 4,000. In actuality, both figures are probably conservative, as the NT records only the men present.[76]

And yet, Jesus said He was humble and people believed Him (and still do). In view of the above outrageous claims, how was that possible? Well, only if they were all true! I remember a TV interview with the outstanding 200m/400m athlete, Michael Johnson, a short time before the Atlanta Olympics in 1996. Amongst other things, Johnson said that assuming he wasn't injured or unwell or made a very bad mistake, he would win both the 200m and 400m because he was simply the best runner in the world over these distances. And, in my opinion, he said all this humbly - because it was based on good evidence and actually true. He did go on to win gold medals at both distances, the 200m in a world record time.

Before continuing, it seems appropriate to give a little more consideration to these *I am* sayings of Jesus. As human beings, we generally tend to say, "I think", because we are often not sure of something or at least know that other people may have different viewpoints. However, we can sometimes say, "I know." This is often in the negative, such as, "I know I can't fly to the moon" or, "I know I can't run the marathon in under two hours" (or maybe two weeks). Positive *I knows* are nevertheless possible, such as, "I know I have two arms and two legs" etc.

What we cannot do, however, is to use *I am* language in its strictest sense. This is because this implies something unchanging, whereas we are always changing. So if I say, "I am a 19-year-old guy with a full head

---

[76] I have met some people who would like to believe in Jesus, but find His more astounding sayings and recorded miracles to be simply unacceptable. Both, however, are continuous intertwined threads that run through all four gospels. Unlike most religions and worldviews, there would not be much of substance left if they were removed – a bit like trying to take the word *Blackpool* out of a stick of rock without demolishing it.

of flowing blonde hair", the obvious reply is, "You might have been once, but you're certainly not now" - too many important cells have experienced unrepaired naturally occurring DNA damage (I looked this up). Saying that I am a 90-year-old man ready to drop dead is also not true – that could be a very challenging future *I am*!

This brings me on to a couple more of Jesus' incredible sayings. The first one is undoubtedly the most outrageous and shocking *I am*, and occurred in a debate with some of those who opposed Him. Jesus actually states, *"I tell you the truth, before Abraham was born, I am!"* (John 8:58) This is not only startling because Abraham, the *Father of the Jews*, lived about two thousand years before Christ entered the world stage, but that the last two words, taken on their own, correspond to the Hebrew word, *Yahweh*. This word (called the *Tetragrammaton* by scholars) is difficult to precisely define but is what God used when replying to Moses' request to know His name; a designation consistent with an entirely unchanging nature. In any event, Jesus' hearers undoubtedly knew what He was talking about. He was claiming to be uncreated God Himself - blasphemy - for which the Jewish punishment was death by stoning. Jesus escaped their attempts to carry this out, but the threat of being killed confirmed His claim to deity.

The second took place when Jesus said to His disciples, presumably to settle and reassure them, *"In this world, you will have trouble. But take heart, I have overcome the world."* (John 16:33) Imagine any *normal* person saying, or even thinking of saying that.

In summary, the record of Jesus Christ is a miracle in itself, and there seems to be little doubt that *it would take more than a Jesus to invent a Jesus.* Not exactly sure how that works theologically, but it certainly makes the point.

There are, of course, various accounts that demonstrate Jesus' incredible wisdom and unrivalled skill in dealing with the more mundane and regular problems of life. These typically involved oppositions from the religious leaders, who were obsessed with ritual, rules, and having a hypocritical, *better-than-you* attitude. Jesus summed up their mindset by telling them that they were worshipping God in vain - letting go of His commands and following teachings that were simply rules taught by men. This still happens today in certain places, under the banner of Christianity.

These comments by C.S. Lewis wonderfully summarise the overall direction of this *perfection* argument, *"I am trying here to prevent anyone saying the really foolish thing that people often say about Him: 'I'm ready to accept Jesus as a great moral teacher, but I don't accept His claim to be God'. That is one thing we must not say. A man who was merely a man and said the sort of things Jesus said would not be a great moral teacher. He would either be a lunatic - on a level with the man who says he is a poached egg or else he would be the Devil of Hell. You must make your choice. Either this man was, and is, the Son of God: or else a madman or something worse."* And, *"You can shut Him up for a fool, you can spit at Him and kill Him as a demon; or you can fall at His feet and call Him Lord and God. But let us not come up with any patronising nonsense about Him being a great human teacher. He has not left that open to us. He did not intend to."* [77]

Although Lewis' remarks are again very strong stuff, they nevertheless do appear to be justified. For example, let's examine, by means of a comparison with Adolph Hitler, his proposition that if Jesus were not the Son of God or a lunatic, He would be the devil of hell. The thing is that, although Hitler was without doubt unbelievably evil, we're now approaching the time when the six million Jews and others killed in his *death camps* would all have died from natural causes anyway. In other words, these unspeakably horrendous atrocities could, in the end, only bring about a temporary earthbound effect. On the other hand, Jesus' words about life after physical death have eternal consequences. If He was, therefore, lying through His teeth about people only being able to

---

[77] C.S. Lewis, *Mere Christianity*. London: Collins, 1952, pp.54-56.

enter heaven through Him, He would inevitably have been more evil than Hitler.[78]

Lewis' argument, known as *The Great Trilemma*, relates to either/or thinking and although many consider it to be very convincing, several challenges have been made over the years. One of these is from Richard Dawkins who reckons that C.S. Lewis should have known better when coming up with an argument such as this and proposes a fourth option whereby Jesus simply made a mistake – What!?

Let me take you back to the summer of 1977 when Audrie and me went around Southern Europe for a month via the train and camping. After the first night camping in Amiens, we needed to take a train to Paris. Aud wasn't in a particularly good mood (something to do with the toilets I think), so I went off to the station to check on train times. Unfortunately, I read the *Arrivals* board instead of the *Departures* board, which cost us several hours. I think Aud has now forgiven me, although we have never been camping again. Anyhow, that was undoubtedly a mistake. What would not be a mistake, is if I were to say to someone today, "Ok mate, just to let you know, before Christ was born, *I AM,* and, by the way, in this world you will have trouble but take heart, *I have overcome the world"*; and then next week tell him, "I'm sorry mate, but I made a mistake last week when I thought I'd always been in existence and had overcome the entire world." That's not a mistake, that's lunacy, Mr Dawkins! (as per C.S. Lewis).

Having drawn attention to eleven of Jesus' amazing claims (there are more, with some, as noted above, corresponding directly to His miracles), it seems appropriate to also include, for comparison, a *top twenty* of quotations from famous and generally profound people – sourced from the internet and in no particular order:

---

[78] *In a YouTube interview about his faith, Bono, the lead singer of the rock band U2, stated that he prayed to Christ as the Son of God because he could not believe the only other possible alternative, in his opinion, of a 'nutter' being able to touch and inspire millions and millions of peoples' lives over a two thousand year period.*

- ❖ Socrates – *"The unexamined life is not worth living."* In other words, we should periodically give thought to things such as: Who are we? Where have we come from? Are we our own bosses? What is our purpose? What are we supposed to be doing as we roam around planet Earth in amazingly well-formed (particularly thinking of myself here) but very short-living human bodies?

- ❖ Bear Grylls – *"Christianity is not about religion. It's about faith, about being held, about being forgiven. It's about finding joy and finding home."*

- ❖ Mother Teresa - *"If you judge people, you have no time to love them."*

- ❖ Dalai Lama - *"Love and compassion are necessities, not luxuries. Without them, humanity cannot exist."*

- ❖ Rumi – 13th century Persian Muslim poet, Islamic scholar, and Sufi mystic - *"There is a candle in your heart, ready to be kindled. There is a void in your soul, ready to be filled. You feel it, don't you?"* (as previously, we all have spiritual needs).

- ❖ Rumi – *"Raise your words, not your voice. It is rain that grows flowers, not thunder."*

- ❖ Churchill - *"Success is not final, failure is not fatal; it is the courage to continue that counts."*

- ❖ Seneca (the younger) - 1st century Roman Stoic Philosopher - *"How many funerals pass our houses? Yet we do not think of death. How many untimely deaths? We think only of our son's coming of age, of his service in the army, or of his succession to his father's estate. How many rich men suddenly sink into poverty before our very eyes, without it ever occurring to our minds that our own wealth is exposed to exactly the same risks? When, therefore, misfortune befalls us, we cannot help collapsing all the more* completely, because we are struck as it were unawares: a blow which has long been foreseen falls much less heavily upon us."

- *George Best* – Irish footballing genius - *"I spent most of my money on women, drink, and fast cars; and the rest of it I wasted."*

- Muhammad Ali - *"He who is not courageous enough to take risks will accomplish nothing in life."*

- Muhammad Ali - *"It's just a job. Grass grows, birds fly, waves pound the sand. I beat people up."*

- Confucius - *"Choose a job you love, and you will never have to work a day in your life."*

- Carl Jung – *"What is a normal goal to a young person becomes a neurotic hindrance in old age."* I could have done with understanding and applying that a bit earlier in my life.

- Sigmund Freud - *The great question that has never been answered, and which I have not yet been able to answer, despite my thirty years of research into the feminine soul, is "What does a woman want?"*

- Bertrand Russell – 19th/20th century British philosopher, mathematician, logician, atheist, and altogether clever bloke – *"Unless you assume a God, the question of life's purpose is meaningless."* Again, without some external and unchanging measuring standard, everything, including purpose, is subjective and cannot be realistically evaluated; and our extremely short lives here on planet Earth do indeed represent infinitesimal blips between two infinite oblivions.

- Albert Camus – 20th century French atheistic philosopher - *"Only the sacrifice of an innocent god could justify the endless and universal torture of innocence. Only the most* humiliating suffering by God could relieve man's agony."

- ❖ C.S. Lewis – *"I believe in Christianity as I believe that the Sun has risen; not only because I see it, but because by it, I see everything else."*

- ❖ Plato – The accuracy of this quotation is absolutely amazing. It occurs in *'Republic Book 2'*, where, during conversation, the *perfectly just man* is described as follows, *"Beside our picture of the unjust man let us set one of the just man, the man of true simplicity of character who, as Aeschylus says, wants "to be, and not to seem, good." We must, indeed, not allow him to seem good, for if he does he will have all the rewards and honours paid to the man who has a reputation for justice, and we shall not be able to tell whether his motive is love of justice or love of the rewards and honours. No, we must strip him of everything except his justice, and our picture of him must be drawn in the opposite way to our picture of the unjust man; for our just man must have the worst of reputations even though he has done no wrong. So we shall be able to test his justice and see if it can stand up to unpopularity and all that goes with it; we shall give him an undeserved and lifelong reputation for wickedness, and make him stick to his chosen course until death ... The just man, then, as we have pictured him, will be scourged, tortured, and imprisoned, his eyes will be put out, and after enduring every humiliation he will be crucified, and learn at last that in the world as it is we should want not to be, but to seem, just."* Of the many parallels and insights that might be chosen, perhaps the most significant is Plato's recognition that, in order to confirm his authenticity, the 'just man' must have the worst of reputations, as per Jesus who was 'crucified with criminals and as a criminal'.

- ❖ Rousseau – 18th century Swiss philosopher and atheist – *"When Plato describes his imaginary righteous man, loaded with all the punishments of guilt, yet meriting the highest rewards of virtue, he describes exactly the character of Jesus Christ."*

- Plato – *"We can easily forgive a child who is afraid of the dark. The real tragedy of life is where men are afraid of the light."* Note the comparison with John's gospel where Jesus says – *"This is the verdict: Light* (Himself) *has come into the world, but men loved darkness instead of light because their deeds were evil."* (John 3:19) How close is this! A second quotation from Plato that is uncannily similar to the NT record of Jesus.

It, therefore, seems evident that Plato wrote, presumably under divine inspiration, two amazing prophecies about Jesus Christ some 350/400 years before He walked on this planet.

Although all the above quotations are excellent, they are simply not in the same league as those of Jesus; particularly the *I am* quotes, which all relate to ontology – the nature of being and, in His case, of being Ultimate Reality/God.

Finally, a couple of my quotations that I prepared earlier, "Everyone has an equal right to their own opinion, but not all opinions are equally right" - particularly thinking here of my revolutionary *Cream Doughnuts Only* diet for losing weight and getting a six-pack. And, from a slightly more adult perspective, "Everything, apart from unconditional love, becomes ridiculous when taken to extremes" - e.g., free speech must be subject to certain limitations, such as the treatment of slander as a *civil wrong* in the UK.

This is the last of my three *bankers* (point 6). It concerns biblical prophecy, and specifically those in the OT that predict the coming, life, death and resurrection of Jesus Christ. Researching the internet revealed the amazing total of approximately 300 OT prophecies that Christ is understood to have fulfilled. However, some of these are rather more obvious than others - probably a bit like the giving of penalties in football, some are *stone-wall* and others are *a bit soft*. Surely biblical exegesis at its finest! Anyhow, be that as it may, I am going to take the very conservative view that there are fifty *stone-wallers*, where there can be no doubt that the prophets are talking about Jesus Christ. This is still, of course, an amazing amount, and who else's birth and life etc., including any religious leader, has been accurately written down hundreds of years before it took place?

Many years ago the Times Newspaper offered a substantial prize to anyone who could name any other individual, past or present, who had fulfilled even half of these (*stone-wall*) prophecies – not surprisingly, there were no takers. For my purposes here, I'm simply going to list ten:

TABLE 1: BIBLICAL PROPHECY FULFILLED BY JESUS (1 of 2)	
Prophecy	Prophet / Scripture / Date
1. Jesus to have existed before His life on Earth – in fact from *eternity*.	Prophet Micah [5:2] (approx. 750 – 685 BC) and as per the start of John's gospel.
2. Jesus to be born in Bethlehem.	Prophet Micah [5:2]
3. Jesus' mother to be a virgin.	Prophet Isaiah [7:14] (similar time to Micah)
4. Jesus to grow up in Galilee (Nazareth was in this province).	Prophet Isaiah [9:1-7]
5. Jesus to be betrayed for the sum of 30 pieces of silver.	Prophets Zechariah [11:12/13] (approx. 500 BC) & Jeremiah [various] (approx. 600 BC)
6. Jesus to experience extreme pain and suffering, in order to bear the responsibility for all mankind's wrongdoings.	Prophet Isaiah [52:13 – 53:12]
7. Description of Jesus' death by crucifixion - "*... a band of evil men has encircled me. They have pierced my hands and my feet. I can count all my bones. People stare and gloat over me. They divide my garments among them and cast lots for my clothing.*"	Psalm 22 [1-31] (traditionally King David - approx. 1000 BC, but certainly before 500 BC, and likely to have pre-dated death by crucifixion). Even on its own, this incredible psalm, which contains multiple fulfilled prophecies, should alert us to the probability of supernatural involvement.

TABLE 1: BIBLICAL PROPHECY FULFILLED BY JESUS (2 of 2)	
Prophecy	Prophet / Scripture / Date
8. More on Jesus' crucifixion - *"He was assigned a grave with the wicked"* i.e., the thieves on the adjacent crosses - *"and with the rich in His death"* - buried in the tomb of a guy called Joseph of Arimathea, who was undoubtedly minted.	Prophet Isaiah [53:9]
9. Even more on Jesus' crucifixion. - *"They will look on me* (the Lord*), the one they have pierced..."*	Prophet Zechariah [12:10]
10. Jesus' resurrection	Psalm [16:10] (King David) & Jonah [1:17] (8th century BC)

The above list is very impressive, and perhaps even sufficient on its own when it comes to putting forward a compelling case for the trustworthiness of both the Bible and Jesus Christ's claims to equality with God. However, there are a couple of questions that seemingly need an answer.

The first of these concerns the possibility that some, or maybe even all, of the relevant OT prophecies could have been written down after Jesus' time on Earth. There are many ways this question could be answered, but, hopefully, the following few comments will suffice.

On the spiritual side, I cite the Apostle Peter's second letter, where he states, *"For prophecy never had its origin in the will of man, but men spoke from God as they were carried along by the Holy Spirit."* (2 Peter 1:21) Nevertheless, as noted previously, the styles of writing normally took into account the natures and life experiences of the various authors – they were not treated simply as human typewriters. So overall, Peter is declaring the spiritual source and resultant integrity of OT prophecy.

From a historical perspective, it is possible to identify the approximate life-spans of the OT prophets by cross-referencing certain known facts, particularly the recorded reigns of the Israelite/Jewish kings and those from surrounding countries (e.g., Prophet Isaiah - King Hezekiah of Judah – King Sargon II of Assyria [see appendix]).

Scholars can also get a good handle on the dating of original documents (known as *autographs*) by utilising *Philology* – a subject relating to languages, and particularly their historical development. The exact meanings of words often change over time, giving strong indications of the relevant period. For instance, a friend of ours recently shocked her nephew by saying that he *looked fit*. She, of course, assumed the traditional meaning, whereas he took it that his aunt was saying he was *hot and sexy*. And as a second *for instance*, the word *gay* has had at least three different meanings during just my lifetime.

In conclusion, even allowing for a degree of redaction (editing), the evidence all points to the prophecies being wholly fixed in form, well before 100 BC.

The second question concerns the fact that, despite the outstanding nature of these prophecies, comparatively few Jews have thus far embraced Jesus as their Messiah or Christ, or Deliverer, or Anointed One, or Chosen One, or indeed, as per the prophet Isaiah, *"Wonderful Counsellor, Mighty God, Everlasting Father, Prince of Peace."* (Isaiah 9:6b) Some of the reasons for this are given in later chapters.

Moving on to the seventh point, the majority of us, including the adherents of most worldviews, take love very seriously and regard it as being of crucial importance to a whole raft of relationships ranging from the physical to the spiritual and from the individual to groups and even nations. The Beatles song, *All you need is love*, is still somewhat of a mantra, with the British Human Rights campaigner, Peter Tatchell, stating on the Jeremy Vine Radio 2 Show (2018) that the love of people, and particularly the disadvantaged, was his main motivation. But where does love come from?

Surely not the *soul of the cosmos*, subsequently discussed in connection with Pantheistic Monism, which is deemed to be coterminous with the universe (having the same boundaries) rather than being transcendent. In other words, for this specific possibility, there would need to be an illogical marrying up of an impersonal god with the highly personal characteristic of love. When it comes to naturalistic or atheistic science, this again seems unlikely to fit the bill due to its *selfish* emphasis on the *survival of the fittest* once random DNA/gene mutations have taken place; an overall process sometimes called *chance and necessity* (see previous comments on empathy).

This leaves a personal being, and, taking account of the situation before any cognitive species, such as *Homo sapiens*, came on the scene, probably comprising more than one person. This is because it is surely impossible for a strictly singular being to be capable of anything beyond narcissistic or self-love – which, of course, cannot be classed as love in a meaningful sense.

So do any of the myriad worldviews entertain the possibility of a supernatural being comprising more than one person? As far as I am aware, the only apparently credible blueprint occurs in Christianity, where Ultimate Reality/God is understood to be a triune being – that is a *Trinity* of Father, Son and Holy Spirit.[79] Of course, some people, particularly those belonging to certain religious cults, simply cannot get their heads around this due to an inability to satisfactorily understand such an entity from a solely human perspective. But that should surely be the case when considering Ultimate Reality – an actuality responsible for creating everything including ourselves. There has to be some degree of mystery; otherwise, as discussed in connection with New Age, each of us could end up believing that we are God.

I find the teaching concerning a triune God, which is contrary to normal earthly expectations, to be very inspirational. We humans tend to plump instead for individual evil *superpowers*, such as *Darth Vader*. So how can we have some insight into Ultimate Reality of this nature? As discussed previously, it is necessary to have a grammatical construct, such as analogy or metaphor. One analogy that seems to be fairly frequently utilised is that of H_2O – that is ice, water and steam are all made up of the same H_2O molecules and yet have very diverse properties.

---

[79] It is recognised that, within the Hinduistic school of Dvaita Vedanta, Brahman represents Ultimate Reality and is usually visualised in three forms, collectively known as the 'Trimurti'. However, this is very different to the Trinity of Christianity, a matter taken up again in chapter eight.

However, there appears to be an alternative, and much better, analogy available. That is to consider six squares of identical size and colour, and imagine that these could be pushed together so tightly that all the boundaries disappear. The result is that a single rectangle is formed, inevitably replacing the squares so that all six lose their separate identities. However, this is a two-dimensional model and if a third dimension is added, a single cube is formed; all the squares thus remaining visible and retaining their individuality. The simultaneous existence of both six squares and one cube is therefore not a contradiction, but rather a very significant progression once this further dimension is added.

Although the latter analogy can inevitably only go so far, it does nevertheless indicate the possibility of both single and multiple co-existences, thereby lending itself to a single being comprising three separate and equal interacting *persons*. It, therefore, follows that any such Ultimate Reality might always have been capable – that is before being involved with created intelligence of any kind - of the actual giving out and receiving of love.

The Apostle John's first letter accordingly includes two very revealing statements, *"God is Love"* (1 John 4:16b) and, *"We love because He first loved us."* (1 John 4:19); again, a proactive God. And then, almost at the start of the Bible, as previously quoted, *"Then God said, 'Let us make man in our own* (spiritual) *image, in our likeness.."* (Genesis 1:26a) The latter short declaration is, therefore, again consistent with the triune teaching of the NT, although it can also be understood as representing an intensification of the attributes and overwhelming transcendence of God; something known as the *Majestic Plural*.

As an addendum to the above, it's important to realise that the God of the Bible is always portrayed as all-powerful, totally self-sufficient, and transcending (uncreated and infinitely superior to) the universe that He has created. This is very different to 'the gods' of contemporary ancient peoples in the Middle East/Mediterranean, who were pictured within and as parts of the created universe - e.g., *Jupiter* as the Roman god of the sky and thunder and *Selene* as the *Moon goddess* in Greek mythology. These man-made gods, normally confined to a specific nation or area, were often *needy*, and typically required human beings to be their slaves and provide them with food and other necessities. Natural events, such as thunder and lightning, were thus usually understood to mean that these capricious gods had suddenly become angry.

The final three points (8-10) all relate to the uniqueness of the person and mission of Jesus Christ – as per Augustine of Hippo, hidden within the OT and unveiled in the NT. One of the main reasons for the specific inclusion of this topic is the general lack of relevant knowledge in the UK and other contemporary Western societies; and even when some facts are known, they can be rather distorted and shallow – *fake news*. People can, therefore, easily believe they have outgrown any need for Christianity, and then dump their understanding of it straight into the rubbish bin. But the gospel of Christ is monumental, awesome and glorious, and surely deserves its *day in court*. This most important of subjects is therefore considered both within and beyond this chapter, with the denouement occurring in chapter eight in conjunction with Judaism.

Point 8 considers the claim of God becoming human, or *The incarnation of Christ*. In other words, the possibility of God reaching in rather than human beings simply reaching out – perhaps the key overall theme of this book. It's vitally important to get a good handle on this, even though the concept is initially foreign to most of us. Three analogies, all intended to provide additional clarification are included below; but first, a little bit of theology is needed.

The previous discussion concerning a triune being or *The Trinity* hopefully sets the background for this, where Jesus Christ, although considered to be God, is also distinct in person from *God the Father* and *God the Holy Spirit*. In other words, God embodies both individual expression and harmonious fellowship. The first two verses of John's gospel are consistent with this general description, stating, *"In the* beginning was the Word, and the Word was with God, and the Word was God. He was with God in the beginning." (John 1:1-2) The Greek for Word is Logos, which the Greek Stoics thought of as the (impersonal) ordering structure behind the universe. They, therefore, considered that the meaning of life was to be found in aligning themselves with this universal and rational principle that governed all things (as per various other worldviews such as Taoism). Even though this viewpoint would have been foreign to the majority Jewish contingent of John's original recipients, he nevertheless confirmed the necessity of this alignment, but then appealed to both Greeks and Jews by the stunning and indeed mind-boggling proclamation that the *Logos* is a person – Jesus Christ – Absolute Truth.

John also subsequently declared that Christ, *through whom all things were made*, took on manhood (the *God-man*, temporarily *"made a little lower than the Angels"* (Hebrews 2:9)) and, for a short period, lived among us. *"The Word became flesh and blood, and moved into the neighbourhood"* (John 1:14a -*The Message version of the Bible* [80]), the true meaning of Christmas, whatever Sainsbury's or Morrison's might say.

This assertion of creation being from God the Father through Christ the Son is consistently taught in the NT and appears to be a logical consequence, given the divine nature of both. Yet it is a truth that, possibly due to the inevitable related mystery, seems to have been given little priority by most Christian teachers and scholars. Of those that have addressed this subject, C. E. Gunton is particularly helpful.[81]

So as a personal entity, Jesus can only be known in very broadly the same way that human beings relate to one another. It is, therefore, not a question of simply getting our words *right*, as it would be impossible to love or form relationships with each other if we believed and defined ourselves as *energy*, *meaning*, or *principles* etc. Three more NT quotes,

---

[80] Eugene H. Peterson, The Message Bible (MSG), Navpress, 2005.
[81] C. E. Gunton, *Christ And Creation*. The Paternoster Press & Wm. B. Eerdmans Publish. Co., 1992.

again confirming Christ's deity, *"He is the image of the invisible God..."* (Apostle Paul, Colossians 1:15), *"The Son is the radiance of God's glory and the exact representation of His being..."* (Hebrews 1:3 – author unknown, but certainly of Jewish heritage) and, *"...they will call Him Immanuel – which means, 'God with us.'"* (Matthew 1:23)

The following quotations from Alister McGrath, based upon both his writings and those of two other distinguished theologians, Eberhard Jungel and Emil Brunner, again confirm the inward reaching of God through self-revelation/disclosure, *"The idea of divine self-revelation implies that unaided human attempts to fully discern the nature and purposes of God are ultimately unsuccessful. Although most Christian theologians hold that a natural knowledge of God* (from nature and conscience, sometimes known as *common grace*) *is possible, any such natural knowledge is generally understood to be limited in scope, in coherence, and in depth. The idea of revelation expresses the basic Christian belief that we need to be told what God is like"* [82] And, *"In its developed sense, revelation does not mean merely the transmission of a body of knowledge but the personal self-disclosure of God within history."* [83]

Finally, *"God could take the initiative away from humans, through self-revelation and a willingness to be known in a historical and personal form, namely Jesus Christ. Theology is thus to be thought of as a human response to God's self-disclosure, rather than the human quest for God."* [84]

So maybe we should take on board the possibility that if we only consider our search for God and take no account of His search for us, we could be looking through the wrong ends of our binoculars.

Moving on to the analogies: The first relates to two cockatiels that were family pets some 25 years ago. Neither the male (Gus) or the female

---

[82] Alister McGrath, also citing Eberhard Jungel. *Christian Theology – An Introduction.* John Wiley & Sons Ltd, 2017, p.136.
[83] Alister McGrath. Ibid.
[84] Alister McGrath, referencing Emil Brunner. Ibid, p.181.

(Tweetie) had been hand-reared and hence were not particularly tame. Tweetie, in particular, tended to be freaked out by any attempt at human contact. Gus, however, was better and it appeared that, at times, he really wanted to perch on our hands or whatever. But he just couldn't quite do it. No matter how softly we spoke to him and how much encouragement he received, he wouldn't land. What he and Tweetie needed was for one of us to be incarnated as a cockatiel. This would then mean that we could give them information way beyond even the wisest and greatest of cockatiels, and thereby convince them that human beings were OK, wanting to care for rather than hurt them.

The second analogy concerns the legendary *Charlie Cat the Cat*. What a magnificent animal! – the *Ginger Governor* and $18^1/_2$ pounds at his fighting weight. A very smart cat, I spent many happy hours teaching Charlie to play *tennis*. It even got to the stage that if I said to him, "Charlie, tennis", he would immediately lie on the floor waiting for me to throw a table tennis ball to him. He would then hit the ball back to me using either paw (some footballers could learn from this), and we got this off to such a fine art that quite often I was able to catch it. And we could, of course, go on for ages because, as we all know, cats are never in a rush or have full diaries. So this game enabled me to form a relationship with Charlie - I knew where he was coming from, and he knew where I was coming from. However, in between our games (think of the time and money I was wasting!), I would generally go upstairs to my office and carry out what I like to think were fairly complicated calculations or involved reports. As far as I am aware, and I'm pretty confident about this, no relationship was possible between Charlie and me concerning my calculations or reports. So with *tennis*, Charlie was getting me at my *easy end*. I believe the same is true for Jesus Christ - He was and, I believe, as far as His relationships with us as human beings are concerned, still is, God at His *easy end*.

In other words, similar to a human mother using *baby-talk* with her small child, so God, in Christ, stoops down to our level and paints a self-portrait which we can understand and leads us towards intimacy. It has to be this way round, the bigger to the (very much) smaller – otherwise, as touched on previously, we might as well expect babies and infants to be solely responsible for learning to walk and talk, and developing into mature and well-adjusted adults. Once we see God in the lead role instead of ourselves and realise it's all about His great desire and ability to make Himself known to us, everything begins to fit.

Thirdly, the movie, *Taken*, starring Liam Neeson; one of the few films where I remained awake from start to finish. He plays a guy who is often distracted by the onerous demands of high-intensity security work, and, as his daughter grows up, she is not sure of his love for her. Then she gets kidnapped in Paris and, after some incredible detective work and amazing physical action (not in Kev's league of course), he eventually finds her. When he does, she suddenly realises that he does love her after all and will literally move heaven and earth to rescue her - so she shouts out in high emotion, "Daddy, you came for me."

That, in a nutshell, is the gospel – it is completely revolutionary - Jesus has come for us and encourages us to call God, Abba, which means *papa*, *dad*, or even *daddy*. And, unlike human fathers, God is the perfect daddy. Yes, God is absolutely awesome and *wholly other*, but He is also passionate about us coming to know Him intimately; it is why He made us, and it is what He delights in.[85]

As a powerful illustration of this, I once watched a DVD which included the story of an Indian pastor who talked to God as, *daddy*. Every morning God woke this guy up at about 4am to give him his *marching orders* for the day. One day he awakens at 4am with a *picture* in his head of a 'Maharajah' to whom he knows he must tell the gospel of Jesus Christ. Recognition is no problem when he does find the 'Maharajah' because God has also given this guy an accurate *picture* of the Indian pastor! That's not religion; it's the kingdom of God.

---

[85] While recognising and hopefully experiencing God's intimate presence, we should not lose sight of His awesome transcendence (He is, after all, still God *Almighty* and not God *All-Matey*); two very powerful truths that most people find difficult to hold in good equilibrium.

This ninth point is vitally important, as it reveals a radical and crucial difference between true Christianity and, apparently, all other worldviews. The recognition of the significance of this paramount distinction does, however, require an appreciation of where human beings stand in comparison with the perfect morality of God. This is discussed at some length in the following chapter, so it seems sufficient at this stage to simply re-emphasise that our wrongdoings or sins have consequences, the most serious of which is a chasm between God and all humanity that requires bridging.

As previously highlighted, adherents to many worldviews appear to recognise, consciously or unconsciously, this separation and consequently believe that some kind of remedy is required. This usually involves the undertaking of certain actions or techniques, sometimes in conjunction with the pursuit of enlightenment. Although, unsurprisingly, the overall variation of these actions is extremely wide-ranging, everything can be summarised by the little phrase, *human works* (or *legalism*). This means that bridging the chasm is deemed to be largely, if not entirely, humanity's responsibility and that we all, therefore, need to achieve certain standards and/or transformations and/or harmonisations and/or enlightenments using solely our own efforts and insights.

Christianity is radically different from the above because it is based on God's grace rather than human effort or works. In the NT, grace means God's love in action towards men and women who simply do not merit such favour and cannot bridge the chasm themselves. Grace, therefore, equates to God building the bridge from His side. Many NT verses demonstrate this – for instance, from the Apostle Paul's letter to the Church at Ephesus - *"For it is by grace you have been saved, through faith - and this not from yourselves, it is the gift of God - not by your own human efforts, so that no-one can boast."* (Ephesians 2:8-9)

The NT, therefore, consistently teaches that, instead of prioritising the need to *do or become something,* the main emphasis for the seeker is rather to *receive* something. Wow! What a great deal - the offer of forgiveness and heaven rather than the need to earn them is surely something that everyone would want. But often we don't; an attitude presumably influenced by a prevailing Western culture that prizes self-made men and women, and believes that we should do all things, including the *spiritual*, our own way and under our control (only perceived of course). Our general tendency is, therefore, to resist the available assistance and outreaching from an all-powerful, all-knowing, and *agape* (unconditional) - loving Father God, believing that any detachment from self-dependence would move us away from the safety of our default comfort zone. But this represents false comfort; as explained in some detail in the next chapter, we cannot fix ourselves and are thus unable to bridge the existing chasm.

By way of confirmation, this is an alternative rendering of the above verses according to The Message, *"Now God has us where He wants us, with all the time in this world and the next to shower grace and kindness upon us in Christ Jesus.*[86] *Saving is all His idea, and all His work. All we do is trust Him enough to let Him do it. It's God's gift from start to finish! We don't play the major role. If we did, we'd probably go around bragging that we'd done the whole thing! No, we neither make nor save ourselves. God does both the making and saving."* (Ephesians 2:7-10 MSG)

It must, however, also be emphasised that genuine conversion should be marked with a desire to become increasingly like Jesus Christ, no matter how imperfectly this truth may be grasped at the time. Otherwise, we can easily abrogate our moral responsibilities, becoming in danger of a gigantic cop-out and making a mockery of the gospel.

If many more Christians, me included, had really got hold of this tenth and final point and managed to live it out (as some undoubtedly have), then our world would be a very different and far better place. Although I've probably had the correct head knowledge in this area for most of

---

[86] The NT refers to both *believers being in Christ* and *Christ being in believers*, a supernatural, reciprocal and ongoing experience, inevitably and understandably shrouded in some mystery. There is, however, no suggestion of believers simply being absorbed into Christ; human individuality is maintained.

the past 40+ years, I'm still struggling to experience its truth on a regular basis. The thing is that no-one is ever expected to live the Christian life using only his or her own resources. It is simply beyond our ability to go it alone, a truth touched on again in subsequent chapters.

A Chinese Christian, known as Watchman Nee, once wrote, *"The distinctive feature of true Christianity is that it compels people to receive."* [87] That is not only upon conversion (as per point 9 above), but *letting God love you and empower you* for the rest of your life. Christians are all called to be ambassadors for Christ; it is a great honour. However, we have no chance of making a proper go of this unless we continually tap into His love, peace, power and everything else, as made available to human beings through the Holy Spirit.

And from the 19th century American evangelist, D.L. Moody, *"You might as well try to hear without ears or breathe without lungs, as to try to live a Christian life without the Spirit of God in your heart."* [88]

Three quotations from the Apostle Paul explain the Scriptural and intended spiritual position, *"I can do everything through Him* (Jesus) *who gives me strength"* (Philippians 4:13), *"Do you not know that your body is a temple of the Holy Spirit, who is in you, whom you have received from God?"* (1 Corinthians: 6:19) and, *"But the fruit of the Spirit is love, joy, peace, patience, kindness, goodness, faithfulness, gentleness and self-control."* (Galatians 5:22-23a) So great energy - bring it on!

But how does this all work out in practice? Does God do everything, and we just passively watch it all happening? Not at all. These are the words of Jesus, as recorded by Matthew:

"Come to me, all you who are weary and burdened, and I will give you rest. Take my yoke upon you and learn from me, for I am gentle and humble in heart, and you will find rest for your souls. For my yoke is easy and my burden is light."(Matthew 11:28-29)

---

[87] Watchman Nee, *Changed into His Likeness*. CLC Publications, 2007, p. 97.
[88] D L. Moody. https://www.azquotes.com/quote/581700

No matter how you look at it, these are great words. Knowing the intimate presence of God is far more precious and valuable than any of our achievements or even receiving the desired answers to our prayers. Are there any equivalents in other worldviews? *Dunno*, but surely unlikely.

A few words of explanation are probably appropriate. Yokes are wooden beams used to link a pair of oxen together as they plough furrows in third world farming. The usual method is to pair up a novice ox with an older more experienced animal who teaches it the ropes. Jesus undoubtedly wishes to do this for us, He being the senior partner and ourselves, the juniors. His yoke for us, individually tailored to our personalities and temperaments, will be the perfect fit. The phrase, *learn from me*, thus makes perfect sense, enabling us to be taken up in the excitement of what God is doing rather than just focussing on ourselves. Part of this may require going outside of our *safe place* and doing things that we would not have previously thought possible, including comforting others experiencing life problems by using the comfort we have received from God during our own.

So that then completes the objective evidence on offer within this particular chapter. How good is it? Well, I like it! and consider that, as a cumulative body, it passes both the *coherence test* (consistent, logical and comprehensible) and the *correspondence test* (realistic link-ups with the world and humanity). Furthermore, using whatever logic remains after my civil engineering brain blew up, the Bible records pretty much what I would expect if God became a human being (very much easier to believe than a man becoming God – *top-down* as opposed to *bottom-up*).

Specifically, He would:

- Have a unique entrance into life.
- Be morally perfect and without fault.
- Have the authority to forgive all human wrongdoing/sin.

- Manifest the supernatural in the form of miracles over every realm of nature.
- Have an acute sense of difference.
- Speak the greatest words ever spoken.
- Be proactive in terms of both human salvation (deliverance/rescue) and divine leadership.
- Have a lasting and universal influence.
- Satisfy the spiritual hunger in men and women.
- Exercise power over death.
- Confirm ancient and detailed prophecies.

Jesus Christ accordingly ticks every box, with, in particular, power over death and an authentic resurrection CV. It is very difficult, therefore, to conclude that He is anything other than the Son of God.

It may be that others could draw up an even lengthier list but, in any event, what more could we realistically expect? The author and itinerant minister, David Pawson (1930-2020), once wrote, *"We need to find the truth that is as true for everybody as for anybody, and the truth that remains true whether it is believed by anybody or nobody."* [89] This surely is it. While again acknowledging that the inevitable mystery makes it impossible to adequately describe *Father*, *Son*, and *Holy Spirit* simply by using human language, there seems to be very little doubt that Jesus Christ, as the unequivocal Son of God, is synonymous with Ultimate Reality. As He said Himself, *"I am the way and the truth and the life"* (John 14:6), three apparent absolutes rather than the politically correct: *a way*, *a truth* and *a life*.

---

[89] David Pawson, *The Challenge Of Islam To Christians*: Hodder & Stoughton, 2003, p.102

Time to return to Karl Barth. Things changed after his earlier scepticism, as again recorded by Holmes and Rook, *"Barth found his answer in Jesus Christ. He never deviated for a second from the conviction that God was utterly beyond any human attempt to understand, but realised that we did not have to reach God: God had graciously given Himself to us in Jesus."* [90]

I also include a couple more of Barth's relevant quotes, this time relayed by Alister McGrath, *"God is known only as God chooses to be known – in other words, in God's self-revelation in Jesus Christ."* [91] And *"There is a radical discontinuity between God's self-revelation to humanity, which leads to faith, and humanity's search for God, which leads to religion."* [92] Shortly before he died, Barth was asked if he could summarise his entire theology in a single sentence. He replied with a line from a well-known children's hymn, *"Jesus loves me this I know, for the Bible tells me so"* - it's not rocket science!

This chapter would not be complete without reference to at least one of Jesus' post-resurrection physical appearances. The following event is reported in Luke's gospel. It is prosaic rather than flowery and has all the appearance of authenticity rather than fabrication. So did it actually happen? I would be simply astounded if it didn't - look at the disciples' amazement and trouble they had in believing it was Jesus (presumably the main reason why the nail marks were left in).

While they (ten disciples – Thomas was elsewhere and, obviously, no Judas) *were still talking about this, Jesus Himself stood among them and said to them, "Peace be with you."*

They were startled and frightened, thinking they saw a ghost. He said to them, "Why are you troubled, and why do doubts rise in your minds? Look at my hands and my feet. It is I myself! Touch me and see; a ghost does not have flesh and bones, as you see I have."

---

[90] Stephen Holmes and Russell Rook, *What are we waiting for?* Paternoster, 2008, p.4.
[91] Alister McGrath, *Christian Theology – An Introduction.* John Wiley & Sons Ltd, 2017, p.63.
[92] Ibid. p.414.

When He had said this, He showed them His hands and feet. And while they still did not believe it because of joy and amazement, He asked them, "Do you have anything here to eat?" They gave Him a piece of broiled fish, and He took it and ate it in their presence.

He said to them, "This is what I told you while I was still with you: Everything must be fulfilled that is written about me in the Law of Moses, the Prophets and the Psalms." (the Tanakh/OT) [93] (Luke 24:36-44)

So what is my level of certainty concerning the truth of the gospel of Jesus Christ? Well, taking into account the objective evidence put forward in just this one chapter together with the times I have been aware of and experienced God's accompanying self-disclosure (such as at my conversion and the very much later *Baptism of love* in the psychiatric unit, as relayed in part 1), I put my confidence in Christ's gospel in the same bracket as my belief that I exist as an individual, conscious being and not as part of another person's dreams or whatever. Alternatively, going back to C.S. Lewis' *Great Trilemma*, the faith necessary for me to believe that Jesus Christ was *not* the Son of God would overwhelmingly dwarf what I need to believe that He is - as per Bono of U2.

This confidence in Jesus' ontology is, therefore, above the faith I exert in both the normal and very important decisions of life, including that previously used in connection with the correctness and accuracy of interpretative reports and calculations (I was never sued in the thirty years duration of my business). This doesn't mean that I've got absolutely everything sorted out – I think it's pretty clear from part 1 that I definitely haven't. It's just that my existing unresolved questions are nowhere near sufficient to have any real impact on my core Christian beliefs. For whatever reason, and perhaps this is a particular gift from

---

[93] Apart from some differences in the order and division of the various books, the Jewish 'Tanakh' is essentially the same as the Christian Old Testament. In particular, both can be considered as having three parts – the Law (the 'Torah'), the Prophets (e.g., Isaiah, Jeremiah), and the wisdom writings (e.g., Psalms, Proverbs), a categorisation confirmed by Christ.

God (because I know that not all Christians can say this), I have not to date had any serious doubts concerning the truth of the gospel since the day of my conversion in April 1977. Thus, although I have admiration for various people from all walks of life and their related achievements, I could never be one of their avid followers – after all, they're only humans, only cockatiels.

In summary, it is considered to be *job done* concerning the nature of Jesus Christ, the associated blueprint being entirely consistent with His claims of Ultimate Reality/God reaching into our world. Furthermore, the objective evidence offered up in this chapter bears witness to the Bible as a reliable and trustworthy *road-map*, and to the fact that, as we read it, we can come to know both ourselves and, most importantly, the real Jesus. It's, therefore, clearly not narrow-minded or bigoted to believe that, although various religions and worldviews may well contain truth within them, only one can be considered as providing both consistently accurate truth and the universal picture. I am, however, more than happy to examine any other plausible Ultimate Reality blueprints; if I'm basing my life on wrong beliefs, I prefer to find out sooner rather than later.

As an example of how we are depriving ourselves when we ignore the gospel records of Jesus Christ, I again refer to my maternal grandfather, Captain E H Slater. What an interesting life that guy had. His father died of sunstroke and was buried at sea when my grandfather was just ten years old. He went to sea himself at the age of fourteen and didn't return until he was eighteen. He circumnavigated the globe twice, once under sail and once under steam. His ship was sunk in the 1st World War, but he survived. He was dockmaster at the strategically very important Swansea Docks during the 2nd World War (no vessel moved in or out without his say-so) and, upon retiring, he headed up *The Mumbles Lifeboat* in Swansea for several years.

I would love to have had an adult conversation with him to find out what it all felt like, and what his innermost thoughts were during those times. But he died shortly before my eleventh birthday, and so the *pictures* I have of him as a boy, youth and pre-retirement man can only be based on my imagination. However, this situation would undoubtedly change if someone discovered his hitherto unknown journals, meticulously kept throughout his life. It would be a real turn-on, because I could then have a greater and more intimate understanding of his character and whole nature. And it would certainly be completely ridiculous if I refused to read these journals, preferring my imagined pictures instead. Yet that is what so many people are doing with the life and ministry of Jesus Christ.

As a summary *heads-up* concerning the next chapter, it's particularly important to remember three things. Firstly, we are all in the same boat; secondly, God reaches out to us all with unconditional love, whereby He loves us because He loves us; and thirdly, His purposes and plans are without equal and, with our co-operation, will ultimately result in each of us becoming the best version of ourselves possible - or to quote Soren Kierkegaard, "Now, with God's help, I shall become myself." [94]

---

[94] Soren Kierkegaard. https://www.goodreads.com/quotes/423155-now-with-god-s-help-i-shall-become-myself

CHAPTER FIVE

**We Are All Sinners and Need a Saviour (the relevance criterion)
"You cannot be Serious Man, You cannot be SERIOUS!" (John McEnroe, Wimbledon, 1981)**

I had originally considered naming this chapter the *Un-Chapter* but then decided that the title was perhaps a bit too cryptic. It is, nevertheless, un-PC, un-Postmodern and un-New Age, with the content also maybe being un-popular. But not, I trust, un-true. This is undoubtedly the hardest chapter for me to write, simply because I have struggled and wrestled with the subject matter over several decades.

As mentioned earlier, I believe the main questions for any worldview or religion should be concerned with truth and relevance. I also stated, at the end of the previous chapter, that I've had no serious doubts concerning the truth of Christ's gospel since my conversion. However, it's been a rather different story when it comes to relevance. Just look at the title of this chapter; the gospel and indeed the whole Bible declare that we are all wrongdoers, or the antiquated and un-PC/un-postmodern word, *sinners*. None of us are therefore fit for heaven and accordingly require a *saviour*. Another un-PC/un-postmodern word. But can this actually be correct?

There are some amazing people out there, of no particular faith, undertaking excellent humanitarian work, and many other equally impressive individuals who are so fantastic and brilliant that simply being in their company is a real privilege and delight. I particularly remember an excellent pole vault coach, who was such an incredible guy and gave me so much time, support and encouragement. Then, of course, there are life's *heroes*, such as members of our emergency services who risk life and limb to save others, with the general public themselves sometimes marvellously stepping up to the plate by courageously confronting certain of life's great challenges and generously helping people less fortunate. Why should all these wonderful (non-believing) human beings need to *come to Christ*? I have therefore written this chapter as much for me as for anyone else.

It would all be so different, and easier to write about, if we could go back a hundred years and more into UK history. But we can't, and we probably wouldn't want to anyway (no welfare system or domestic central heating, plus the delights of outside toilets – if you were lucky). Back then, if you asked non-believing people living in this country why they were not Christians, you would probably have received two quite different answers. The first, which may have applied to perhaps 50% of those questioned, would be pretty much the same as that put forward today – that is, "We don't need the Christian gospel with its emphasis on repentance and forgiveness, because, quite frankly, we're essentially good rather than bad persons." This reply is often followed with comments like, "I'll always help anybody, I'm hard-working, I never mean anyone any harm, I may not be perfect but I always do my best etc..." There's no doubt that I would have subscribed to this view in pre-conversion days.

The second reason, which is comparatively rare these days, goes something like, "I am such a bad person; there is no way I could be forgiven by a good God for all the wrong things I've done." Our society has changed so much in the past century or so, and most of us *good British citizens* now believe that everything's cool on the moral front. The gospel of Jesus Christ, when it's thought about at all, is therefore commonly viewed as basically irrelevant – a solution to a problem we simply do not have any more. And, of course, should we feel any guilt from our various misdemeanours, we can usually dismiss this fairly easily by simply watching The News, "Look at that evil murdering paedophile and the raging fanatical terrorist – we've got to be so much better than them."

Accordingly, the word *sin* has only minor significance in our current society's vocabulary. If it means anything at all to many UK citizens, it probably relates to our eating too much chocolate or something similar. In other words, it is more or less completely trivialised. Or perhaps, as is quite often the case in politics, we label our various misdeeds as 'mistakes' when they are eventually discovered. Alternatively, for some folks brought up under a particular religious persuasion, the thought of sin equates directly to guilt and pain and is therefore almost immediately dismissed. And still others may prefer to treat this word as an *anachronism* – that is something completely out of date such as the 'twin-tub', famously used by my mother for decades after washing machines had been invented (whatever happened to the mangle?).

So did we have it all completely wrong 100+ years ago? Are we now simply better educated and more informed, particularly concerning global matters and other worldviews, so that words like *sin* can be consigned to the infancy or perhaps adolescence of our evolution?

Before going any further, it seems important to include a few thoughts concerning the whole subject of *justice*. It may be recalled, from chapter two, that C.S. Lewis once said that there is provision for our every desire. Well, we certainly desire and, on occasions, even crave justice. For the murdering paedophile, the raging terrorist, Adolph Hitler, Joseph Stalin, Idi Amin, Saddam Hussein, Robert Mugabe et al. And if they have escaped being called to account and severely punished for their crimes in this life, then we hope that, in some way, they will get their just deserts after death. It's, therefore, not surprising that the newspaper headline, *May they rot in hell* or similar, still seems to crop up fairly regularly. So anyway, there's good news and bad news. The good news is that God is a God of justice and is far more concerned about this than we humans are. The bad news relates to where He sets the bar and how this might drag us all into the equation.

It has already been pointed out that we only experience a historical *snapshot* of the society we live in, and that the popular attitudes and beliefs of the time may or may not be correct and reliable. But, of course, we normally seem to take it for granted that *our* society is so much more sophisticated and *on-the-ball* than those that have gone before (and perhaps will follow). But why should it be? Is a no plausibility structure society better than enlightenment-based or Christian revival–based societies? Surely a very relevant question; one that most of us probably don't even think to ask. True Christianity, when sensitive to the customs and traditions of different cultures and generations and, most importantly, when empowered by the Holy Spirit, is capable of transcending the associated distinctions; resulting in teaching and enlightenment relevant to all people groups past, present and future. In order to be faithful to the complete gospel message, this teaching must set out the Christian position regarding the universal and timeless *human condition*, as illustrated by the following selected quotations and related comments.

Taking these in chronological order, and commencing with the OT prophet, Jeremiah, who lived around 600 BC. He said, *"The heart is deceitful above all things and beyond cure. Who can understand it?"* (Jeremiah 17:9) This is very different to the often-heard phrase, *His/her heart is in the right place*, but the shock to my system from the events of recent years has led me to believe that Jeremiah got it spot-on. Before this, I had a very different and much higher opinion of myself. As discussed in part 1, my *external unreal me* was generally very significantly above my *internal real me*, resulting in looking down at some of the people with whom I had contact. So, probably not before time, I've had my eyes opened.

When we come to Jesus, it seems that He simply takes it for granted that none of us is *good*. In Matthew's gospel (and similar in Luke's) He says, *"If you, then, though you are evil, know how to give good gifts to your children, how much more will your Father in heaven give good gifts to those who ask Him…..?"* (Matthew: 7:11) These sentiments thus appear to be the exact opposite of how we think about ourselves as people living in present-day Western society. Most of us believe that we are *good people, who can do some bad things*, whereas Christ clearly says we are *bad people who can do some good things*. If I understand Jesus aright, the fact that I once did a good and praiseworthy act by saving a woman from drowning (Majorca 1992) is irrelevant to my basic character, which may not be up to much. I think there is little doubt that Jesus Christ would have very few clients if He was a psychologist in our society today.

Referring once more to C.S. Lewis. Back in the early 1940s, he wrote, *"A recovery of the old sense of sin is essential to Christianity. Christ takes it for granted that men are bad. Unless we feel this assumption of His to be true, though we are part of the world He came to save, we are not part of the audience to whom His words are addressed."* [95] And from the same period, not sparing himself, he came up with the following conclusion: *"In my most clearsighted moments not only do I not think myself a nice man, but I know that I am a very nasty one. I can look at some of the things I have done with horror and loathing."* [96]

Coming virtually up to date, I cite Terry Eagleton, Professor of English Literature at The University of Lancaster, and regarded by many to be Britain's most influential present-day literary critic. Eagleton talks about the *"lamentable state of humanity"*, and says he means by this *"...the prevalence of greed, idolatry and delusion, the depth of our instinct to dominate and possess, the dull persistence of injustice and exploitation, the chronic anxiety which leads us to hate, maim and exploit, along with the sickness, suffering and despair which Jesus associates with evil."* [97] He also points out that there has been no human culture to date in which virtue has been predominant - particularly relevant to social justice, the prioritisation and pursuit of which the Bible emphasises throughout.

---

[95] C.S. Lewis. https://quotefancy.com/quote/781605/C-S-Lewis-A-recovery-of-the-old-sense-of-sin.

[96] C.S. Lewis, *Mere Christianity.* 1952, MacMillan in New York, – adapted from a series of BBC radio talks between 1941 and 1944.

[97] Terry Eagleton, *Reason, Faith and Revolution – Reflections on the God Debate.* Yale University Press, 2009, p.24.

That then represents a microcosm of the Christian take on the universal human condition, which it considers to be sinful and in urgent need of regeneration/spiritual renewal. The Christian Church is, of course, called to preach this message but, as mentioned in chapter three, can easily be affected more by the prevailing values of UK and Western society than vice-versa. This situation, which has now existed for many decades, is accurately summarised by a quotation from Francis Schaeffer, a renowned 20th century American theologian and philosopher. He said: *"I have come to the conclusion that none of us in our generation feels as guilty about sin as we should or as our forefathers did. I think this basically is the problem of living in a psychologically oriented age."* [98]

So what is this psychological orientation? Returning to my earlier question concerning the possibility of our general indifference to sin being mainly due to evolving beyond a past somewhat primitive worldview, I now answer in the negative. Indeed, as per Francis Schaffer, I consider that modern psychology, in conjunction with other secular influences such as Postmodernism, has cultivated a UK/Western society whereby comparatively few people are willing to accept responsibility for personal sin. To emphasise the validity of this viewpoint, I refer to the modern secular psychologist, Paul Gilbert, and his book, *The Compassionate Mind*. In this book, Gilbert talks about becoming very distressed while watching a TV programme on the horrors of the Holocaust and concentration camps. As per the title, he does indeed seem to be a compassionate man and, not surprisingly, ends up weeping. In fact, he becomes so upset that he's tempted to turn off the programme.

Quoting Gilbert verbatim, he says, *"I was glad I didn't. In the discussion that followed, people expressed the usual simplistic ideas about good and evil, but then one person pointed out that this had little to do with good and evil and everything to do with our brains, what they are capable of and the social contexts that pattern them – that we must give*

---

[98] Francis Schaeffer, *Letters of Francis A. Schaeffer: spiritual reality in the personal Christian Life.* Westchester, Ill: Crossway Books, 1986, p.123.

up believing that we have full control of our minds when history shows time and time again that we don't – it's an illusion – in groups, we can do all sorts of terrible things (not sure how he defines 'terrible' here). *That sentiment is the road to compassion. My understanding of the pure despair in this tragedy and my realisation of what we are up against from our evolved minds, and how we can be so easily led by our 'old brain/mind' passions, gave me new insights and greatly affected me."* [99]

Wow - how to reply to that? In your face or what! Anyhow, my first thought is that if this opinion is considered in conjunction with the naturalistic outlook of atheistic science where human beings are essentially random accidents, then why bother with things like law courts? OK, we're clearly up on your average lion who, the day after mauling someone to death, is hardly likely to turn up at the Royal Courts of Justice with his defence barrister. But when you get right down to it, Gilbert is surely agreeing with the above hypothesis that (virtually) nothing is ever our fault.

So then, doesn't anyone have to take *any* responsibility for the truly gargantuan amount of bad stuff that goes on in our world? And that really is no overstatement – imagine taking all the horrendous and unpleasant reports out of The News – what would be left? And would anybody be interested? I've checked myself out on this, and my default position is undoubtedly to go first to the bad news (after the Sport of course, which, in any event, often falls into this category for Torquay United supporters). Finally, Gilbert talks of the 'road to compassion' - how compassionate is this to the Jewish people?

So that's my go at it. A better and more comprehensive explanation is given by Os Guinness in a YouTube video (published 30/04/10) who, during a Q & A session at an American University, responds to one student's proposition that evil is not within a person but only on the outside. I again quote Guinness' answer verbatim. *"What you're*

---

[99] Paul Gilbert, *The Compassionate Mind*. Constable & Robinson Ltd., 2013, pp.223-224.

describing is the fruits of the 18th century Enlightenment, which doesn't believe in evil, doesn't believe in sin or responsibility; so looks to things like more psychology, better politics, higher education, and this will solve the problem. And clearly, 20th century evil has blown a huge hole in that. Now when you meet people who still believe in it, I think this is the way to approach them – they have never met real evil. Let me give you an example. The great poet, W H Auden, came to faith through meeting evil. He was a socialist, atheist and left-wing radical……He came to America to escape Nazism. But one evening watching a documentary in New York saw Hitler's troops entering Poland bayonetting (Jewish) women and children, and most of the German audience were on the side of the Nazi Stormtroopers and cried out in the darkness, 'kill them', 'kill them', egging them on. And Auden said: 'In two minutes my whole worldview was turned around. On the one hand, I knew we were evil. I was looking at something that no psychology, no education and no politics could ever change. This is radical evil.' But then he said: 'I realised, as a European intellectual, I'd spent all my life removing the absolutes – everything's relative. But I wanted to say that Hitler was absolutely evil. So he said: 'I left the cinema a seeker after an unconditional absolute, and I met Christ.'"* [100]

Although the views of most people would probably still be closer to those of Os Guinness, the essence of Paul Gilbert's psychology, as concluded by Francis Schaeffer, is undoubtedly filtering down insidiously into Western society.

One of the things that completely blew Auden away, as he refers to elsewhere, is the fact that the German audience in the documentary were not soldiers under orders, but *ordinary* people seemingly acting spontaneously out of their own free will. OK, since coming to power in 1933, the Nazi propaganda against the Jewish people had become ever more vitriolic, including the mass circulation of much anti-Semitic literature such as Hitler's fanatically racist, *Mein Kampf* (published

---

[100] Os Guinness, *Are we responsible for evil?* YouTube, 30/04/2010.
https://www.bing.com/search?q=Are+we+responsible+for+evil+%2b+Os+Guinness&FORM=SSRE

1925/26); but still...celebrating the bayonetting of women and children! And what about the possibility that we, the citizens of UK 2020, could have acted in like manner given similar circumstances? There are several places in the NT where inner hate is considered to correspond to murder; thus indicating that, when there seem to be no repercussions, people, and particularly men, are capable of all sorts of evil.

To continue, there is a well-known saying, *power corrupts and absolute power corrupts absolutely,* but is it perhaps more accurate to say, absolute power allows an already corrupted nature to show itself for what it really is? So could this line of reasoning be a valid explanation for why some of the worst Nazi offenders, who carried out atrocities of their own volition and subsequently escaped judgement, seem to have been *pillars of society* (doctors, lawyers, scientists etc) in Germany both before and after World War II? Is it possible that these examples represent a case of certain individuals' *real internal me's* temporarily being allowed to go external? Who really knows what is in any of us? – Heinrich Himmler (1900 – 1945) was a chicken farmer before he became head of the Nazi SS and Gestapo.

We can also extend this argument to the sex scandals surrounding Harvey Weinstein, Bill Cosby and other high-profile celebrities, plus Westminster, the seat of British Parliament, where' there have been recent allegations concerning a whole range of inappropriate sexual behaviour by male MPs. All of the foregoing involved power, opportunity and, again, an absence of foreseeable repercussions. How many of our male population would have behaved in like manner given similar opportunities? All acts of impropriety (and indeed every type of wrongdoing) start in the mind, which is consistent with Christ's teaching, *"You have heard that it was said, 'Do not commit adultery'. But I tell you that anyone who looks at a woman lustfully has already committed adultery with her in his heart."* (Matthew 5:27-28)

I guess it's pretty clear where I'm going with all of this. The OT accordingly states the following, *"But the LORD said to Samuel, 'Do not consider his appearance or his height, for I have rejected Him. The LORD does not look at the things man looks at. Man looks at the outward appearance, but the* LORD *looks at the heart'."* (1 Samuel 16:7) This is hardly great news; because I strongly suspect that, like me, most of us specialise in judging our outward actions – it's simply so much easier and less painful. However, as referred to previously, the recent extreme events, although directly resulting from illness, can also be traced back to rotten matter deep down in my soul.

So, *God looks on the heart* - that is He examines what is actually going on inside of us, the bit that we usually keep hidden from others. And this hidden bit is not small. The American writer and pastor, R.T. Kendall, in his book *Totally Forgiving Ourselves*, believes that we reveal to the outside world perhaps only 10% of our actual personalities. So, *"When we see each other we see only 'tips' of icebergs."* [101] I have no idea whether this 10% assumption is correct or even close to the mark, but again refer back to the realisation that the *external unreal me* I've put out there has often been very different to and much better than the *internal real me*. Usually, it's only those very close to us, such as our spouses or partners, that get to know much about our inner selves; and even they don't know what we may be holding back or what is unknown to us ourselves. Any inadvertent disclosures can, therefore, cause us to feel vulnerable and maybe even agitated. Social media is rarely a help in these matters, usually revealing more of our hidden and ugly stuff, and making it more difficult to climb down when specific *bust-ups* are known about by all and sundry.

Why is there often so great a difference between our inner and outer selves? I think it is usually our pride that wants others to think the absolute best of us - that we are *top people*, really well sorted, and great to be with. We, therefore, generally manage to successfully conceal the not so nice stuff that *lurks beneath* from those with whom we come into contact. However, these hidden flaws, weaknesses and sins can easily surface at potentially stressful times, such as buying/selling houses, weddings and at Christmas. These types of events, we sometimes say,

---

[101] R.T. Kendall, *Totally Forgiving Ourselves*. Hodder & Stoughton, 2008, p.42.

bring out the *worst* in us (or, at least in others); but what about the possibility that they actually bring out the *real* in us? And, assuming we accept this, can we properly hide behind the little phrase, "It's only human nature!" Yes, it is - but doesn't that simply confirm what we're like, rather than being any sort of legitimate excuse? Look at how mad some of us get when we've been *cut-up* by some idiot driver. Even the merest thought that they might try to justify this *despicable* action by appealing to their inescapable human nature will, rather than helping, probably make us even madder.

On a somewhat lighter note, I have sometimes, when people said that they were essentially *good* and thus in no need of repentance/forgiveness, asked them if they would be happy to show me, if this were possible, a video of their thought life during the preceding week. Almost without exception, they all said no, but, as previously, that's the bit which is most important to God. I suppose, for the sake of honesty, I ought to mention the only time a person has said that they were happy with revealing their inner thought life to all and sundry. This was *Fats Freddie*, at one of Matt Williams' Christmas meals. He simply told me to, "bring it on", although he had been drinking quite heavily at the time. Interestingly, Fats Freddie never admitted to being overweight, always insisting that he was simply *under-height*. At the last reckoning, Freddie needed to be 7ft 6ins tall for his weight to be classed as normal.

The NT provides comprehensive descriptions of our misdeeds and flaws with the following discussion utilising two opposite perspectives – the sins of omission (failure to do certain good things and often internal) and the sins of commission (bad stuff and often external). A famous passage from the Apostle Paul's first letter to the church at Corinth, often read at weddings, can be used in conjunction with the first. It's about love and says this, *"Love is patient, love is kind. It does not envy, it does not boast, it is not proud. It is not rude, it is not self-seeking, it is not easily angered, it keeps no record of wrongs. Love does not delight in evil, but rejoices with the truth. It always protects, always trusts, always hopes, always perseveres. Love never fails."* (1 Corinthians 13:4-8a.)

Quite a common test to see how we are getting along with this is to replace the word *love* with our name. *Graham is patient, Graham is kind* etc.... I think I'm so far off this pace for it actually to be funny if it wasn't so serious. As it happens, I have even begun to question whether I know how to truly love; generally considered to be the most important human attribute and the focal point of genuine Christianity. A bit too harsh? – maybe – but certainly worth thinking about.

Coming at it from the opposite perspective, the following comprises the conflation of very short sections of the Apostle Paul's letter to the church at Galatia and his second letter to Timothy, *"The acts of the sinful nature are obvious: sexual immorality, impurity and debauchery; idolatry;.....hatred, discord, jealousy, fits of rage, selfish ambition, dissensions, factions and envy; drunkenness, orgies, and the like. I warn you, as I did before, that those who live like this will not inherit the kingdom of God."* (Galatians: 5:19-21) And, *"There will be terrible times in the last days. People will be lovers of themselves, lovers of money, boastful, proud,* [102]*abusive, disobedient to their parents, ungrateful, unholy, without love, unforgiving, slanderous, without self-control, brutal, not lovers of the good, treacherous, rash, conceited, lovers of pleasure rather than lovers of God - having a form of godliness but denying its power."* (2 Timothy 3:1-5)

I can even add to this catalogue of bad stuff: arrogance, judgmentalism, hypocrisy, hubris, resentment, bitterness, lying, deception, impatience, stealing (including tax evasion - *cash-jobs* etc.), manipulation (by physical and psychological means), greed, gossip, mockery, holding grudges, complaining attitudes, coveting other people's jobs, spouses, houses etc. (don't even get me started on football clubs!).

---

[102] The term *proud* in the context of the above comprehensive list of individual sins refers specifically to socially undesirable pride, such as that relating to an inflated ego and hubris – i.e., it is assumed to have only limited ontological significance, something that is discussed separately. There is, furthermore, a positive side to this type of pride, such as that associated with doing a good job or being excited about what our kids have achieved.

So a fairly gobsmacking list. Nevertheless, I recognise many of these sins, past and present, in myself, in families (*umpteen* with at least a couple of members refusing to speak to each other, plus a few divorces), in politicians, and in so-called *celebrities* (the worse the behaviour, then usually the greater level of interest). And, magnifying it all up: in wars, genocide, human trafficking, sextortion, sexting, exploitation, corporate corruption, grave injustices at societal and international levels, and so on. And, if pressed, most people will acknowledge that they are familiar with some, or perhaps many, of the above individual sins and that they actually would like to live better lives. Let's face it, we don't even live up to our own standards, let alone God's!

The thing is that besides sin being an offence against God and others, it really hurts us. Again, quoting from Paul Backholer, *"…but it (the Bible) also reveals that it (sin) dramatically lowers the quality of life for the sinner and the lives of those around them. Sin destroys relationships, tears apart families, costs us our peace, steals our long-term happiness and gives birth to unnecessary pain. Sin brings with it loss of trust, loss of self-worth, heartbreak, fear and anger etc., whilst degrading and devaluing humanity."* [103] God wants to save us from all that. Isaiah describes His feelings, *"I am the Lord your God, who teaches you what is best for you, who directs you in the way you should go. If only you had paid attention to my commands, your peace would have been like a river, your righteousness* [104] *like the waves of the sea."* (Isaiah 48:17b-18)

Returning to the thought that past generations were much more aware of sin than we are, and the possibility that they may have been correct. In the early part of the 20th century, *The London Times* newspaper ran a competition called, *What is wrong with the world?* There were various entries, many of them very long. However, the winner was G.K.

---

[103] Paul Backholer, *How Christianity Made The Modern World*. Faith Media, 2009, p.106.
[104] Biblical *righteousness* is an extensive subject that has produced copious amounts of related literature. In its simplest form, as far as human beings are concerned, it conveys the basic idea of being in a right relationship with God and behaving accordingly.

Chesterton, who simply wrote, *"Dear Sir: Regarding your article 'What's Wrong with the World?' I am. Yours truly, Chesterton."* [105]

Going back very much further to the 1st century AD and, having already looked at the life of the Apostle Paul, who considered himself to be the *worst sinner of all*, how about the Apostle Peter? This is an incident recorded by Luke. Peter and some of the other disciples have spent a long night fishing and caught absolutely nothing. Anyway, after sitting in Peter's boat for a while teaching the gathered crowd on the nearby beach, Jesus tells him to take the vessel out into deep water and let down the nets for a catch. Now it's important to remember that Peter was a professional and highly knowledgeable fisherman, whereas Jesus wasn't. So when Peter more or less tells Jesus that this would be a waste of time, it seems reasonable to assume that his pride might have been hurt and that he may even have been a bit miffed. Nevertheless, because it's Jesus, he follows His instructions to the letter.

The result? – a catch of fish so large that Peter and those in his boat have to get the help of other fishermen simply to land it! So what's Peter's reaction to all of this? Does he lead the applause for Jesus? Or does he even get a little bit sulky? – After all, fishing is his domain and not Jesus'. No, none of these. Peter actually falls at the feet of Jesus and says, *"Go away from me Lord; I am a sinful man."* (Luke 5:8) So what is going on? I believe that Peter suddenly and shockingly became aware of the fact that he was actually in the presence of very God, who could see right into the depths of his inner being and the residing sin he always kept hidden. He, therefore, felt completely exposed and freaked out – he simply had to put some distance between himself and Jesus.

When it comes to personal experience and recalling Os Guinness' comments earlier in the chapter, I have undoubtedly met real evil. I know what it's like to look into the eyes of an extremely wicked person who had caused our whole family much agony and heartache and to be

---

[105] G.K. Chesterton. *Goodreads*. https://www.goodreads.com/quotes/18818-dear-sir-regarding-your-article- what-s-wrong-with-the-world.

met by a stare of such defiance and venom that it seemed to come directly from hell. I also know what it's like to have my resultant prayers (later that day) being answered, at least in part, by God. This was not a *Why Us* prayer, as I already knew that many people suffer terrible experiences, which seem to be nonsensical and unjustified, the only common denominator being that they all live, or have lived, in this very imperfect and sinful world. No, my prayer was basically along the lines of, whatever my faults, I had to be so much better than that individual and was, therefore, a *good* person.

Now, I very rarely get *pictures* or *visions*, but I had an amazing one then. I saw two light bulbs: one belonged to the perpetrator and was very dingy and dirty - about 40 watts; the other was mine and much brighter - about 150 watts. So I initially believed that I was doing OK. However, seemingly from nowhere, this thought then *exploded* in my mind, *But the comparison is the sun*. So what if the moral comparison is not the sun, SUN, but the son, SON? - that is the perfection of Jesus Christ – who's up to that? What if the life of Jesus turns out to be the level at which God actually sets the bar? Something else to ponder.

Yes, it's something to ponder all-right, but I'm sure it wouldn't take most of us very long before this type of pondering turned to questions, and then, quite possibly, to anger. What exactly is being implied, and how can we make sense of it concerning our own lives?

My take on this is that the light bulbs represent our *internal real me's*, and how they may play out and be judged when it comes to eternal consequences – fundamental to this chapter. This, of course, is something that's ultimately between each individual and God, although a few associated comments are made at the end of chapter eight. However, it's crucially important, concerning the here and now, to understand that God is certainly not saying that this evil person should be allowed to go unpunished; there must be justice.

Sometimes I feel that UK society is itself getting rather woolly in this area, with burglars every so often receiving longer prison sentences than murderers and, on occasions, the criminals seemingly being treated more as *victims* than the victims themselves. I never want to write anybody off, but attempted rehabilitation of convicted criminals should be done in the right way, and certainly never at the expense of individuals who have been harmed, and maybe broken, by their actions.

And can people who have committed terrible crimes, resulting in awful pain and suffering, ever be forgiven by the victims or their families? My answer is, yes, because I've actually seen it done. However, this incredible accomplishment was greatly helped by God's involvement and even then took many years, maybe a decade. Sometimes I think that Christians, because they are so aware that God wants them to forgive, try to do this almost immediately after the most horrendous of circumstances, resulting in denial and long-term mental health problems. There have, of course, been people who have consistently forgiven right from the start. Gordon Wilson,[106] whose 20-year-old daughter Marie died in his arms during the 1987 Enniskillen Remembrance Day bombing, comes to mind, but we should never put any timeframe for forgiveness on those grievously suffering due to others. Ultimately though, forgiveness, or at least continued attempted forgiveness, will help the mental health of victims more than stubbornly holding onto unforgiveness, no matter how justified it may seem.

Otherwise, they are allowing the culprits, who suffer no resulting discomfort themselves, to live *rent-free inside their heads*.

When you can't forgive someone,
pray for them.
It may not change them, but it
will always change you.

---

[106] The amazing forgiveness of Gordon Wilson (a man having a strong Christian faith, and not a sectarian) that he extended to the provisional IRA bombers who killed his young daughter is seen as a pivotal point in the Northern Ireland peace process, whereby love began to replace hatred and eventually led to the Good Friday Agreement in 1998.

This next observation concerns a probably even greater hindrance to experiencing true fellowship with God than any of the previously listed copious sins. It concerns ontological pride or what I shall call, *Identity Theft*. However, unlike the common usage of this little phrase, it's us ourselves who do the thieving. This is one of the things that has exercised my mind big-time, and it is bound to take quite a lot of unpacking. Nevertheless, because of its importance, it simply cannot be ignored. I hope the following explanation does it justice.

Starting with C.S. Lewis, who wrote, *"According to Christian teachers, the essential vice, the utmost evil, is Pride. Sexual immorality, anger, greed, drunkenness and all that, are mere flea bites in comparison. It was through Pride that the devil became the devil. Pride leads to every other vice: it is the complete anti-God state of mind."* [107] Lewis is here referring to this ontological pride or identity theft which, although not entirely unrelated to socially undesirable pride, differs significantly in both nature and magnitude.

Most of us, including me much of the time, live out our lives as if we are the creators rather than highly intelligent, but still dependent, creatures. We accordingly talk about our own lives and our rights as human beings, all the time insisting that we're the boss and it's *our* life steering wheel, accelerator, and brakes. We want to be in control and do exactly as we please, thank you very much. *We're the daddies*; a view we can perhaps hold on to as long as we are able to convince ourselves that no transcendent being exists and we're, therefore, totally free to determine who we are and what we can be (an increasingly heard mantra in modern Britain). It's therefore evident that our default position, conscious or unconscious, is to think of ourselves as *Suns* with all other people being less important *planets* orbiting around us. As per the band, Tears for Fears *"Everybody Wants To Rule The World"* (or at least their tiny bit of it).

---

[107] C.S. Lewis, *Mere Christianity.* New York: Simon & Schuster Touchstone edition,1996, p.109.

The thing is, and I've made considerable efforts in previous chapters to establish this: *There is a God and we're not it*. Or rather Him. Nor are we the principal actors, with everyone else simply being *bit-players*. No, it is God who is the playwright, principal actor, director and producer — it's His show! To quote from a bygone age, *We need to know our place*. Wholly inapplicable and cruel when concerned with other human beings, but right-on when dealing with God.

So how are we as modern Westerners going to be able to get, or even want to get this perspective? There are certainly a lot of potential obstacles in our way. For a start, as noted earlier, even though we're only tiny creatures whose lives are *but a breath*, we yearn to remain (at least in our perception) independent beings, thinking that this is the best, most enjoyable, and safest option for *doing* life. It's not because, despite His awesomeness, God, as noted previously, is at heart an agape-loving Father who wishes for all of us to experience the great benefits that come from knowing Him personally.

Then there are the *big three* societal obstacles of Postmodernism, Political Correctness and New Age, with at least the science that reaches us from the TV sets being almost 100% atheistic. And finally, there are the Christians themselves! And I'm not particularly talking about the *churchgoers*, but rather some of us who dare to believe that we are *Ambassadors for Christ*. It's perhaps a bit like Marmite[*] with, at least as far as many non-believers are concerned, the strongest argument for Christianity being those Christians who receive and then share God's love in action, and the strongest argument against Christianity being those (apparent?) Christians who become self-righteous, cliquey, and even unkind.

I suppose some might argue that, because of all the potential obstacles, they're quite justified in claiming that they never hear from God. However, as I look back at my own life and hear about the experiences of others during their pre-Christian days, this again confirms that God continually attempts to communicate with humanity utilising both the visible creation and conscience; enabled to hear His distinctive inner voice as it penetrates right down into peoples' souls. This voice has a ring of truth and authenticity about it and reminds us of our true position in creation if we would only listen.

Furthermore, is the idea of being responsible to God so counterintuitive to our society? Aren't there some clues to the contrary? I believe there are – some strong ones. For instance, all good parents expect and demand obedience from their children, particularly when they are very young when disobedience may lead to an accident or even death. It also hardly needs to be said that if children are not properly and lovingly disciplined, they are unlikely to develop into mature and well-rounded adults.

When we come to God, all this inevitably *ramps* up. Firstly, although we do take part in a pleasurable activity (hopefully!) at the very beginning of our children's lives, that is in actuality the only *creation* we are involved in. The designation of *creators* is, therefore, no more valid than describing us parents as *car designers/makers* simply because we know how to put the fuel in.

Secondly, our children grow up and, at some stage, normally overtake us. This, of course, cannot happen with God; we are simply never going to even remotely approach an omnipotent (all-powerful), omniscient (all-knowing), infinite, eternal, ever-present, agape-loving, transcendent, triune, divine Creator. So we will forever be subject and responsible to Him. That, without doubt, is our rightful (ontological) position as created beings or creatures, and it is fantastic news that, unlike Darth Vader or some other humanly imagined abominable super-power, God is Love and, again, only wants the best for us. And to repeat, if we could work God out and put Him in a box inside our brains to perhaps give ourselves a bit of misplaced comfort, He certainly would not be transcendent or worth the name.

Continuing with this whole question of knowing God and our consequent responsibilities, there are a few indicators that can help us understand our true position in creation. For instance, we usually don't like it if we meet a real *big-head* who goes on and on about how successful he is as a *self-made man*. We might think something like, "If you'd been born in North Korea or Sudan, you certainly wouldn't be a self-made man." We also don't like it (well women certainly don't – us guys might be ogling too much to take offence) if a very good-looking woman really knows it and struts her stuff accordingly. Additionally, if I'm meeting some of Rachel's friends for the first time, what would they think if I said something like, "Really pleased to meet you and, by the way, I'm the most intelligent person you will ever come across in your entire lives?" Well, presumably they would immediately class me as a *Total Pratt* and quickly move on to someone living in the real world. But, just for a moment, and this will test the imaginative powers of those who know me to the limit, what if I was the most intelligent person that they would ever meet? Would anyone be pleased in this instance if I bragged about it? No, they absolutely would not - because they'd know that I had nothing to do with how my brain was made. I did not make myself, and that applies to the other two examples as well. I've already discussed the self-made man, and the beautiful woman could equally have looked like the *back of a bus* for all she had to do with it. I am 67 years old, and it was not until I was 62 years old that I first thanked God for being *something – a human being made in His spiritual image* - rather than never having existed at all.

If God has indeed given all of us our individual lives, then it naturally follows that we are answerable to Him. He must have every right to expect this. When we ignore and resist Him, we're being rebellious and disobedient - like feral kids. And maybe, in some respects, I'm particularly qualified to talk like this. Because what is the worst way we could repay God for this great gift of life? Well, clearly, by attempting to commit suicide; albeit that, as is probably usually the case, there were certain mitigating factors. It's simply fantastic that forgiveness and giving people new starts rank so high in God's scheme of things. He never gives up on us no matter how far we stray. Incidentally, these sentiments are completely opposite to the sometimes heard phrase, *God only helps those who help themselves* – not in the Bible and wholly untrue.

However, despite the above clues, there seems to be little doubt that the whole concept of identity theft remains foreign to most of our society. I, therefore, include one final example. Many years ago, I sat in for my friend and fellow civil engineer, Matt Williams, and ran his practice for five weeks while he was visiting friends in Canada. My recollection is that all went fairly well, and I certainly can't remember any major cock-ups. However, picture the scene when Matt returned if I'd said to him something like," No problems when you were away, Matt, but I need to tell you that your practice is now my practice, your former clients are now my clients, and I also now own the office building." For this imaginary scenario then, I would have taken the whole business away from its rightful owner.

This is what we have done with our lives. We've denied God's rightful position at the centre of our being, and gone down our own selfish paths where everything revolves around a *self* we all call *my*, the fragility of which must be hidden and protected at all times.

This insistence to, as per Frank Sinatra, do it *My Way*, without any reference to the Creator of our entire physical, psychological and spiritual makeup, again aptly demonstrates what is meant by *Identity Theft* or *Sin* with a capital *S*. Our sins have already been described in some detail, but Sin is the creature, *I*, put squarely in the middle of my life instead of Creator God. It is *I–land* where I rule, it is, *I–first* and indeed sometimes, *I-the-one-and-only*. And the *I* is so powerful – it appeals to our self-importance and pride, causing us to even, on certain occasions, almost rather die than admit to being in the wrong. So I'd go stronger on this than Elton John, *sorry* doesn't just *seem* to be the hardest word, it *is* the hardest word.

I-land is often a very unhappy place. Consider how frequently we hear of successful people in the film and music industries, those with great wealth (check out the billionaire J. Paul Getty's family and some of the lives of big lottery winners), and many other famous individuals experiencing much grief and disillusionment. Why? Because it's almost as if their *I* in the middle has been welded into place. So often those around them (many of whom may well be sycophants and hangers-on), social media, and the various gossip magazines have praised these people to the hilt creating, amongst other things, ego-related stresses and accompanying symptoms.

As an illustration of this, the American author Philip Yancey writes about interviewing two types of people – the highly successful, rich and famous, including sports and film *stars* in one group, and human beings whom he calls *servants*, such as doctors and nurses working among leprosy patients in India, in the other. He found that the first group of *idols* were as miserable a collection of people he'd ever come across, and also that, while he had been ready to honour and admire the *servants* from the second group, he was amazed to find, upon meeting up, that he envied them.[108] But this is the way that God has made us – to find fulfilment in looking outwards to other people's needs as much as we look inwards to our own.

God has also created us to find ultimate fulfilment in worshipping Him. As it says in the very trendy! *Shorter Westminster Catechism, "The chief end of men and women is to glorify God and enjoy Him forever."* However, some might say, "Doesn't that indicate God's a bit *needy*, and that our worship, therefore, panders to His ego?" I suppose it might if He was a human being but, of course, He's not. He no more needs our worship than the sun needs someone to say that it's hot or Mount Everest that it's high. As if our feeble praise could make Him bigger, or the sun hotter or Mount Everest higher.

God wants our worship because He desires for us to know Him, the *Ultimate Reality*. And the only way we will get to know Him is to look up - because if we are always looking down (and maybe comparing ourselves favourably with those around us), we will never be able to *see* this glorious being who transcends absolutely everything. Then, and after 40+ years, I'm still a beginner in all of this, any form of genuine contact, from quiet reassurance to blowing our socks off (as per my *Baptism of Love,* described in part 1) will change us and lead onto celebration and, possibly, even ecstasy as the kingdom of God becomes

---

[108] Philip Yancey, *The Jesus I Never Knew.* Zondervan, 1995, pp.117-118.

real in our lives. And we will begin to discover that, ultimately, worship is not so much about what we do for God, but what He does for us.

Many people today, when they think about it at all, seem to believe that Christianity is all about keeping laws, rules and regulations, and not doing lots of stuff - especially if it's enjoyable. In seventies' lingo, *What a drag!* There is, however, some justification for this viewpoint. In the first place, there are certain Christians who live up to, or we could say down to, these negative opinions, and, secondly, there is a strong historical aspect. Specifically, the key provision to a treaty titled the Mosaic Covenant was the Ten Commandments (the *Decalogue*), given to the Israelites for their particular attention and instruction, and linking, directly or indirectly, with a further 603 commandments which together comprised the *Torah* or *Law* (alternatively, *Mosaic Law* or *Law of Moses*). These numerous commandments, contained in the first five books (the *Pentateuch*) of the OT/Tanakh, formed the basis of the moral, ceremonial (religious), and judicial (governance/civil) life pertinent to the ancient Israelite community.

The *Torah/Law*, dating back to the $14^{th}/15^{th}$ century BC, was undoubtedly relevant to the time of Christ and there were also multitudinous oral teachings (known as the *Oral Torah*), handed on from generation to generation, arising out of a practical need to interpret this Law in such a way that it could continue to be lived out at the everyday level as Jewish culture changed over time.

So what was the attitude of Jesus Christ – the *God-man*, when it came to weighing up the importance of a mind-boggling plethora of written and oral laws/rules of the day, compared to His repeated emphasis on intimacy and personal relationships between God and mankind? His response to this question is something that we should still learn from today. When asked, He did not even point to the Ten Commandments but reduced everything down to just two summary commandments. Wow, that's pretty amazing and also pretty good! Only a couple of commandments; what could possibly go wrong? And it's even better when we find out that, as long as we faithfully keep these commandments, we can do whatever else we like. So what are they? Maybe adultery has been left out after all.

Jesus got to the *spirit* behind the Law, and every other legitimate rule/regulation, by stating, *"Love the Lord your God with all your heart and with all your soul and with all your mind and with all your strength."* And *"Love your neighbour as yourself."* (Mark 12:30-31) Unconditional love such as this results in complete freedom, at individual, corporate, and world levels; because where it's present, there's no need for laws. Hang on then – that's a bit of a shock, and probably not what most of us had in mind.

So let's skip the first commandment for the moment and concentrate on the second, which does at least have clear relevance to the citizens of present-day Western societies. Perhaps the first question that comes to mind is, Who is my neighbour? As far as it goes, I seem to get on pretty well with those living round about me but, even then, I cannot imagine any unconditional love coming into the equation. Unsurprisingly, this question was asked of Jesus, who gave us the fairly well-known parable of *The Good Samaritan* (although Christ never actually called him *good*). The thing is that the Jews back then hated the Samaritans in probably the same way that most of today's Jews living in Israel seem to hate the Palestinians.

And in both cases, this hatred appears to have been/be reciprocated. So for a Samaritan to go to the aid of a severely beaten up Jewish guy who, incidentally, had already been ignored by a couple of Jewish religious leaders passing by, would almost certainly have been unconscionable and indeed offensive to Christ's Jewish audience. In other words, the Samaritan's *love* was way out there, far beyond their own (and no doubt, most of ours); although, of course, consistent with Jesus' instruction to, *"Love your neighbour as yourself"* And, elsewhere, to actually *"Love your enemies and pray for those who persecute you..."* (Matthew 5:44 - the *Sermon on the Mount*, His longest recorded public discourse)

It may additionally be useful to interpret the phrase *loving your neighbour as yourself* by considering how we try to look out for, care for, and comfort ourselves as we go through life, rather than thinking about *lovey-dovey* stuff. Contained within this commandment is the requirement to be radically open to others different to ourselves by reaching out beyond our *own people*, thereby taking on board what may well be unusual and unconventional in the context of our own lives. This is undoubtedly something that was an intrinsic part of Christ's ministry.

Anyway, how about loving God? – rather tricky if we don't know Him, which I guess applies to many of the present UK population. But the great thing is that God will help us to know and love Him if we just ask. To repeat this quotation from the Apostle John, *"We love because He first loved us."* (1 John 4:19) God seeks our response as His universal, and perhaps rather *unsettling*, voice reaches out and appeals to us all. So, how are we going to respond - positively or negatively?

Whatever the answer to this question, it is self-evident that none of us, as we stand on our own two feet, can get anywhere near the underlying implications and resultant outworking of the standards that Jesus sets in His two summary commandments. I doubt if there has been even one day out of the approximately 24,500 I've spent on the planet so far when I have consistently exhibited unconditional love for God or those around me. OK, there have probably been a few occasions as I have gone along in life, but certainly nothing more. And if this goal seems too high and unrealistic, then it's important to again remember that we have all done and thought many things we knew to be wrong and could have avoided had we so wished.

To reiterate, we don't even live up to our own standards, which incidentally, are often far less onerous than those expected of others. It is so much easier to pick up on, and maybe even magnify, the faults of other people while ignoring or remaining blind to our own shortcomings. Yet, in this enveloping *no-blame* UK culture, they are probably doing the same to us. After all, most of us seem to believe that we can live other peoples' lives better than they can.

The foregoing thus confirms and fleshes out the initial *Un* - designation of this chapter. In summary, we are *sinful creatures* rather than *cool creators*, whose complete lives, physical, psychological and spiritual, have been given to us by God;[109] the very nature of whom has been revealed in a form that we can understand – that is in Jesus Christ. We simply do not belong to ourselves and God has every right, therefore, to judge us on how we have lived; an underlying belief common to many worldviews, albeit varying in particulars. So what can we do about it? Well, apparently nothing. As sinners, we're all part of the problem and are thus about as likely to be successful in building a bridge to God as being able to lift our bodies off the ground using just our own arms (my mother told me that she frequently attempted to do this when very young – it doesn't work!). The obvious corollary, therefore, is that the bridge spanning the chasm between the perfection of God and ourselves, with our numerous varied and often serious imperfections, has to be built from God's side. Much as we might like to think we can merit heaven by our own efforts, the truth is we simply cannot fix ourselves and thus need a saviour, Jesus Christ. Self-help won't do, we need a divine rescue.

None of our inabilities to fix ourselves has, of course, taken God by surprise. There are simply so many prophecies relating to His rescue plan, some of which have been previously highlighted, going right back to Genesis at the beginning of the OT. And, in the garden of Gethsemane (not far from ancient Jerusalem) shortly before He was arrested and then crucified, Jesus prayed, *"And now, Father, glorify me in your presence with the glory I had with you before the world began."* (John 17:5) In other words, He was confirming His pre-existence and, indirectly, His role in creation, and anticipating the forthcoming resurrection and ascension back into heaven. This is again picked up on by the Apostle Paul at the start of a letter to Titus, another of his 'converts', where he refers to faith in Jesus Christ as follows, *"...- a faith and knowledge resting on the hope of eternal life, which God, who does not lie, promised before the beginning of time..."* (Titus 1:2)

---

[109] "Know that the Lord is God. It is he who made us, and we are his..." (Psalm 100:3a)

Just to clarify, 'hope' in the Bible normally relates to waiting for something that has already been planned and is bound to happen, unlike the less certain meaning of this word generally implied in our present culture.

The word *gospel*, meaning *good news*, is perhaps best explained at its everyday level by a couple of analogies. The first one concerns a guy found guilty in court for a crime that is severe enough for the imposition of a large fine. The judge is a very kind person and, knowing that the convicted man is going to find it almost impossible to come up with the necessary *readies*, really wants to let him off; but he can't – he's the judge! So he sentences the guy accordingly but subsequently, as a private citizen, pays the large fine himself.

The second analogy concerns a little kid who, while playing, smashes a very valuable and treasured family vase. Because his parents love him and he is very upset, they immediately forgive and comfort him by saying that everything's alright and he doesn't need to blub. But if they want the vase repaired or replaced by a similar piece then someone, either the parents or the insurance company, has to cough up. The child, of course, is unable to contribute in any meaningful way.

When it comes to God, He is faced with the same problem, but on a hugely magnified scale. As previously highlighted, mankind, including us all, has run up a massive 'bill' resulting from numerous wars, atrocities, and every kind of personal and corporate sin imaginable during the whole history of the human race. And on top of this, there's all the damage we have done to the planet and its wildlife. We have certainly not been good stewards of God's creation. Because God is Love, His overwhelming desire is to wipe the slate clean and excuse every single person and indeed whole countries. But He can't simply write off all this sin; because, like the human judge, He also has to act with justice – someone has to pay. As pointed out in the previous chapter, one of the crucial differences between Christianity and other worldviews is that God Himself picks up the tab and pays for the whole shebang – that is He acts in amazing grace.

And how does the related scheme work? What are we told about it? It's perhaps not generally realised, but *progressive revelation* is one of numerous consistent threads running through the whole Bible. I guess this is an unfamiliar phrase to many, so here's an example. I remember, as a small child, being taken by my parents and grandparents to a place called Rhossili on the beautiful Welsh Gower Coast. The associated cliffs tower over the bay, and I remember saying that I could safely jump onto the beach several hundred feet below. And the reason for this confidence? – Because sand is soft. It's easy to imagine what drastic action would have been undertaken on my behalf if I'd attempted to make this leap. I recall that my grandmother was a rather severe lady, so I suppose it might have been fun to see her sprint flat out. But, as the years went on, we could have had a much more mature conversation (not surprisingly, we didn't) concerning how a gravitational acceleration of 32ft/s^2 (9.81m/s^2) towards the centre of the Earth's mass would have resulted in a wholly destructive force on a human body falling from high cliffs onto a *soft* sandy beach. So this then is progressive revelation – nothing changed over the years concerning the beach, the height of the cliffs or the gravitational acceleration, but my understanding of the various factors involved certainly did.

That's how it is with God's progressive revelation of His plan for the welfare and rescue of the human race, which in some ways mirrors our growing up. Revelation through OT prophecy commences in the form of a rather abstruse announcement in the very early part of Genesis, with the overall message gradually being made clearer by commandments, promises, teachings, symbolic practices and events played out principally in the lives of Abraham, the Father of the Jews, Moses, their human deliverer and giver of the Law, the Prophets, and, finally, Jesus Christ, the fulfilment of the Law and *Saviour of the World*. So much of the OT points to Christ and indeed the required elements of His messianic role.

However, the people living before His physical entrance into this world (or in areas where the gospel had not yet reached) would have had nothing like the insight currently available in the West concerning God's redemptive scheme - the Bible's principal storyline. It's, therefore, important to emphasise that God's judgments, consistent with His character, are always based on what people know, not on what they don't.

Once it's understood that attempts to curry favour with God by solely human endeavours are, and always have been, based on wrongly perceived self-sufficiencies with no prospect of successful outcomes, the ministry of Jesus Christ and its absolute necessity as a divine rescue, makes sense. Specifically, we need to depend on Christ's sacrificial death and confirmatory resurrection, together with His perfect fulfilment of the Law (both the spirit and the letter), all done on our behalf. He is the perfect and all-sufficient one, not us! This is the New Covenant, as implied previously by point 9 of *An Objective Spine of Evidence*.

Not everyone gets this, and I quote from the former Labour MP, Tony Benn's wife, Caroline, who wrote, "*...because the Christian ethics, if interpreted as I had done, are really inhuman, and it is only the saints and martyrs who can hope to keep them.*" [110]

Leo Tolstoy, the 19th/20th century Russian writer, seems to have gone down a similar path to Caroline Benn but, in his case, kept going. I quote from his book, *What I Believe*, "*And, when I had understood this, I asked myself why I had never followed Christ's doctrine, which leads to salvation and happiness, but had followed a contrary teaching that had brought me nothing but suffering. There could be but one answer to that question – the truth had been hidden from me.*" In the same passage, Tolstoy refers to, "*the doctrine of Christ, which was rational, clear, and in harmony with my conscience...*" [111] His thinking at that time, particularly influenced by the Sermon on the Mount, is understood to have had a significant effect on the beliefs of Mahatma Ghandi.

Theologians often define the overall mechanism of the New Covenant as the *Divine Exchange*, or, Jesus Christ becomes what we are so that we might become what He is. As the Apostle Paul put it in his letters to the Galatians and Colossians, "*I have been crucified with Christ*" (Galatians

---

[110] Tony Benn, *Dare To Be A Daniel*. Hutchinson London, 2004, p.144.
[111] Leo Tolstoy, *What I Believe, 2000 Edition*. Adamant Media Corporation, chapter 11.

2:20a) and *"Since, then, you have been raised with Christ..."* (Colossians 3:1) Thus, in some mysterious way known fully only to God, believers become so completely united and identified with, and indeed in, Christ that it's as if we've also died and been raised with Him. More directly, *Jesus Christ* wasn't simply *crucified and resurrected for us,* He was *crucified and resurrected as us!* So in the same way that breaches of our country's laws become irrelevant once we have died, our deaths (in Christ) nullify and remove all our many wrongdoings in this life.

Furthermore, as noted above, the perfection of Christ's life, including His faultless keeping of the Law, is irrevocably attributed to each believer. Thus, when God looks at our lives He sees no indications of even remnant sins, but rather perfected human beings. This then is our *legal position* – that is we are *justified in Christ.*

As further confirmation that the foregoing transaction depends solely on Jesus Christ's accomplishments on our behalf rather than our own efforts, I refer to Billy Graham when he was asked what would happen if, despite his great preaching ministry, he was still not quite good enough to make it into heaven. Graham replied that if his acceptance into heaven depended 99% on Jesus Christ and 1% on him, then he would not make it, but as it depended 100% on Christ, he would be OK.

I suppose someone might consequently ask, "Well then, can't we just keep on deliberately doing wrong stuff and repeatedly come back to God for His automatic forgiveness?" (as still seems to occur in certain parts of the Christian Church). I believe the answer to this is that genuine conversion results in immense and ongoing thankfulness to God, as per the soldier who dives on an exploding bomb to save his mates. And it should also result in an increasing desire to love and know Christ better, becoming more like Him as we follow His lead. As in the case of anyone we truly love, we would rather please than displease Him by the way we live our lives.

Yes, it is still true that Christian believers do have to come back to God for forgiveness on a fairly regular basis, but this should be with regret and a genuine desire to be changed for the better; to become more like Christ. If it is other, say like putting a coin into a *forgiveness machine*, it's what the German theologian and martyr, Dietrich Bonhoeffer, called *cheap grace* and is therefore probably meaningless.

Virtually all the discussions thus far have related solely to what is essentially only the first part of our total salvation. But there is more, as particularly accentuated within the letter to the Hebrews, *"....because by one sacrifice He has made perfect for ever those who are being made holy."* (Hebrews 10:14)

Going back to the guy who has had his fine paid by the generous judge, he immediately becomes, in the eyes of the law, a free and upright (perfect) citizen. However, being reprieved in this manner has not necessarily changed his character for the better, which may take many years. So it is for us; as soon as we are justified and spiritually born again as *new creations* - a one-off event - then a second and long-term procedure called *sanctification* begins. This involves God, through His Holy Spirit, taking hold of our imperfect and flawed lives and working in, and with, us so that we are gradually purified and transformed inwardly. This is a process that the Apostle Paul calls "the *renewing of your mind"* (Romans: 12:2), which continues until finally, probably upon physical death, moral perfection (true holiness, as per Christ) is attained.

The Apostle Paul confirms this *process of sanctification* in his letter to the church at Ephesus, *"For we are God's workmanship, created in Christ Jesus to do good works, which God prepared in advance for us to do"* (Ephesians 2:10) – that is *after* our conversion to Christ. Interestingly, the Greek word for workmanship, *poiema*, can also be translated as *work of art* or *masterpiece*. I hardly think of my life as being either of these (I think Audrie will back me up here); but God is the master-craftsman and so, if I'm willing, I guess they will ultimately be appropriate. We should, therefore, welcome the thought of this experience – it really is *Great News*.

Although God accepts us where we are, He, nevertheless, wants to help us so we don't stay there. A bit like loving parents, no doubt chuffed to bits when their tiny offspring manage their first wobbly steps and squeak out their first barely coherent word or two, being decidedly underwhelmed if no further progress occurs in, say, the next twenty years. God wants to assist us to develop, grow, and mature as we follow and become more like Christ – *our wholly satisfying purpose, our wholly satisfying eternal destiny.* As the Apostle John says in his first letter, "We know and rely on the love God has for us." (1 John 4:16)

So again, we have to flip it, and realise that it is God Himself who is proactive in both restoring and sustaining flawed, and often broken, human beings – Hebrews again, *"Let us fix our eyes on Jesus, the author and perfecter of our faith, who for the joy set before Him endured the cross..."* (Hebrews 12:2a) Again, the whole thing starts with God and His side of the chasm.

Nevertheless, it would be wrong, on the one hand, to think that all of this is divorced from our particular plans and dreams or, on the other, that our future lives will be without troubles and difficulties. Christ's gospel does not promise a future without problems, but rather that these can be overcome by knowing the presence and peace of God, something I am beginning to experience more frequently as I get back on the right road. I'm also again realising that God knows the best routes for all of us, even though this may sometimes not be apparent in the short-term. He always recognises what is appropriate – we don't, and oftentimes need saving from ourselves.

It is also very important to stress that Christ frees us from any related guilt or shame. As I wrote in part 1, the awful happenings up to and including the *railway lines* incident were all too much for *little Graham Martin*, and it seems most unlikely that I could be recovering so well without this freeing knowledge.

The unique nature and supreme importance of Christ's gospel are hopefully now coming across. I've already talked about how numerous people have told me, "Well, it's great if Christianity helps you Graham but, quite frankly, it's simply not for us." I have also had other conversations, and perhaps sometimes thought this myself in pre-conversion days, when people have said something like, "Christianity (or more probably, 'religion') is OK as long as you don't let it dominate your life. If you *must* have it, keep it to little doses forming only a small part of your overall character – in that way, you will be able to remain a balanced person."

Of course, that's all well and good if the Christian gospel is not Almighty God's *one and only rescue plan to save a broken world.* BUT IT IS! And thus turning down Christ's free offer of salvation and eternal life is a much more serious proposition than, say, turning down a lifeboat rescue when on the point of drowning. Surely this latter predicament wouldn't engender a reply such as, on behalf of Postmodernism, New Age, PC or some other *ism*, "Saving my whole body is too drastic and fanatical, just save a bit of me."

The above illustration can also be extended to show the basic difference between believers and non-believers. Believers have at some stage become aware of their need for forgiveness and trusting God, as per the drowning person who realises his or her dire situation and the need to grab the hands of and rely on those trying to rescue them. Immense thankfulness should undoubtedly be the appropriate reaction for rescued individuals in both situations; and it's also clear that neither scenario relates to simply saying the right words or claiming you're a better person than anyone else. No drowning person is ever refused entrance into a lifeboat because they have not memorised the correct *rescue mantra* ("I'm sorry, but those aren't the words I have on the card"), and no rescued person is ever thrown back into the sea simply because their life doesn't match up to those of their fellow rescuees. What the words spoken at conversion should accordingly be representing, again however imperfectly understood, is a godly sorrow concerning how we have lived our lives and a determination to give them back to their rightful owner, Creator God – that is, as previously, a personal response to an unconditional offer.

One final analogy: In the autumn of 1973, I had a very bad pole-vaulting accident when I landed on my back onto a concrete kerb serving as one of the edges to the all-weather surface runway (you don't have to be an expert to know that it's so much more pleasurable to end up in the landing area – the *soft bit*). Athletes immediately stopped training and came over to see if they could help (when you are in that much pain, embarrassment means nothing). Anyhow, it was assumed that I had broken my back, and therefore no one dared move me. After some time, an ambulance appeared, driving around the 400m running track. Even in my extremely pained condition, it still seemed very surreal. Running tracks are meant for athletes, not ambulances. If this vehicle was on the running track, then something had gone severely wrong. God Himself, our Creator, in the person of Jesus Christ, has stepped on to the *running track* of the world - totally surreal, and again meaning that something has gone severely wrong (with the whole of humanity). Furthermore, as described in graphic detail in the next chapter, God in Christ has let His created humankind treat Him horrendously just so that we can inherit all of His amazing promises.

In summary, the gospel of Jesus Christ contains monumental benefits for all humankind, with its principal focus resulting in *plebs* like us receiving individual, conscious, and wonderful eternal life, commencing at the time of our conversion, along with the immortality to be found only in Him. There are no *heavenly* weighing scales and no pass mark necessary for us to be part of this entirely God-designed and accomplished salvation plan - it is, thankfully, about our own wills and related decisions rather than having to achieve certain standards, transformations or enlightenments.

Neo-atheists, such as Richard Dawkins and the late Christopher Hitchens, take a wholly opposite stance on all of these matters and consider that Christ's crucifixion represents an immoral act, whereby (if true) a gleeful god punishes a pain-seeking human being. But they press the analogy much too far by failing to recognise that the triune nature of God corresponds to an inherent degree of integration and intimacy between Father and Son that is simply way beyond anything we can imagine here on Earth.

In his second letter to the Corinthian church, the Apostle Paul says the following,*"For God was in Christ, reconciling the world to Himself, no longer counting people's sins against them."* (2 Corinthians 5:19 [NLT] [112]) We fathers cannot have that kind of intimacy; however close we may be, we cannot *be in* our sons. So even though as parents we can sometimes *feel* our children's pain, it is surely beyond us to satisfactorily conceive the possibility of the colossal suffering of the Son of God being matched by the colossal suffering of God the Father. Nevertheless, we can certainly celebrate and enjoy the resulting great triumph, which heralded in, amongst many other benefits, hitherto impossible unions and intimacies between God and human beings.

The Spirit of Jesus Christ is able, if we are willing, to change us on the inside, whereas religion and/or esoteric knowledge and/or incredible factual understanding all pander to our pride, and thus can only change us from the outside (i.e., superficially). This observation is also relevant to certain socio-economic political ideologies, such as Communism, the dominant forms of which are based on the ideas of Karl Marx and supposedly attempt to create stateless, classless societies governed by the working masses (the *proletariat*). However, this philosophy never seems to have been put into practice at a meaningful level, the greedy, selfish, and power-hungry natures of those that make it all the way to the top resulting in them grabbing most of the spoils for themselves.

Ultimately, the only society that will work fairly, and indeed perfectly, will have to be composed of perfect people. In other words, like Jesus Christ; and that, in a nutshell, is where God's consummate and unstoppable plan is headed. And we will not be clones or stereotypes or lose our individual identities, but beings whose moral characters have been transformed into the likeness of Jesus Christ. That society, based on perfect love and absolute unselfishness, is simply the only one that is viable in the long-term. Anything else will just be a repeat performance of the chaos and suffering we see around us all the time.

---

[112] The New Living Bible (NLT), Tyndale House Publishers, Inc., 2004.

CHAPTER SIX

Jesus Christ – A Unique Being with a Unique Mission

It seems particularly appropriate to start this chapter with a brief description of the final stages of C.S. Lewis' conversion to Christ at thirty three years of age, based mainly on quotations from his highly acclaimed book *Surprised by Joy*. [113] For clarity, Lewis never liked his first names of *Clive* and *Staples*, and therefore insisted upon being called by his adopted nickname of *Jack*.

Inspired by his reading, Lewis' personal philosophy had been slowly approaching theism (belief in a god) under another name: he came to believe in a universal spirit without yet calling it God. He knew that his position was confused. He likened the following process to being hunted down by God, or even being defeated by Him in a game of chess.

Lewis had several Christian friends at Oxford, including Hugo Dyson and the Catholic J.R. Tolkien, with whom he often argued philosophy and religion. A chance remark by another acquaintance, T.D. Weldon, caused Lewis to rethink what he still was calling 'the Christian myth'. Weldon, known for his cynicism, thought that the evidence for Jesus's life and resurrection was remarkably good. Lewis read the gospels and was struck by the thought that they did not sound like fiction: the writers seemed too unimaginative to have made the whole thing up; the gospels read more like reports than stories.

Lewis' father, Albert Lewis, died in early 1929, and Jack believed he could feel Albert's presence after his death. At this time Warren (Lewis'

---

[113] C. S. Lewis, *Surprised by Joy*. Geoffrey Bles (UK), Harcourt Brace (US), 1955.

brother, and usually known as *'Warnie'*) *and Jack were both thinking of becoming Christians, although church attendance was still unappealing to Jack and he still did not accept many aspects of Christian theology. He recalled,* "You must picture me alone in that room at Magdalen (College), *night after night, feeling, whenever my mind lifted even for a second from my work, the steady, unrelenting approach of Him whom I so earnestly desired not to meet. That which I greatly feared had at last come upon me. In the Trinity Term* (April – June) *of 1929, I gave in, and admitted that God was God, and knelt and prayed: perhaps, that night, the most dejected and reluctant convert in all England."* [114] However, this episode represented only a partial conversion, and it was Tolkien's friendship that finally brought him to his encounter with Christ.

On September 19, 1931, Lewis, Dyson and Tolkien took a night-time stroll and began a conversation about myth. They walked and talked until morning. Tolkien convinced Jack that myths were God's way of preparing the ground for the Christian story, which brought to fulfilment whatever truths were to be found in other religions and worldviews (as specifically highlighted in relation to Plato). *Dyson's contribution was to impress upon Jack how Christianity worked for the believer, liberating them from their sins and helping them become better people. His remaining arguments were being demolished. Jack Lewis was about to be checkmated.*

The final stage in Jack's conversion to Christianity took place three days later and was typically unconventional. He and Warnie were travelling by motorcycle to Whipsnade zoo, "When we set out I did not believe that Jesus Christ is the Son of God, and when we reached the zoo I did." [115] This full conversion experience took him by joyful surprise - hence the book, *Surprised by Joy.*

---

[114] C. S. Lewis, Surprised by Joy. Chapter XIV. Goodreads. https://www.goodreads.com/quotes/681434-you-must-picture-me-alone-in-that-room-in-magdalen

[115] C. S. Lewis, https://libquotes.com/c-s-lewis/quote/lbd0l6z

Lewis also realised that his old experiences of 'joy' had been pointers, reminding him that he was made for another world: he now reinterpreted them as longings for heaven, for God. [116]

The foregoing reveals two things that Lewis and his friends, J R Tolkien and Hugo Dyson, finally all agreed upon. Firstly, there were Christian truths within certain mythical or true stories encountered in various religions and worldviews which, although not an end in themselves, acted as signposts preparing the way for the historical Jesus Christ and, most significantly, His crucifixion and resurrection. This would, of course, be consistent if Jesus does indeed represent *The Big Picture*.

Secondly, the gospels were written as unimaginative factual records and thus cannot be thought of as belonging to any type of fictional literature. The development and explanation of the relevant parts of these records form the main thrusts of this chapter, with the overall objective being to demonstrate that they represent authentic and reliable history.

A significant part of this exercise is to draw out the main characters involved in Jesus' trial and crucifixion and to show where they were coming from (as amply demonstrated by the Scriptural accounts). In some ways, their personalities and related actions turned these events into a kind of soap opera as they were played out. The following account is based on the four gospel records and a classic book called *The Day Christ Died* by Jim Bishop.[117] It is accordingly in general harmony with the many similar endeavours undertaken to date, albeit that the different perspectives and audiences relevant to the NT writers make it unviable for modern authors to be in total agreement on every peripheral detail and aspect.

Jesus Christ was born in Palestine at a time when the country was in bondage to the Romans. This Empire, under Caesar Augustus in Rome, ruled, amongst others, nations around the Mediterranean Sea and in

---

[116] C.S. Lewis, *Surprised by Joy*.
https://www.bbc.co.uk/religion/religions/christianity/people/cslewis_1.shtml
[117] Jim Bishop, *The Day Christ Died*. Greenwich House, 1984.

Europe, North Africa, Syria and Egypt. Palestine, much of which bordered the Mediterranean Sea to the west, was very small, with a maximum length (North to South) of approximately 150 miles and approximately 90 miles (West to East) at its widest. The total population comprised some three million citizens. The capital was Jerusalem, situated in the southern part of the country, with an estimated permanent population ranging between about 50,000 and 75,000 citizens. However, large influxes of pilgrims, some being put up for free by the city residents and others encamped in surrounding fields, increased this number several fold at the time of major religious festivals such as the *Passover and Feast of Unleavened Bread*. The very limited length of the enclosing perimeter wall, at barely three miles, confirmed the small size of this ancient city.

Not surprisingly, given its size, the Romans treated Palestine as a rather unimportant part of their Empire and, probably for that reason, allowed the Jews *freedom of worship* and the right to follow their laws as long as these did not conflict with the interests of Rome. This meant that the country was basically a *Theocracy* - that is effectively governed by the religious leaders.

The Jews also had a king. Originally these had been warrior leaders such as King Saul and King David (still revered today as Israel's *best-ever* king). However, the military roles of these kings were ended by the various empires that had conquered Palestine (including the Macedonians/Greeks under Alexander the Great), of which the Roman Empire was the latest.

At the time of Jesus' birth, the first of the Herod's, King Herod the Great, who was based in Jerusalem, had 'reigned' in Palestine for almost forty years with two or three more to go.

Herod the Great was basically in it for what he could get. He had no interest in religious matters and happily bent his knee, as a *puppet king*, to Rome who named him, *King of the Jews*. He was a vicious tyrant, who married a total of ten times and murdered various members of his family, including wives and sons, on whims and suspicion. Caesar Augustus said that it was safer to be Herod's pig than one of his sons. By the time of his death, Herod had become acutely paranoid and even decreed that certain religious leaders be murdered to make sure there were tears in Jerusalem coincident with his passing (orders that were apparently ignored).

Anyhow, on the upside! Herod did oversee, wholly or partially, various successful building projects, the most magnificent of which was the rebuilding and extension of the Jerusalem Temple[118] on the eastern side of the city, the main focus of worship in Palestine, However, these stupendous construction works, lasting about eighty years in total, turned out to be in vain; shortly after their completion, the Temple was destroyed by the Romans under General Titus, an event prophesied by Christ shortly before His crucifixion.

It seems fair to conclude that the Jews hated the Romans (a not unusual position for any subjugated people) and that this was reciprocated by the occupying soldiers. The two societies could not have been more different. Jewish lives were stringently regulated by religion, and they took the worship of the one God, *Yahweh*, extremely seriously. Of the very many rules to which they were beholden, the keeping of the Sabbath was of paramount importance; something that had a significant bearing on the events surrounding Jesus' death.

The Sabbath was a day of rest when (essentially) no work could be undertaken between sunset on Friday and sunset on Saturday. There were also *special* Sabbaths associated with certain festivals, celebrations etc; such as the *Passover Sabbath*, which did not necessarily fall within the usual Friday/Saturday slot - although it appears that the one relevant to Jesus' crucifixion actually did.

The Passover Sabbath constituted the first day of the festival, with the Feast of Unleavened Bread, the following six to seven days. The

---

[118] When not specifically named, the *Temple* always refers to the Jerusalem building.

integrated event, which commemorated the deliverance of the Israelites from Egypt under Moses, was of huge importance to the Jewish people and certainly the biggest occasion in their calendar. The *unleavened bread* had both metaphorical (leaven or yeast often associated with sin) and practical (fleeing Israelites couldn't wait for any leaven put into the bread to rise) implications. For ease, the entire festival is subsequently referred to as the Passover, with many pilgrims, coming from far and wide, often enjoying the seven to eight days as a holiday.

The Jews additionally abhorred nakedness and considered that all women should be suitably covered. There was even, at the time of Christ, a group of religious leaders nicknamed the *bruised and bleeding Pharisees*, as they always covered their eyes at the approach of any woman, resulting in them walking into walls and other structures - I'm not making this up.

In marked contrast, the Roman World was laid-back, indulgent and highly civilised. They had their pagan gods, but don't appear to have taken them very seriously, some historians reckoning that the Romans were more interested in cleanliness than worship. Women's apparel depended upon their wealth and class, but it seems that all were much less restricted in their dress sense than the Jewish women. Sex was accordingly much freer in Roman than Jewish society, although there were rules, especially for girls. This sexual freedom for adult women was attested by the Roman Poet, Ovid (43BC – AD18), who said, *"Pure women are only those who have not been asked."* [119] He also quipped, *"A woman is always buying something."* – no change there then!

There were also amphitheatres in both Rome and Jerusalem where *the Games* took place, Herod apparently being involved in commissioning the latter. The Games in Rome were very brutal, and included gladiatorial fights to the death plus various animal fights. There are accordingly records showing that a single morning's *entertainment*

---

[119] Publius Ovidius Naso

comprised four hundred tigers fighting to the death with elephants and bulls and that the dedication of the *Colosseum* involved the deaths of 5,000 animals. The Roman citizens loved it all, whereas in Jerusalem where the Games were in actuality less severe, the Jews were angry and offended by the amphitheatre and usually looked away when walking past.

Probably the greatest expectation and excitement in most Jewish homes, which had been the case for many hundreds of years, concerned the prophetically promised coming of *Messiah* – translated as *Christ* in Greek. As already noted, this word has various meanings such as Deliverer, Anointed One, and Chosen One, with an even more powerful and comprehensive description being found in the book of Isaiah (lived approximately 750 to 685 BC).

> *For to us a child is born,*
> *to us a son is given,*
> *and the government will be on His shoulders.*
> *And He will be called*
> *Wonderful Counsellor, Mighty God,*
> *Everlasting Father, Prince of Peace*
>
> *Of the greatness of His government and peace*
> *there will be no end.*
> *He will reign on David's throne*
> *and over His kingdom,*
> *establishing and upholding it*
> *with justice and righteousness*
> *from that time on and for ever.*
> *The zeal of the LORD Almighty*
> *will accomplish this.*
>
> (Isaiah 9:6-7)

This all-conquering *Messiah* was, therefore, the expectation of most Jews in the run-up to Christ's incarnation – that is someone who would physically deliver them from the Romans, thereby ushering in a golden age of great joy, peace and justice for the Jewish nation. There accordingly seems to have been little account taken of the prophecies concerning the Messiah's initial mission (see the selected ten in Table 1). This was, by His sacrificial death as a *suffering servant*, to *purchase* the spiritual deliverance of all peoples from their bondage to sin. Jesus' related *mission statement* is given in probably the most famous verse of the whole Bible, John 3.16, where He says, *"For God so loved the world that He gave His one and only Son, that whoever believes in Him shall not perish but have eternal life."* References to this verse can still sometimes be seen on banners at the Olympics and World Cup tournaments. Jesus also summarises His *mission* elsewhere by saying that He did not come to be served, but to serve and give His life as a ransom for many. The second part of Jesus' mission, prophesied in both the OT and NT, concerns his, still future, second coming as Conquering King.

Mary and Joseph lived in Nazareth of Galilee, a village (or possibly small town) located towards the northern end of Palestine and some 75 miles to the north of Jerusalem and Bethlehem. For much of Mary's pregnancy there appeared to be no possibility that Jesus would be born in Bethlehem, as prophesied by Micah (2nd prophecy). However, at apparently the last moment (at least as far as Mary and Joseph were concerned), Caesar Augustus decided that, for tax purposes, a census had to be undertaken so that he could know how many subjects he had in Palestine and where they all came from. Each person, therefore, had to return to the town of the original *Father* of the family, which, for Mary and Joseph, was King David of Bethlehem. So they had to make the long journey to Bethlehem, which probably took about five to six days by donkey, presumably staying at cheap inns along the way. Hardly the greatest preparation for childbirth, which seems to have occurred almost immediately upon arrival.

Most people know the story, but the lack of an available room for Christ's birth was due to the fact that numerous people who could trace their family back to King David had already returned to Bethlehem for the census. Soon after Jesus' birth, the family had to escape to Egypt (as refugees), as King Herod, true to form, decreed that all baby boys of two years and under living in and around Bethlehem were to be murdered. This incredibly cruel edict was again heavily influenced by Herod's well-advanced paranoia, resulting in him becoming threatened and freaked out by the reported birth of a new *King of the Jews*. Very similar to Pharaoh ordering the murder of all male babies at the time of Moses.

Herod had first found out about the birth of Christ from the *Magi*, possibly astrologers from Persia or Southern Arabia, the NT record giving no suggestion of *three kings* and also indicating that their visit took place some months after the birth. It's interesting that the gifts they brought all had symbolic meaning: Gold because He was a king, Incense because He came as a priest - the *God-man* to *stand-in-the-gap* by providing the bridge to reunite mankind with God, and Myrrh, a burial fluid, because He came to die.

Following Herod's death, two or three years after Jesus' birth, his *kingdom* was divided up between three of his sons and, possibly, a daughter. The situation changed again only a few years later when the Romans instituted a succession of *procurators* (*prefects*) to govern the provinces of Judea (Judah), Samaria and Idumea, a region named after the former as a political categorisation. There was accordingly a certain tension and power struggle between the Jewish religious leaders of the time and the various procurators, particularly as Judea contained Jerusalem where most of the real action took place.

A short time after Herod's death, Mary and Joseph returned to Nazareth where Jesus grew up. This then confirmed the 4th prophecy. The only record we have about His early life concerns a visit with His parents to Jerusalem to celebrate the Passover. This was when He was about twelve years old, and He stayed behind after the finish of the event to discuss religious matters with the teachers of the law (*scribes*). There is this related comment in Luke's Gospel - *"Everyone who heard Him was amazed at His understanding and His answers"* (Luke 2:47); so something pretty special was obviously going on at a very early stage of His life.

It is difficult to form a definitive opinion concerning formal education in 1st century Palestine, but it appears to have comprised religion, reading, writing and arithmetic, and been compulsory for all children from six to at least eleven years old. No formal education beyond eleven years of age seems to have been available for girls, with some of the boys also leaving school at this time to learn a trade (such as fishing – as per a number of Jesus' disciples), while the more academic ones (possibly the disciple and gospel writer Matthew, a former tax collector) continued with their studies. If they demonstrated good progress in religion, they might go on, at the age of 16/17 years, to study with a scribe or *rabbi* (at that time, a fairly informal title, bestowed on the basis of wisdom and knowledge). For example, the Apostle Paul studied under the eminent Jewish rabbi, Gamaliel.

Forward now to the start of Jesus' mission, commencing at about the age of thirty when He was baptised in the River Jordan by *John the Baptist*. This baptism was performed, as today, in conjunction with a person's repentance of their sins, and was therefore unnecessary for Jesus Himself, as the faultless man. There are several reasons why Jesus insisted upon this baptism, perhaps the most important being that, as our perfect substitute, He needed to align Himself completely with humankind's sin and failure. Broadly speaking, the majority of Jesus' three year ministry seems to have taken place in and around Galilee, with a number of visits to Jerusalem, plus at least one requited visit from a contingent of the capital's religious authorities, leading up to its climax in that city.

It is hardly surprising that as time went on, Jesus, who sometimes even healed on the Sabbath (scandalous!), became an increasing problem for the religious leaders in Jerusalem. They were simply no match for His great wisdom, especially when accompanied by miracles.

It's probably useful to give a couple of examples. The first concerns a run-in with a group of these leaders, specifically selected to trap Jesus into saying something stupid or contentious. Their question concerned whether or not it was right to pay taxes to Caesar. This seemingly put Jesus in an impossible position. If He said Yes, He would lose the affections of the Jewish people, with their allegiance to God (Yahweh), who they recognised as their proper king (not Caesar, who they hated). If Jesus said No, then He could be crucified for advocating rebellion against Rome.

So Jesus asks one of those questioning Him for a coin (a *denarius*). Pointing at it He says, *"Whose portrait is this? And whose inscription?"* –*"Caesar's"* they reply. *"Then"* says Jesus, *"Give to Caesar what is Caesar's and to God what is God's."* (Mark 12:13-17) This very concise reply may not sound quite so amazing almost 2,000 years on, but it really is brilliant and a complete knockout – in any event, such words are hardly those of a lunatic or even an unbelievably evil man.

The second example concerns the well-known raising up of Jesus' friend, Lazarus, after he had been dead for four days (John 11:1-44) - still quoted by football commentators when teams come *back from the dead.* This happened at Bethany, a few miles from Jerusalem, and did much to seal Jesus' fate – that is it intensified the fears of the religious leaders, some of whom knew, or at least knew of, Lazarus. In particular, they were becoming increasingly alarmed by the fact that so many of their Temple members were leaving to follow Jesus. Indeed, why would people listen to them spouting on about religious law, when this man could make the blind see or even raise the dead before the gaze of so many? And if there was any sort of uprising or rioting caused by resultant factions within the Jewish people, then this would lead to Roman intervention and a probable lessening of their permitted authority.

There is also something rather incredible about this miracle which is sometimes missed – that is Jesus' attitude before He raises Lazarus. I think that most human beings, me included, would have had two quite different reactions immediately before this event. Either we might weep over the extreme sadness of the occasion and our frustration or anger over our helplessness, or, if we actually knew we could bring Lazarus back from the dead, then celebrity status would be the name of the game – "get me on camera three, it shows my best side." But Jesus does both – He weeps, and then raises Lazarus.

My interpretation of this is that Jesus was frustrated, angry and upset over all the sin, suffering and death affecting humanity (particularly, at that time, of the great distress of those who had come to mourn Lazarus), and this caused His tears. Unlike ourselves, He had no great ego to satisfy, and was therefore only concerned that His observers realise He was speaking the very words of God, and then hopefully act on them. Or to summarise the above, this is an occasion where we can see both the God and human essences of Jesus Christ; which would, of course, be expected for the *God-man*. Again, as per John Stuart Mill, how could the disciples or anyone else have made up a character such as this?

While on the subject of Jesus' miracles, it seems pertinent to point out that, as might be expected for *God in the flesh*, these encompassed and overcame all of our physical laws.

He accordingly exhibited power over:

- The Weather, by instantaneously dismissing a raging storm, saying *"Quiet! Be still!"* in Mark 4:37-41
- Gravity, by walking on water and ascending into heaven, as reported in Matthew 14:22–27 and Luke 24:51-52
- Food and drink, by feeding the five thousand in Luke 9:12-17 and changing water into wine in John 2:1-11
- Illness, disease and disabilities, by healing all diseases, the lame and the blind - as particularly prophesied by Isaiah
- Demons, by casting them out using only a few words as seen in Mathew 4:24, 8:16 & 9:32-33. Jesus' deliverances involved no histrionics and it is also clear that He differentiated between the demonised and epilepsy - there have been some bad mistakes in this area down the ages.
- *Death* itself, through His own resurrection, confirmed thoughout the NT, and the raising up of others, including Lazarus in John 11, the widow of Nain's son in Luke 7:11-15 and the daughter of Jairus, a synagogue ruler in Luke 8:51-56.

Much of the above occurred on multiple occasions, with John's gospel ending with this hyperbole, *"Jesus did many other things as well. If every one of them were written down, I suppose that even the whole world would not have room for the books that would be written."* (John 21:25)

Why then, given Jesus' incredible miracles, culminating in the raising up of Lazarus, and His amazing teaching to boot, did the religious leaders refuse to believe that He was the *Messiah* or *Christ*? In actuality, quite a few of them did, but knew they would lose face and position if they confessed their faith – that is, *"they loved praise from man more than praise from God."* (John 12:43)

However, the majority, who lived and breathed their religious status, probably never got this far, preferring instead to back up their stance of unbelief from messianic prophecy. Specifically, they knew that the Messiah had to be from the line of King David and be born in his home town of Bethlehem (Jesus, of course, ticked both boxes), but actually thought He originated from Nazareth in Galilee. These leaders thus believed Him to be simply *Jesus of Nazareth*; although it seems that, if they'd been prepared to do a little research, they could have found out the truth by consulting the public records of genealogies, understood to have been held in the Temple. They might perhaps also have known that the Messiah was to grow up in Galilee (again, 4th prophecy) although, given the spiritual climate, it may well have been difficult to spot the connection at that time.

The approach of the annual Passover could only have made things worse for the religious authorities, who must have been all too aware of the *awful* prospect of Jesus' ministry going ballistic once exposed to so many extra people.

So on to the *soap opera* concerning the events surrounding Jesus' trial and crucifixion; and involving the following main players:

- **Tiberius Caesar** – The Emperor of Rome, the big boss. At the time of Jesus' confrontations with the authorities in Jerusalem, he was about 70 years old. He apparently suffered from acne and found it almost impossible to show emotion, being known as *The Mask*. Tiberius supposedly ruled in conjunction with a Senate (the dominant branch of government) but had become pretty much an all-powerful tyrant by this time. He appointed Pontius Pilate to be the Procurator of Judea on the recommendations of Sejanus, one of his advisers, and Claudia Procula, Pilate's wife and (apparently) the granddaughter of Caesar Augustus. Tiberius liked to keep his officials in almost constant fear and dread, and would willingly have removed Pilate from office given half the chance.

- **Pontius Pilate** – The Procurator in office at the time, probably middle-aged, with sufficient Roman troops to enable him to keep law and order in Judea. Although, because it was the *done thing*, he bent the knee to the Roman gods, he was an atheist and also absolutely despised the Jews. He is portrayed as an ambitious and fairly intelligent man, but with no other particular attributes to mark him out for distinction. Thus, despite his apparent intellect, Pilate was essentially weak and could be indecisive. Pilate normally resided in Caesarea at the northern end of Palestine's coastline but came into Jerusalem for important events such as the Passover, where he usually stayed, with a guard of Roman soldiers, at Herod's Upper Palace[120] situated on high ground at the western side of the city. These visits at the times of Jewish festivals and similar were probably deemed necessary because the Jews, fired up with religious fervour, sometimes got over-excited and could riot.

---

[120] Herod's Upper Palace refers to King Herod the Great, and was one of the main buildings constructed during his *reign* over Palestine. The writings of the Jewish historian, Josephus, maintain that this building was Pilate's official residence when visiting Jerusalem, although scholarly opinion is divided with some favouring the *Antonia Fortress* in the northern part of the city. The matter is, in any event, of limited importance.

- **Caiaphas and Annas** – Palestine, as effectively a theocracy, was governed by the religious leaders unless they fell foul of the Roman Empire. Top of the pile was the High Priest, Caiaphas, although it appears that much of the real power was held in the hands of his father-in-law, Annas, who had also been the High Priest in his day and may have been partly responsible for getting Caiaphas the job. Caiaphas was thus constantly striving to keep Annas sweet.

   The two men lived fairly close to each other in Jerusalem and were united in their hatred of Pilate and Herod (see below). Although these men had probably never come face to face with Jesus, their subordinates would have kept them informed of the problems that He continued to cause the establishment. They probably initially thought that His ministry would soon blow out; after all, there had been several other apparent messiahs who had never got very far and generally ended up being killed. But the raising up of Lazarus in the nearby locality had proved to be *the last straw*. Caiaphas, who was driven by his need to retain status and authority plus the general *status quo*, therefore declared that, for the continued stability of the Jewish nation, Jesus had to die and, if at all possible, before the Passover.

   There were, however, significant problems in actually carrying this out. If the religious leaders attempted to arrest Jesus in the day, where He was often preaching in the Temple grounds, they might well have caused His many supporters to riot. And then, if they went for a night arrest, they were not sure of Jesus' movements and also had doubts that He could be correctly identified in the dark. They were, therefore, in quite a predicament and had no clear way of alleviating their anxiety by *quietly* arresting Jesus before the Passover commenced.

- **The Great Sanhedrin** – The word *Sanhedrin* means *Assembly* or *Council*. There were sanhedrins in various cities across Palestine, but all their laws and decisions had to be ratified by the all-powerful *Great Sanhedrin*, located in the Jerusalem Temple (subsequently referred to as the *Sanhedrin*). The Sanhedrin comprised the High Priest as the presiding officer and seventy *members*, *elders*, or *judges* - prominent men from local society and of various religious persuasions within the Jewish faith. The Romans allowed the Sanhedrin to have supreme authority when it came to religious matters and a moderate degree of power in relation to civil affairs. The Sanhedrin could pass the sentence of death on Jews, or even on Gentiles (non-Jews) who were not citizens of Rome, but such sentences had to be reviewed by the current Roman Procurator and confirmed. If the latter was the case, the convicted person was often crucified by the Romans instead of the usual Jewish method of stoning to death.

Caiaphas, with the support of Annas, had significant control over the Sanhedrin and could often lead them in a particular direction when judging criminal and civil cases, both of which rarely took more than a day or two to complete. Nevertheless, there had to be adherence to certain rules, which were particularly strict for criminal cases. These included the following: the Court could not sit at night, a false prophet or blasphemous person (the prospective charge against Jesus) had to be judged by the full membership of 71, the witness statements had to agree, no account could be taken of any statements made by the defendant, and a guilty judgement plus the consequent sentencing had to be carried out on consecutive days. The obvious conclusion is that a court case against Jesus needed to allow two days before the Friday/Saturday Passover Sabbath commenced.

- **Herod** – The particular Herod at this time was Herod Antipas, who *ruled* the provinces of Galilee to the north (Jesus' home province) and Perea to the east, commencing his *kingship* (strictly Tetrarchy) upon the death of his father, Herod the Great. Like his father, Herod Antipas was also a puppet king under the Romans, cared little for the Jews' religious practices, and was basically in it for what he could get. He was probably also a bit unhinged, given his father's record of murdering people, including wives and sons, upon a whim and his alleged subsequent roaming of corridors shouting out their names. As in the case of Pilate, Herod was not based in Jerusalem; residing at the Hasmonean Palace, close to the centre of the city, during religious festivals such as the Passover.

The fact that Herod Antipas' *kingdom* was separate from Pilate's jurisdiction in Judaea initially made it unlikely that the two men would both become involved with Jesus. However, Pilate made a monumental error when he had been in office for less than two years. This concerned his judgment that Jerusalem needed an improved water supply during the summer months. Not surprisingly, given his reciprocal hatred of Caiaphas and Annas, he decided to wind them up by extracting the monies needed from the Temple's treasury. This infuriated the Jews who rioted. Pilate subsequently sent in some of his troops who attacked the Jews and left many dead.

Unfortunately, he had not attacked the rioting Jews, but some visiting Jewish pilgrims from Herod's Galilee province in the North. Pilate was too proud to admit his mistake, resulting in ongoing animosity between himself and Herod. Indeed, Herod tried to get even by repeatedly sending letters to Pilate's boss, Tiberius Caesar in Rome, telling him that his Procurator was doing a lousy job.

- **Judas Iscariot -** 2,000 years on, who calls or even considers calling their son, Judas? I certainly haven't heard of anybody, with my best attempt being to name *Judas Priest*, a heavy-metal band of the 1970s/80s (this has absolutely no theological relevance, but does demonstrate my music knowledge). Judas was the treasurer for the group of thirteen men and was intermittently lining his own pockets by stealing a proportion of the money.

Jesus knew this and also that he would be the man to betray Him; and yet, all through His three-year ministry, He loved and treated Judas the same as the rest of the disciples. The reason we know this is because when Jesus announced at the *Last Supper* that one of them would betray Him, the other eleven disciples had no idea who it was – *"Is it I, Lord?"* (Matthew 26:22b ESV [121]) That has simply got to be agape/unconditional love.

How much Judas believed Jesus to be the Messiah is not known, but he must have seen many miracles. However, the fact that the religious leaders wanted to have Jesus killed had reached the streets and, amazingly, Jesus Himself had even said on several recent occasions that He had come to Jerusalem to die. I think we can take it for granted that whatever faith Judas had in Jesus, it certainly would never have stretched to a resurrection after three days. Indeed, as noted earlier, it seems clear that none of the disciples got hold of this truth until after the event had taken place. Judas, therefore, probably concluded that, once Jesus had been crucified, Caiaphas would round up all the disciples and have them crucified or stoned - after all, that was what usually happened to followers of false messiahs after the main player's demise and eradication. He also knew that the authorities had problems in arresting Jesus during both the day and night-time hours.

Judas was intelligent and street-wise; if he could offer the service of betraying his leader at this time, he would get into the religious leaders' *good books* and thus probably not be killed or even arrested after Jesus' death. Additionally, if he played it right, he might be able to make a few quid for himself. So, as is still fairly well known, Judas went to the religious leaders and agreed to betray Jesus for the sum of thirty pieces of silver (5th prophecy).

---

[121] English Standard Version (ESV) Bible, Crossway, 2001.

It appears that by the time Caiaphas became aware of Judas' willingness to betray Jesus, there were already no more than 24 hours before the start of the Passover Sabbath – that is the arrest had to take place on that Thursday/Friday night. Caiaphas would then have gone, as a matter of urgency, to Herod's Upper Palace to request the assistance of Pilate's troops. He probably did this for two main reasons: firstly, to make the arrest look, in the eyes of Jesus' followers, more like a Roman matter and thus avoid possible riots, and, secondly, the enlisting of Roman aid at this time would result in Pilate also becoming embroiled and consequently make it difficult for him not to confirm any decision of the Sanhedrin to have Jesus killed. No details of this meeting are known, but it seems that Pilate agreed to send a whole detachment (at least 120 soldiers) who then teamed up with the Jewish Temple guards and various religious officials plus, maybe, a few spies known as *Herodians* – lax Jews who supported Herod Antipas.

Why Pilate, who of course hated Caiaphas and Annas, actually agreed to this level of assistance is a bit of a mystery, because the obvious upshot is that he would have seen refusal as a welcome opportunity to frustrate or humiliate them. However, the Roman governor, who presumably knew nothing of Judas Iscariot's involvement or even who he was, may have thought that this party would have been unable to find Jesus (possibly made more difficult by camping pilgrims), resulting in great embarrassment for the two religious leaders. Alternatively, if Jesus was found and there were lots of followers and supporters with Him, Pilate probably being unaware that the entire group totalled only twelve men, then he dared not risk a humiliating defeat.

Following the Last Supper, the whole group (less, of course, Judas) make their way to the Garden of Gethsemane a little way up the Mount of Olives, a short distance to the east of the ancient walled city. En route, Christ has prophesied that all His disciples will later run away and that Peter would disown Him three times before the cock crowed at the crack of dawn. Jesus is in great agony of spirit, so much so that Luke, who was a doctor as well as a historian, talks about His sweat becoming like *"clots of blood trickling down upon the ground;"* (Luke 22:44 DSB[122]) now a well-known condition called Hematidrosis, occurring when abject fear is piled upon abject fear. Jesus knew exactly what horrific events lay immediately before Him (imagine that), causing the recoiling of His inner self. However, as He pleads with God, He uses words that we might not expect. He actually *says, "My Father, if it is possible, may this cup be taken from me. Yet not as I will, but as you will."* (Matthew 26:39) So what cup is He talking about?

The cup Jesus is talking about is God's 'Cup of Wrath'. What! How can that possibly be right? It's surely hard enough for most of us (certainly in Western societies) to accept that we are sinners in need of some sort of rescue plan; and this particular little phrase smacks of draconian punishment, conjuring up all sorts of related negative feelings and imaginations, none of which are surely worthy of a God whose defining essence is unconditional love.

God's wrath is a difficult concept for most people in our society, including me, to understand. Perhaps the most important thing to realise is that, when attributed to God, this intense emotion is never capricious or representative of arbitrary losses of control, but is always linked to measured and correct responses to serious situations. In other words, God's wrath may be thought of as *righteous anger*; entirely appropriate and necessary when dealing with the massive amount and frequently horrendous nature of humankind's sin. Indeed, it would be unreasonable, unjust and impracticable for a God of love *and* justice to ignore and refuse to judge sin and wrongdoing. Human sin, which, as we have seen, resides in all of us, creates a colossal deficit in the heavenly moral/spiritual *law courts*. It is accordingly imperative that settlement is made in full, and clearly not by us human beings. We are the reason for the imbalance and, as previously noted, would be no more successful than my mother when she tried, as a little girl, to lift herself off the ground by using just her own arms.

---

[122] Henry M. Morris, *The Defenders Study Bible KJV*, World Publishing, 1995

So Jesus Christ, as God and the future flawless human being, says (or rather, has already said), *"I will do it. I will pay the price."* It has to be Him – only the *Logos* or *Word of God* has the authority and capability for a task such as this. Only He can completely settle up on our behalf. Jesus is thus agreeing to the required full identification with humanity in order that He can become our authentic substitute and the consequent sole bearer of God's wrath for global sin, past, present and future. It is a massive, massive version of the soldier who falls on an exploding bomb to save his mates. This is a terrifying prospect for Jesus, and it's not surprising that, given the extreme physical and other tortures to be endured and their universal significance, His earthly ministry repeatedly stressed an immense either/or decision that lies before us all. For example, *"Whoever believes in the Son has eternal life, but whoever rejects the Son will not see life, for God's wrath remains on Him."* (John 3:36) Heavy-duty stuff then, and something that should undoubtedly shake us up. This subject is again taken up at the end of chapter eight.

The truly horrendous physical punishment to be suffered by Jesus is only part of the payment for humankind's sin. It has to be completed by Him also experiencing excruciating psychological and spiritual pain due to utter abandonment by Father God as the totality of the world's sin is judged, condemned, and *consumed*, in order that the ransom for human sin can be paid in full. As it says in the NT, *"God made Him who had no sin to be sin for us..."* (2 Corinthians 5:21) and *"...so that by the grace of God He [Jesus] might taste [spiritual] death for everyone"* (Hebrews 2:9)

So all of this physical, psychological and spiritual agony to be experienced by Jesus is to wholly dissipate God's *Cup of Wrath*, and win enormous earthly and heavenly benefits for the entire human race. Can any human being really grasp the cosmic suffering undergone by Jesus Christ to give us this opportunity for heaven and the future joys of eternal life?

A very relevant comment from C. S. Lewis, who could see further than most of us: *"When we SAY that we are bad, the 'wrath' of God seems a* barbarous doctrine; as soon as we PERCEIVE our badness, it appears inevitable, a mere corollary from God's goodness."[123]

Getting back to the main plot; Judas knew that Jesus regularly went to the Mount of Olives after dark, and correctly leads the large raiding party, carrying torches, lanterns and weapons, to the Garden of Gethsemane. He walks over, kisses Jesus on the cheek, and then says *"Hail master"* to make sure that they all know this is the leader they have been told to arrest. Jesus says *"Judas, are you betraying the Son of Man with a kiss?"* (Luke 22:48)
Jesus then says to the rest of them, *"Who is it you are looking for?"*
"Jesus of Nazareth" they reply.
"I am he" says Jesus. (John 18:5-6)

There is then the extraordinary reaction whereby a number of the arresting party draw back and fall to the ground. The words of God, even when clothed in a human body, are still very powerful. It is also another of Jesus' *I am* sayings. Some re-grouping takes place and, following another assertion that He is indeed *Jesus of Nazareth*, Jesus is formally arrested by the soldiers. As He had prophesied, amid the chaotic scenes, all His disciples run away.

Although it is not possible to be precise, the available information suggests the time is in the region of 2am on the Friday morning. Jesus is then led, via a noose hanging loosely around His neck and His hands tied behind His back, back to the city. This march takes a roundabout route, avoiding the Beautiful Gate, the main Temple entrance immediately adjacent to the eastern city wall, just in case they encounter any of Jesus' supporters. The journey begins His physical torture, as He is frequently pulled, shoved, and kicked along the way. The group finally arrive at their chosen destination, the large house belonging to Caiaphas thought to have been located in the southwestern corner of the city. [124]

---

[123] C.S. Lewis, *The Problem of Pain.* New York: HarperCollins, 1940, pp. 50-52.
[124] This journey seems to have been almost two miles. Although Jesus has still to make various gruesome treks within the walled city, these will be shorter (less than a mile) due to the ancient Jerusalem's small size.

Caiaphas has a quick look at Jesus and then orders, as a diplomatic move, that He be sent to the nearby house of his father-in-law, Annas, for him to have the first examination. This also gives him a bit of time to get as many Sanhedrin members as possible to his own house for a special emergency meeting. No phones, internet and I-pads back then, but it is likely that most of the members live nearby, and Caiaphas has plenty of servants. He also asks them to get as many false witnesses as possible to testify against Jesus, quite probably by saying that they had heard Him proclaiming Himself to be the Son of God/Son of Man[125] (Blasphemy) in the Temple grounds. Annas, more than happy that Jesus has now been captured, asks a few low-key questions and then sends Him back to Caiaphas for a more rigorous interrogation.

By about 4am, it is likely that Caiaphas has got his full quota of 71 members or at least most of them. A few of the Sanhedrin's main laws have already been referred to, and it seems that Caiaphas is prepared to break any or all of them simply to get Jesus tried, convicted and killed before the start of the Passover Sabbath at sunset when no work will be possible for 24 hours – even he can't do anything about that. Anyway, he starts the trial, or some might say pre-trial, of Jesus more than an hour before sunrise. Right away he has problems because, one after the other, the stories of the witnesses collapse under questioning. More witnesses are called, and the same thing happens.

Caiaphas is trapped and, as much in desperation as anything else, starts to question Jesus – *"Are you not going to answer? What is this testimony that these men are bringing against you?"* (Matthew 26:62) Wry smiles from some of the members because they know that Caiaphas has not got enough for a conviction and that, under the Law, Jesus is not required to say anything. Although they probably feared and hated Jesus, most are likely to have taken their roles as judges quite seriously and did not want innocent persons to be wrongly condemned.

---

[125] The title *Son of Man*, most frequently used by Christ when referring to Himself, can be considered as synonymous with both the *Son of God* as the heavenly exalted one (Daniel 7: 13-14) and His universal role as the representative *Son of all humanity*.

Caiaphas has one final shot at it. Looking straight at Jesus and almost pleading, he shouts, *"I charge you under oath by the living God: Tell us if you are the Christ, the Son of God."* (Matthew 26:63) He knows that as long as Jesus does not speak, then the Sanhedrin has to acquit – and he, Caiaphas, has lost. He looks hopefully at Jesus again, not expecting any reply; but incredibly, at the most critical time of all, Jesus decides to speak *"Yes, it is as you say."* (Matthew 26:64) - alternatively, *"I am"* (Mark 14:62)

Wonderful relief for the High Priest – when all was lost, Jesus had actually condemned Himself. As is appropriate for this type of crime, Caiaphas rips the front of his tunic in two and shouts out *"He has spoken blasphemy! Why do we need any more witnesses?" "Look, now you have heard the blasphemy. What do you think?"* (Matthew 26:65-66a) It is not necessary, at this stage, to take a vote. A crime had taken place right in front of the judges, and they reply in chorus *"He is worthy of death!"* (Matthew 26:66b)

Jesus could have said so many things to reverse this verdict. For instance, "The Law forbids you from trying me at night" or "The witness statements have to agree" or "You cannot judge and pass sentence for a criminal case on the same day" (as they would have to do if He was to be killed before the start of the Passover Sabbath). He might even have said that without His admission, not acceptable evidence under law, they would have no case against Him. But He doesn't. He just stands there and says nothing. And when Caiaphas announces that the court is now in recess until after dawn, He does not attempt to defend Himself as several of the judges leave their seats to blindfold Him, spit in His face, clench their fists, and hit Him, saying, *"Prophesy to us Christ., Who hit you?"* (Matthew 26:68) Jesus is then taken out of the house and led by some of the servants into the stone courtyard, where He is to stand while being closely guarded.

Peter and John have followed Jesus at some distance, and are now in this courtyard, John's family having some influence with Caiaphas. Peter is huddled up near to a fire. He is frightened and has forgotten Jesus' prophecy that before the cock crows, he will deny his leader three times. He is challenged and twice denies being with Jesus or indeed of having any knowledge of Him. He is then accused a third time of being one of Jesus' followers, and the accuser also cites the fact that his Galilean northern accent, clearly distinct from a Jerusalem brogue, gives him away. He then denies it a third time, and immediately a cock crows. Jesus turns around from His guarded position in the courtyard and looks straight at Peter (presumably with great compassion). Then Peter remembers what Jesus had said to him, and goes outside of the courtyard to weep bitterly. The men who are guarding Jesus again apply a blindfold and begin to beat and mock Him, shouting *"Prophesy! Who hit you?"* (Luke 22:64)

Very early in the morning, probably at about 6am, Jesus is taken from the courtyard at Caiaphas' house to the Temple, the usual meeting place of the Sanhedrin, which is now properly reconvened in daylight. They have, of course, already had an informal and unorthodox trial (to say the least!), and Caiaphas now wants to make everything as legal as possible. All 71 members are therefore present and, given the outcome of the night trial, they vote unanimously and swiftly in favour of a guilty verdict, followed by the immediate sentencing of Jesus to death. They conveniently *forget* the law that they cannot pronounce a guilty verdict and sentence the criminal on the same day - their schedule is just so tight, with little more than 12 hours to the start of the Passover Sabbath. Anyhow, who is going to object? Certainly not Jesus, who has come to die and, of course, has no defence counsel.

However, these religious leaders are not yet home and dry; this decision still has to be ratified by Pilate. They also know that to get Pilate's full attention, Jesus' alleged offence must be re-oriented in the direction of Tiberius Caesar, as the Procurator is unlikely to have much interest in Jewish blasphemy laws. They do, however, have the one previously engineered ace in their pack of cards - that is they have already involved the Roman leader by persuading him to send a whole detachment of his soldiers in connection with Jesus' arrest. Any backtracking by Pilate now, and Caesar will be informed of his Procurator's involvement and, particularly, of his misappropriation of the Empire's troops by sending them out on an entirely useless mission.

A decision is also made to take along with Caiaphas and a number of priests (probably *chief* priests, but, for ease, will simply call them priests) some of the Temple guards and other Temple employees. These *extras* will shout against Jesus in the presence of Pilate, and are to be dressed in normal clothes so that no set-up is suspected. They are, additionally, to take their cues from the priests so that their loud protests against Jesus are used to maximum effect. This whole party accordingly sets off for Herod's Upper Palace to petition for Roman confirmation of their death sentence.

Pilate, of course, is hardly likely to simply rubber-stamp this request; he hates Caiaphas and Annas and has lost to them before when they have reversed his decisions by appealing directly to Tiberius Caesar. He also knows that if the Jewish leaders have accomplished the successful capture of this man, Jesus, and their Sanhedrin has condemned Him to death, they will turn up with the prisoner needing his formal validation on behalf of the Roman Empire. So if this is the resultant outcome, he is determined to make their lives as difficult as possible.

Judas has also kept watch from a distance, and probably had his best sight of Jesus during the journey from Caiaphas' courtyard to the Temple. He is, therefore, shocked and appalled at the battered and worn-out appearance of his former leader, resulting from the various beatings and other energy-sapping episodes occurring during the night and early morning hours. Judas loiters in the general vicinity of the Temple and, soon after the Sanhedrin has passed its official verdict, asks one of the Temple messengers about the outcome. The messenger tells him that Jesus has been found guilty of blasphemy, and will be crucified that morning. Judas feels deep remorse; not because he believes that Jesus is indeed the Messiah, but rather that he knows Him to be the gentlest and sweetest person he has ever encountered, and someone who has never done him any wrong.

This should not be happening! It was way too harsh. Perhaps Jesus did deserve some kind of punishment for upsetting the religious establishment here in Jerusalem, such as banishment from Judea, but surely not this. Not crucifixion. In an attempt to reverse the decision, or at least get the death penalty changed, he goes back to the priests and elders in the Temple and offers to refund his payment. He tells them, *"I have sinned,...for I have betrayed innocent blood."* (Matthew 27:4) These religious leaders couldn't have cared less; nothing concerning Jesus can be reversed, so Judas throws the thirty pieces of silver on the ground and then goes off and hangs himself.

The priests and the *rent-a-crowd* plus, of course, Jesus, arrive at Herod's Upper Palace. Caiaphas has gone on before them and already requested an audience with Pontius Pilate. The Procurator, no doubt to aggravate Caiaphas and the priests, takes his time but eventually comes down a flight of steps and sits on his *judgement seat*, situated near to the whole accusing party standing immediately beyond the courtyard gates. These Jews will not go inside the grounds of the *pagan* palace at this time because they do not want to become *unclean* and thus unable to worship in the Temple during the Sabbath. How hypocritical and nuts is this! They are all managing to keep a religious external observation, while at the same time attempting to get an innocent man condemned to death!

Pilate looks at Jesus, who now stands alone just inside the courtyard gates and near to the large accusing group, and finally says loudly *"What charges are you bringing against this man?"* (John 18:29) Pilate had of course been intrinsically involved with Jesus' arrest during the previous evening and would have known perfectly well that the charge was one of blasphemy against the Jewish God, *Yahweh*, which he personally couldn't give two monkeys about. However, as immediately becomes plain to Caiaphas and the priests, he wants to be as difficult as possible, starting by feigning ignorance.

The crowd then roar back so loudly at Pilate's question that Caiaphas and the priests have to wait before answering. *"If he were not a criminal",* they say, *"we would not have handed him over to you."* *"Take him yourselves and judge him by your own law"* Pilate retorts. *"But we have no right to execute anyone,"* they reply. (John 18:29-31)

Pilate, who is already beginning to get a bit irritated by these initial exchanges, then gets up from the judgment seat and starts to walk back up the steps into the palace. Caiaphas and the priests are desperate, and one of them, by distorting Jesus' wonderful answer concerning Roman taxation, shouts out, *"We have found this man subverting our nation. He opposes payment of taxes to Caesar and claims to be Christ, a king."* (Luke 23:2)

For the first time, Pilate is bothered. He would not have been too worried about blasphemy, any demented nutcase or a swindler might claim that; but when a responsible group of citizens resorted to words like *subversion* and *taxes* and *Caesar*, they were charging the prisoner with a serious crime against Tiberius and the Empire. He goes back inside the palace and orders that Jesus be sent to him for a private consultation.

Pilate looks at a pathetic figure of a man, shorn of all dignity, and asks Him various questions about this acclaimed kingship and His kingdom. Jesus tells him that He is indeed a king, but His kingdom is not of this world. Pilate then gets into a sort of existential conversation about what is *truth*, becoming so exasperated by Jesus' brief replies that he goes out once more (with Jesus accompanying him) to sit on the judgement seat. *"I find no basis for a charge against this man,"* (John 18:36-38 & Luke 23:4) he says, and then smiles contentedly to himself while the priests repeatedly strike their foreheads and the rent-a-crowd go ballistic.

The priests fight back *"He stirs up the people all over Judea by His teaching"* they say *"He started in Galilee and has come all the way here."* (Luke 23:5) A now agitated Pilate suddenly perks up. He'd not been aware that the prisoner had originally come from up-country, and quickly realises he has a convenient way out. Herod is in town for the Passover, so Pilate instructs that the prisoner be taken, with a Roman Guard as even more back-up, to the Hasmonean Palace.

The priests can hardly believe their ears and are livid. The mock Messiah was a Jew, who had been charged with both blasphemy and a crime against the Roman Empire while in Jerusalem. How then could He be tried by Herod, whose authority was confined to Galilee and Perea? Added to all this concern was the fact that the Passover Sabbath would soon be upon them, and they knew that Pilate was enjoying their stress over possibly running out of time.

Anyhow, Pilate is the highest authority in Judea, no time now to attempt to go over his head by protesting to Tiberius Caesar in Rome. So Jesus has to be taken to Herod Antipas. Pilate thinks he is really getting on top. In one ingenious stroke, he has removed himself (or so he thinks) from a very delicate criminal case, made friendly and respectful overtures to Herod who is now embroiled himself, and put the pressure right back onto Caiaphas and Annas. Pontius Pilate returns to his office well chuffed with the situation. [126]

The big party of marchers arrive at the Hasmonean Palace. Only the priests, Jesus and the Roman guards are admitted. Herod is extremely pleased to see Jesus. He treats Him cordially as a guest and hopes to see, along with his friends and advisors whom he has also invited, a few demonstrations of His power. He asks Jesus to perform. Perhaps a small feat of magic? or a thunder and lightning show? or even a bit of levitation? Jesus does nothing and also gives no replies to Herod's questions. Herod is angry. The behaviour of Jesus is an affront to his royal dignity. He had promised a magic show to his friends, and the magician has disappointed and humiliated him. He looks at the sorry state of Jesus and reviles Him from His head to His toes.

Then he suddenly has an idea and feels a bit better. He instructs an aide, who leaves the room and then comes back with a garish red garment. Herod puts this over Jesus' shoulders and ties it at the collar - he knows that Jesus has said He is a king, so why not dress Him up as one! Herod gets his intended response. The result is comical, and almost everyone laughs or smiles. Jesus makes the most sorrowful and ridiculous king any of them has ever seen. The priests, however, are agitated; they think all of this is a total waste of time. They cannot, of course, prove blasphemy

---

[126] There were several languages spoken in 1st century Palestine, but it seems likely that all the brief exchanges between Pilate and Jesus and the Jewish religious leaders were held in Koine (common) Greek, a tongue understood by most of the different ethnicities and normally used to facilitate government, commerce and scholarship in the Roman Empire. A form of Aramaic, inherited from the Jews' captivity in Babylon, was the most common everyday language in both Palestine and the neighbouring nations, with the slowly dying Hebrew apparently only remaining familiar to some of the Jewish religious leaders and students. Coming from Rome, Pilate's mother tongue would have been Latin.

in Galilee, and hope that Herod will quickly send Jesus back to Pilate with the announcement that He is indeed a blasphemer in His home province. Herod does return Pilate's courtesy by sending Jesus back to him but, to the priests' despair and even though he despises Him, does not find any fault in Jesus worthy of punishment.

So back again to Herod's Upper Palace for a second audience with the Roman Procurator on his judgment seat. Pilate is pleased that Herod has returned his favour by allowing him, on behalf of the Roman Empire, to determine the final fate of *Jesus of Nazareth*; the whole episode resulting in Pilate and Herod becoming friends. He is also pleased that Herod has agreed with his opinion, and found no fault in Jesus worthy of punishment. Pontius Pilate, therefore, believes he has finally won. The priests, however, have no intention of giving up and have retained their rent-a-crowd to shout for Jesus' crucifixion. As Pilate tells them that both he and Herod have found no fault in Jesus and that he simply intends to discipline Him by Roman scourging (extreme flogging) before setting Him free, there is an ear-shattering bedlam as the rent-a-crowd, again under the direction of the priests, shout for vengeance.

Pilate again finds himself in a corner, and feels even more uneasy when he receives a note from his superstitious wife, Claudia Procula, telling him, *"Don't have anything to do with that innocent man, for I have suffered a great deal today in a dream because of Him."* (Matthew 27:19) However, he suddenly remembers that there is an annual custom at the inception of the Passover to release a single Jewish prisoner. He is also informed that a political prisoner called Barabbas is being held for instigating a riot, during which he had committed murder. Pilate, therefore, makes a naive and yet another major judgment error by offering the crowd the choice of releasing either this man or Jesus - *King of the Jews*.

He thinks this is a no-brainier - surely they will go for Jesus who has, in Pilate's eyes, committed no crime. Unfortunately for Pilate, he has completely misjudged the make-up of his audience. By this time, Caiaphas and the priests plus their rent-a-crowd, all brain-washed to shout for Jesus' crucifixion, have been joined by the political friends of Barabbas equally keen for him to be released. They, therefore, shout in unison for Barabbas to be freed. Pilate is shocked. *"What shall I do, then, with the one you call the King of the Jews?"* he asks despondently.

"Crucify Him!" they roar back.

"Why? What crime has He committed?" Pilate asks.

The crowd, who are unlikely to have been told of Jesus' alleged crime, shout back even louder, *"Crucify Him!"* (Mark 15:12-14)

Pilate accordingly releases Barabbas and, still playing for time and trying to save someone who has no interest in being saved, sends Jesus off to be scourged, hoping that this will somehow satisfy His accusers.

Roman scourging was called the *Halfway Death*, as it was supposed to stop just short of this occurrence. However, death was not particularly unusual, and sometimes those scourged became insane. It was not always administered in addition to crucifixion, and it appears that the two thieves, destined to be crucified with Jesus, were not subjected to this particular form of torture. The punishment was invariably carried out by a Roman *lictor*, who used a short circular piece of wood, to which were attached several strips of leather. Sown into the ends of these strips were chunks of bone or pieces of pottery or iron. The complete instrument was known as a *flagellum*. There was no set number of lashes (stripes) to be meted out, and no specific rules concerning the parts of the body to be hit.

Jesus is on His feet, but bent over and tied securely to a short column. The lictor approaches and takes up a position about six feet behind Him. The flagellum is brought all the way back and then rapidly whipped forward making a dull sound as the strips of leather plus the jagged ends smash against the back of Jesus' rib cage and curl around the sides of His body, causing cuts and grazes to His back and across His chest. This process is repeated again and again until the Tribune (Roman army officer) calls a halt to proceedings as he believes death to be imminent. Jesus becomes unconscious towards the end of this hideous punishment and is brought back to awful consciousness by buckets of cold water being thrown over Him. His entire body screams in agony.

It was the custom for the attending Roman soldiers to be allowed to *play a few games* with the victim. Some of them accordingly find a purple robe to dress Him in and make a crown of thorns, which is pressed into His skull. He also has a heavy reed sceptre (a royal staff) placed in one of His hands. He is, therefore, once again costumed as a comical king, an exaggerated version of Herod's escapade. The soldiers kneel before Him in mock homage, and yell *"Hail, King of the Jews!"* (Matthew 27:29) They again spit in His face and slap Him, with some snatching the sceptre out of His hand and thrashing His head and body with it.

When the soldiers have finally tired of their games, Jesus is taken for a third and last time to Pilate sitting on his judgement seat, again close to the priests and the accompanying rent-a-crowd immediately beyond the courtyard gates; although some of the latter have now probably left to perform Temple duties relating to the rapidly approaching Passover Sabbath. Barabbas and his followers have left in triumph. He is a very lucky boy, released simply because of his inadvertent role as a pawn in Pilate's conflict with the Jewish religious leaders. Nevertheless, the remaining crowd is still sufficient to roar and cry out for the blood of Jesus if this is required. Pilate silences the murmuring of the crowd and shouts out, *"Look I am bringing Him out to you, to let you know that I find no basis for a charge against Him."* (John 19:4)

Jesus is brought out from behind a couple of soldiers, still wearing the crown of thorns and the purple robe. The crowd gasp; this person is a shocking sight, beaten to a pulp and barely recognizable as a man. It is hardly surprising – since His agony in the Garden resulting in Him sweating blood, Jesus has been repeatedly hit, shoved, kicked, spat at, scourged to within a few breaths of His life and has had a crown of thorns violently jammed into His head. Added to this, He has been continually mocked and fiercely questioned and has had no food, water or sleep, having been required to either stand or walk for the entire period. His awful appearance is, in fact, clearly consistent with the descriptions given in both the OT and Plato prophecies.

Pilate can see the initial horror on the faces of the crowd and tries to take advantage of their pity and compassion. He points to Jesus and shouts, *"Behold the man!"* (John 19:5 ESV) The priests, however, soon wrestle back control and again lead the crowd in a chorus of, *"Crucify! Crucify.'"* (John 19:6)

Pilate is still not happy. He desperately wants victory over the Jewish religious leaders and also feels nervous, maybe more affected by his wife's dream than he thinks. He again takes Jesus back into the palace for even more questioning. Jesus says little, and what He does say gives Pilate nothing substantive to work with as far as any possible acquittal is concerned. Back then to the priests and the crowd. The people shout out, *"If you let this man go, you are no friend of Caesar. Anyone who claims to be a king opposes Caesar."* (John 19:12)

Pilate pretends to be shocked, *"Shall I crucify your king?"*

"We have no king but Caesar" they reply. (John 19:15)

This represents an upping of the ante and is sheer irony; everyone hates Caesar and wants only God as their king. However, the threat of Jesus Christ is such that, just to have done with Him, they are prepared to engage in hypocrisy and lies.

That is enough! Pontius Pilate, Procurator of Judea on behalf of the Roman Empire, gives in and calls it a day. He has a basin of water brought to him, washes his hands in front of the crowd, and says *"I am innocent of this man's blood; it is your responsibility"*
All the people respond *"Let His blood be on us and our children!"* (Matthew 27:24-25)

This washing of hands was a Jewish rather than a Roman practice, but still, from at least a human perspective, exempted the Procurator from all blame (which would have given Pontius an easier time with his missus) – all responsibility being transferred to the Jews and, in particular, their religious leaders. This saying has lasted very well; even now people sometimes say things like, "I wash my hands of the whole business."

So Caiaphas and Annas have *won*, if you could call it that. They finally have authority to crucify Jesus Christ. So much of the early morning shenanigans could, however, have been avoided if Pilate had routinely confirmed the Sanhedrin's decision to put Jesus to death. In actuality, it seems that he did automatically rubber-stamp the sentencing to death of the two thieves due to be crucified with Jesus (8th prophecy) but, of course, there was no political one-upmanship over Caiaphas and Annas to be gained in these cases.

One thing that Jesus' protracted trial clearly demonstrates is that human nature has not materially changed over the past 2,000 years. The principal players involved in procuring His death sentence exhibited fear, insecurity, resentment, pride, hypocrisy, judgmentalism, lies, greed, jealousy, mockery and brutality. To bring it up to date, you would only have to add the gruff remark, "I need to have a word with you bruv", and you've got *EastEnders* (I know Grant Mitchell's not in it any more).

Following on from this dire character assessment, it is clear that the culpability for Jesus' death lies entirely with mankind and certainly not with God. Yes, God did completely transform the very wicked free-will actions of those responsible into the greatest triumph the world has ever seen, but this was due to His all-knowing foresight concerning the salvation of the human race. God never motivates people to do bad things.

So Jesus is to be crucified and die as a common criminal. Barely conscious, He has the purple robe taken off Him and is dressed in His own clothes for the journey to the cross. Three *trees*, for Jesus and the two thieves, are obtained from the Roman supply room. Each is the *crosspiece* of the cross, the *upright* already standing at the place of execution and being used many times. The crosspiece, which weighs about 30-40 pounds, has to be shouldered by each of the convicted men as they make their way to the general area of the execution site, a rocky outcrop known as *Golgotha* in Greek and *Calvary* in Latin (means *place of the skull*).

At some point on the way, despite probably being intermittently whipped to keep Him going, it becomes clear that Jesus is simply too exhausted to carry the crosspiece any further, and it is given to a fairly beefy bystander called Simon of Cyrene to complete the journey to the execution site. The precise location of this is not known; but it would have been somewhere slightly beyond the city wall and in a very public place, such as close to a road, so that the victims were subjected to maximum humiliation and degradation, and onlookers were deterred from similar criminal offences.

Once at the execution site, Jesus is stripped of His clothes, and, despite the Jews hatred of nudity, it is probable that the Roman soldiers show no leniency, crucifying Him naked, as were the thieves on either side of Him. Jesus still, however, retains the crown of thorns on His head. He is then laid down, on top of the crosspiece positioned beneath His neck. Long iron nails are hammered into this timber member from the little hollow spots on the outsides of both wrists, the hands themselves being incapable of supporting the weight of a human being without being ripped apart. Four soldiers, two on each side, lift the crosspiece, dragging Jesus by His wrists until the mortise hole can be slotted onto the in-situ upright (no more than eight feet above the ground). His whole body must have writhed in agony. Once in position, the legs are bent upwards and one foot is secured over the other by (probably) using an even longer iron nail hammered through its heel into the timber upright. [127]

Jesus Christ is crucified. It is about 9am on the Friday morning. As per the modern songwriter, Graham Kendrick, *"Hands that flung stars into space to cruel nails surrendered."* [128] This then confirms the 7th prophecy.

Various people are watching the execution, one group comprising several Jewish religious leaders who again mock Jesus and challenge Him, if He is indeed the Christ of God, to come down from the cross so that they can believe in Him. He can, of course, do this but it would wreck the *rescue mission*. Passers-by and the soldiers also mock Him, with a few of the military acquiring His clothes by either choice or gambling (again, 7th prophecy). Finally, there is a small group of five

---

[127] By comparison, this is just so pathetic; but I once, while on site, stood on a nail pushed up through a plank of wood. The nail made a slight mark on the top of my foot, so it more or less went all the way through. The pain, during perhaps the two or three seconds it took me to get the nail out, was unbelievable. How Jesus, and of course the thieves, managed to speak during this horrendous ordeal is completely beyond someone like me – who, of course, ended up in A & E.

[128] Graham Kendrick, *The Servant King*. ThankYou Music, 1983

supporters standing close to the cross - His mother, her sister Salome, Mary Magdalene, Mary the wife of Cleopas and the young disciple, John.

Death by crucifixion is a drawn-out affair. The wounds on their own are insufficient to result in death, but cause the three men to writhe in agony. The bodies of all three sag down into V-shaped positions where breathing is not possible. This means that they have to periodically lift themselves up to the top of the cross by pressing down on the nails through their feet. It is an excruciating process, a word that derives from this torture.

At 12 midday, when Jesus has been on the cross for about three hours, darkness comes over the land and lasts for about three hours. A copy of a now-lost original quotation (50-55 AD) from Thallus, a pagan historian who attempted to naturalistically explain away the darkness, indicates that this occurrence was well known at the time.[129] Indeed, there are understood to be records of this phenomenon, and its possible connection to Christ's crucifixion and resurrection, as far afield as China. [130] [131]

Jesus is now beginning to weaken more rapidly than the two thieves, who have not been subjected to agonising treatment prior to crucifixion.

From the cross, He speaks out a total of seven utterances, all of which are incredible and have been the subject of many books. I am, however, going to mention just two. The first takes place at about the same time as the soldiers are choosing or gambling for His clothes. He says, *"Father, forgive them, for they do not know what they are doing."* (Luke 23:34) This is, therefore, Jesus' heart for, not only the soldiers, but everyone involved in this gross and hideous miscarriage of justice. There could not be a better demonstration of what is meant by love, unconditional love, occurring in the midst of extreme agony across the

---

[129] Josh McDowell & Sean McDowell, *Evidence That Demands A Verdict*. Authentic Media Ltd., 2017, p.149.

[130] https://ugetube.com/watch/chinese-emperor-guangwu-given-signs-of-jesus-039-crucifixion-and- resurrection-mp4_pmjaOWs4DWjyLpU.html?msclkid=fed9c021cf9a11ec9d2275509580e8e1

[131] https://proselytiserofyah.wordpress.com/2022/03/24/chinese-witnesses-of-jesus-resurrection/?msclkid=2295acc8cf2111ecbf5f5f94aac0703b

three realms of physical, psychological and spiritual. It, therefore, gives us an intimate insight into the amazing character of God.

At about 3pm, Jesus, knowing that His mission is now complete, wills Himself to die and cries out triumphantly, as His penultimate utterance, the Greek word, *"Tetelestai"* (John 19:30), which means *It is finished* or *Paid in full*. In NT times, *Tetelestai* was often written on a receipt to confirm full payment, and, coming from the lips of Jesus at the time of His death, it is sometimes referred to as the greatest word ever spoken. In this context, it is an all-encompassing word – Jesus Christ dies as a substitute for the sins of the whole world, as per His mission statement in John 3.16 - the Jews, the Muslims, the Buddhists, the Hindus, the Sikhs, the Christians, the Post-moderns, the Existentialists, the New Ageists, and the adherents of all other worldviews including Atheists. As He gives up His spirit an earthquake occurs, fracturing the rocks in the general vicinity and splitting the massive veil between the Temple's Holy Place and the *Holy of Holies*. [132]

This highly symbolic occurrence is consistent with Jesus' claimed Messiahship, and ushers in a new, more fully revealed, all-embracing and further-reaching dispensation of grace (the New Covenant), whereby personal relationships with God could now extend to all humanity and be more intimate and continuous than had been possible under the Mosaic Covenant of the OT (see chapter eight). The splitting of the Temple veil would, however, have been kept secret from the normal punters. So Jesus dies at Golgotha, a location just outside the city wall; this external position symbolising His complete separation from God and all people, as is necessary for His sacrificial death to be the consummate and final answer to human sin.

The religious leaders are getting worried that the three men will not die and be removed from their crosses before sunset when the Passover Sabbath kicks off (big, big problem to these guys). They, therefore, send a messenger back into the city to ask Pontius Pilate to order the

---

[132] The *Holy of Holies* was a small cube-shaped room symbolising the very presence of God, now made accessible to all people as metaphorically illustrated by the destruction of the Temple veil.

officiating Roman Centurion to expedite matters. This is agreed, and two of the soldiers are instructed to use a timber board, known as a *crurifragium*, to break the prisoners' legs - yet even more excruciating pain. This meant that they would subsequently be unable to push on the nails through their feet to struggle up to the tops of the crosses where breathing was possible. Death by asphyxiation would, therefore, follow fairly rapidly. This awful process is carried out on the two thieves, but when they come to Jesus they discover that He is already dead. One of the soldiers has a spear and thrusts it into one of Jesus' sides, which causes an outflow of blood and water. There are several different explanations concerning exactly what this represents, but the most likely is that these fluids relate to the rupture of the heart. In any event, there is absolutely no doubt that He is well and truly dead. The Romans knew how to kill people.

Pilate is approached late in the afternoon by a rich guy called Joseph of Arimathea, who arranges for the body of Jesus to be placed in his newly formed family tomb (8th prophecy). The entrance to the rocky tomb is sealed by a large stone. This is not a boulder but a very heavy, cut circular stone disc located in a groove. Once in the 'closed' position, it will take several men to move it. The next day, upon the Jewish religious leaders' request, a Roman Guard is posted. Jesus Christ is then supernaturally resurrected on the third day (Sunday), His subsequent meetings with the disciples and other believers being categorically reported. Indeed, contrary versions of this event have all fallen woefully short in both credibility and longevity, with the floundering of these attempts resulting in some of the antagonists becoming Christians themselves. One such was Frank Morison, advertiser, author and atheist, whose extensive research ended up with him writing, much to his surprise and original intention, an excellent and highly acclaimed pro-Christian book titled, *Who Moved The Stone?*' [133]

Who then was responsible for Jesus' death? the Jews? – Yes; the Romans? – Yes; you, me and everyone else? – Yes. I reckon if I'd been around at the time, I would have joined in and shouted for the

---

[133] Frank Morison, *Who Moved The Stone?* Faber & Faber Ltd., 1983.

crucifixion of Jesus Christ. There is a painting by the Dutchman, Rembrandt, called the *Raising of the Cross*, where he shows the scene as the crucified Christ is manoeuvered into position and also paints himself into the picture as one of those taking part. In other words, Rembrandt knows that he is a sinful man and is deliberately identifying himself with the individuals directly responsible for the crucifixion of Christ.

Anyhow, what to do about all this? Returning to my pole vault accident in the autumn of 1973 - what would have happened to me if, as I lay on the ground, I'd said I was OK and that the ambulance guys were simply wasting their time? That would have been too stupid to even envisage - I was in a desperate state. But that is what so many people are doing with God's Rescue Plan. It was undertaken at such a huge cost, but most of the time we just use the name of Jesus Christ as a blasphemy.

This Jesus is not some fictional character, He didn't get crucified for fun, His gospel is not simply a good way to live (although it includes that), but the whole package is the answer to the problem all human beings have – that is sin, both perceived and, even more, hidden. It is the only *correct pill* because it deals with this sin, the *universal cancer*. We cannot afford to ignore a remedy as brilliant as this. It will not be offered again after physical death. As it says in the letter to the Hebrews, *"How shall we escape if we ignore such a great salvation."* (Hebrews 2:3a)

Genuine repentance and giving our lives back to God, in faith and to the best of our ability is, as previously, the way to acceptance and entrance into heaven and eternal life. In other words, we acknowledge Him as our boss and rescuer – in Christian speak, as *Lord and Saviour*. There is no risk, because *God is Love* and He wants us to have a fulfilled and abundant life. As Jesus said, *"I have come that they may have life, and have it in all its fullness."* (John 10:10) In pre-conversion days, I always thought that God would ruin everything if I handed my life over to Him but, actually, it's been the reverse. Despite all my flaws and problems, He has stuck by me and been utterly reliable. And I have never once regretted the brilliant decision I made in April 1977.

God is love beyond our understanding, and He has become intimately involved in the pain and suffering in the lives of human beings in an immense, extraordinary and, ultimately, restorative way. I end by quoting the last verse of a poem called *Jesus of the Scars* by Edward Shillito.[134]

> *"The other gods were strong; but Thou wast weak;*
> *They rode, but Thou didst stumble to a throne;*
> *But to our wounds only God's wounds can speak,*
> *And not a god has wounds, but Thou alone."*

---

[134] Edward Shillito, *"Jesus of the Scars."* As cited by John Stott. *The Cross of Christ: 20th Anniversary Edition*. InterVarsity Press, 2006 pp. 335-337.

CHAPTER SEVEN

Science and Related Philosophy

Exactly what contribution to the science profession can be made by a guy who just about struggled through first-year maths of an honours degree course in civil engineering and took three attempts, albeit that the first two were pretty half-hearted, to pass GCE O-level physics? Quite clearly, nothing. However, the position appears to be rather different when it comes to the *philosophy of science*, which deals with what can be deduced from the findings of science. *Scientism* is one example of this, being broadly defined as the belief that science can or will be able to answer every single question relevant to the human experience.

As a brief heads up, this does seem rather unlikely; because science, although often adept at answering the *how* questions, relates to a domain where the *why* questions are commonly irrelevant. For example, science can tell me how much cyanide I need to put in someone's cup of tea in order to poison them but can have no opinion on why I may wish to do this. Right from the start, I must acknowledge that much of my insight into this topic has been gained from Professor John Lennox, who, besides expertly engaging in various video-recorded debates with die-hard neo-atheists such as Richard Dawkins and the late Christopher Hitchens (*YouTube*, and certainly worth watching), has authored or co-authored many books. Of these, the most relevant here is a small but highly instructive publication titled: *God And Stephen Hawking - Whose Design Is It Anyway?* [135]

---

[135] John Lennox, *God and Stephen Hawking – Whose Design Is It Anyway?* Lion Hudson plc, 2011.

Probably the most important point to emphasise from the beginning is that there is, in reality, no fundamental conflict between science and religion; there are simply too many scientists on both sides of the debate. For example, Francis Collins, the American scientist and geneticist who headed up the Human Genome Project (project manager overseeing the work of more than 2,000 scientists) is a committed Christian, whereas James Watson, another American scientist and geneticist who, along with Francis Crick, Rosalind Franklin and Maurice Wilkins, discovered the structure of DNA, is an atheist. These are, therefore, two outstanding scientists who have made it right to the top of their profession with completely opposing worldviews. And it is also pertinent to point out that it's necessary to have faith (for instance, in the repeated reliability of various laws and principles) to be able to *do* science, and that many Christian beliefs, as seen earlier, can be shown to be evidence-based. Yes, there is certainly a conflict, but it's between atheism and theism.[136]

Unfortunately, this message does not appear to be getting across to the general public; primarily due, or so it seems, to the neo-atheists on the one side and members of the *Creation Science* movement on the other. I have no wish to criticise the latter, but their ideology, or at least certain parts of it, goad the neo-atheists into an unnecessary contest.

Irreducible Complexity is a case in point. This can be summarised by stating that where there is no current generally accepted naturalistic explanation [137] concerning the formation of a certain feature, then the conclusion must be made that this has been directly created by God - that is the *God of the Gaps* theory. But the creationists could be setting themselves up for potential problems in the future when further

---

[136] Theism is the belief in the existence of a Creator God (or possibly gods), who intercede(s) in the running of the universe. Atheism is, of course, the total opposite. And in this context, the terms *universe* and *cosmos* always relate to that which can be observed.

[137] The above reference to *naturalistic explanations*, although a typically atheistic phrase and assumed as such elsewhere, is here concerned specifically with how something develops once the process has commenced. It does not mean that God didn't start it all off.

scientific knowledge might reveal seemingly plausible naturalistic explanations for certain hitherto irreducibly complex organs.

As it happens, there is a much stronger argument than *God of the Gaps*, which is based on what we do know rather than on what we don't. This involves the principle of *agency*, where God is the (sovereign and personal) agent, separate from and transcending the laws of nature; which, in any event, can only predict, govern and describe rather than create or cause anything to happen in the first place. For instance, take the game of snooker, which, despite my best intentions, I usually end up watching for hours on end when the World Championships are on the box. The thing is that the game cannot start until a snooker player imparts a force into the cue ball, via his arm and held cue. Then, and only then, will the laws of motion come into play.

To continue, the American George Bailey Brayton (1830-1892) is generally recognised as the leading pioneer of the commercial liquid-fuelled internal combustion engine; a machine necessarily subject to and reliant upon the relevant laws of internal combustion. Let's then imagine the scenario where I have always been completely crazy about internal combustion engines (hardly believable, but never mind); so much so that I have read and written countless related books and, even when blindfolded, can carry out their assembly in next to no time. I am, therefore, *the daddy* when it comes to internal combustion engines, knowing more or less everything there is to know about them.

Would my great understanding then mean that George Brayton (a personal agent) had never existed? Clearly a ridiculous question. And which is the most important – George Brayton or the laws of internal combustion? Again, a ridiculous question. And yet these questions belong to the same category of argumentation that the neo-atheists are so confidently putting forward. Firstly, once we know, or think we know, how some entity came into being, this automatically negates the need for a Creator God. And secondly, that it is necessary to choose between a personal agency and impersonal sets of scientific laws.

The founders of modern science such as Isaac Newton, Michael Faraday and James Clerk Maxwell, all of whom were committed Christians, never thought this way but realised that their discoveries simply shone further light onto God's creation. Indeed Isaac Newton, probably the greatest of them all and the writer of many scientific papers, wrote even more papers on theology. In recent times, it is understood that Francis Collins became ecstatic and awestruck when he and his team finally completed the mapping of the human genome, containing over three billion pairs of nitrogenous chemical bases (forming the longest *word* in the world) in the nucleus of every human body cell, exclaiming, *"I am reading the language of God."* He later wrote a highly acclaimed and popular book called, unsurprisingly, *The Language of God*.[138]

Christianity and science are simply not mutually exclusive, with Alister McGrath, a true polymath, stating, *"The scientific narrative of the origins of the cosmos is not the same as the Christian narrative of creation; the two can, however, be intertwined, like a dual helix, to offer a more satisfying vision of our universe."* [139] Yet the pseudo-debate generally known as *creation versus evolution* still rumbles on. As far as I'm concerned, the majestic universe on show is simply awe-inspiring and results in a take-home message of, *God did it and we are not accidents*. And maybe the second part of this phrase provides a clue concerning the relative longevity of this pseudo-debate. It seems to me, from reading various accounts of academics who have become Christians, that it is usually not their great learning that has been the biggest obstacle to them coming to faith. They had just previously wanted to remain autonomous (in their own eyes), with no responsibility or accountability to God, however likely His existence.

While not wishing to appear discourteous, there are a couple of terms that some scientists of an atheistic disposition, knowingly or unknowingly, seem to hide behind. These are *infinity* and the *big bang*. As a brief reminder, attention has already been drawn to the fact that our brains, although unbelievably wonderful, weigh only about 3lbs and are, therefore, inevitably limited. Most pertinently, they are simply not

---

[138] Francis Collins, *The Language Of God*: Free Press, Simon & Schuster, plc, 2006.
[139] Alister McGrath, *Christian Theology – An Introduction*. John Wiley & Sons Ltd, 2017, p.151.

equipped with the *infinity gene* meaning that science cannot, of itself, provide the necessary knowledge to discover and know an infinite being.

I remember once watching a TV programme where four extremely talented scientists set out to tackle *infinity*. They all soon became obsessed with this issue, forgetting to eat or go to bed, and then *went mad* before dying prematurely. The fact that these scientists ended up losing the plot appears to be an almost inevitable outcome; finite minds, no matter how brilliant, will undoubtedly be overloaded by the whole concept of infinity. For instance, consider the *big bang* theory, as very briefly summarised below, and the Bible's Genesis account. Both agree that time itself started and that before this there was no time. But this statement is using *time* as a measure to distinguish between these two conditions! Thus, whatever 'before time commenced' really means, we simply cannot visualise it without an *infinity gene*. Similarly, both agree that space itself was created at the beginning of time as the universe expanded – but what did it expand into? – again, we require an infinity gene.

Probably the ultimate scientific how question is "How did the universe come about?" For several centuries this was not a particular problem for scientists, because it was generally assumed that the universe had always been here, more or less unchanging with time. End of. However, by the mid-1960s, the continuing expansion of the universe and a resultant start point had been proved to the general satisfaction of the scientific community, corroborating research colloquially known as the big bang theory dating from the first half of the century.

This theory maintains that approximately 13½ billion years ago an infinitesimal *site* or *point,* many orders of magnitude smaller than a single atom but containing an unbelievable amount of energy, was the location of a massive 'explosion'. With time, this translated into the creation of all the billions of stars plus planets in our galaxy and all the billions of galaxies in the universe. Without getting into any deep thinking, it surely takes a lot more faith to believe in this all "just happening" than it does to believe that a transcendent grand designer, such as God, "spoke it into existence." However, the term *big bang* is often trotted out by some scientists as if it were the most obvious thing in the world. In reality, the possibility of this phenomenon producing our ordered universe by *chance* or *accident* is so low that it should be viewed as *non-existent* (see below).

This brings us back to the strong anthropic principle, as touched on earlier, and again quoting Alister McGrath, *"The universe that emerged out of the big bang, on an anthropic reading of things, was already governed by laws that were fine-tuned to encourage the rise of carbon-based life-forms"* [140] (as per all living entities). More specifically, three of the four core constituent elements - carbon, nitrogen, and oxygen (the other being hydrogen) – of the biochemical compounds necessary to produce life can only be created at the centres of stars, particularly large stars; and without the incredible precision tuning of the above laws, these could not have formed. So who put these laws in at the very beginning? (note: no possibility here for any associated long-term *evolution*).

Staying with the strong anthropic principle, Roger Penrose, an outstanding English mathematical physicist who has worked on black holes with Stephen Hawking, has calculated the statistical probability for the existence of what he calls the *very special initial state* of the universe as being less than 1 part in $10^{10^{123}}$. [141] Quite frankly, that's a simply unbelievable number. However, to properly demonstrate this, I need to talk about "something to the power of" which, although still incredibly sexy, is not everyone's cup of tea. So the following inset boxes will hopefully explain everything!

---

[140] Alister McGrath, *A Fine-Tuned Universe.* Westminster John Knox Press, 2009, p.118.
[141] Roger Penrose, *Incredible Precision in the Organization of the Initial Universe.*
https://evolutionnews.org/2010/04/roger_penrose_on_cosmic_finetu/

Talking Big Numbers (1 of 2)

It may come as a surprise to some, but numbers often don't play that big a part in maths, although they are, of course, typically required as the end product. However, in this particular case, numbers are centre-stage. And, because it's all that's needed, only numbers related to ten are considered.

How many ways are there of writing the number one million? Well, obviously by doing what I've just done, or 1,000,000 or 10*10*10*10*10*10, or 10^6, which is actually ten to the power six. It therefore follows that whatever power the number 10 is raised to, it will always correspond to however many times it has been multiplied by itself and be able to be expressed by the figure 1 followed by the same number of zeros. So, one billion or ten to the power nine – that is 10^9 = 1 followed by nine zeros = 1,000,000,000.

And how long would it take to write the number one million or 1,000,000? Six zeros and thus only a few seconds – no sweat. But what about writing out $10^{1,000,000}$ in full, equating to a million zeros? That's obviously quite a different proposition. Anyhow, I've worked out that, writing at one zero per second, it should take about $11^1/_2$ days, assuming no toilet breaks.

So when we see a number with two exponents, such as $10^{10^{123}}$, this equates to 1 followed by 10^{123} zeros – that is a thousand, million, million, million, million, million, million, million, million, million, million, million, million, million, million, million, million, million, million, million ('million' written 20 times) zeros.

Indeed, Penrose says that $10^{10^{123}}$ represents too big a number to be written out in full, even if you could write a zero on every single atom (he actually infers sub-atomic particles, but the difference is not that important) of the observable universe. He then adds: "You'd be way short. You'd never do it that way. There's not enough room to put all the zeros in." So how far short is "way short" – Let's see.

Talking Big Numbers (2 of 2)

Now the observable universe is pretty big – approximately 93 billion light years, so we're told. Or, if we can travel at the speed of light (186,000 miles per second – the equivalent of going to the moon in approximately one second), it would take about 93 billion years of 'Earth-time' to go from one 'end' to the other (longer, and maybe not even theoretically possible, if one allows for an expanding cosmos).

And how many universes of similar size to our own would be required to write the number $10^{10^{123}}$ out in full? Well, it's estimated that there are about 10^{80} atoms in our universe, or, for ease, let's say $10^{100} = 10^{10^{10}}$. We thus have to simply divide by this figure. And when dividing exponents, we actually subtract the divider. So, we now have $10^{123} - 10^{10}$ zeros = 10^{113} – that is a zero on every atom of approximately 10^{113} universes of a similar size to our own is needed!

Finally, writing $10^{10^{123}}$ out in full at one zero per second takes 10^{123} seconds, although for a number this big it could equally be years! (i.e., dividing by 31,536,000 to covert seconds to years has essentially no effect).

Conclusion: $10^{10^{123}}$ is an insanely large number; but, nevertheless, still negligible when compared with infinity!

For future reference, negative exponents are simply the inverse (upside down) of the positive ones. So, just as one billion is equal to 10^9 or 1,000,000,000 (9 zeros), one billionth is equal to 10^{-9} or 1/1000,000,000 (9 zeros) or 0.000000001 (note: only 8 zeros before the figure 1 – a 'nano').

Thus, if it's assumed that Penrose is broadly correct (and most scientists working in this field seem to believe he is) in calculating the likelihood of our ordered universe occurring by blind chance as being less than 1 part in $10^{10^{123}}$, it follows that the above non-existent classification must be justified. Furthermore, as highlighted in *Talking Big Numbers*, even the insanely large $10^{10^{123}}$ is itself negligible when compared to infinity. Automatically proffering the word *infinity* in an attempt to give legitimacy to the probabilistic occurrence of Penrose's very special initial state is thus surely untenable, and the existence of a transcendent grand designer therefore appears to be the logical conclusion. Nevertheless, certain atheistic scientists, as noted earlier, have proposed alternative interpretations, involving entities such as quantum mechanics, a multiverse, and the weak anthropic principle.

The essence of the latter is that we can arrive at certain conclusions concerning the laws of the universe from the fact that we exist. When all is said and done, we're here! And thus the universal laws are not so much incredibly fine-tuned as simply being inevitable precursors of the existence of the universe as it is and our individual lives as they are.

To pursue this possibility, let's return to the initial expansion of the universe and, specifically, 10^{-36} seconds after the big bang, when a strong anthropic event known as *cosmological inflation* is believed to have taken place. This related to an infinitesimally short phase of approximately 10^{-35} (0.00000000000000000000000000000001) seconds when the universe apparently multiplied its size by a factor of 10^{30} (1,000,000,000,000,000,000,000,000,000,000).[142] Or, in more everyday language, an expansion, according to Stephen Hawking, roughly *equivalent to* a 1cm diameter coin suddenly blowing up to about ten million times the width of the Milky Way (for clarity, not the chocolate bar). [143]

To me, that looks more like *"In the beginning God created the heavens and the earth."* (Genesis 1:1, first ten verses of the Bible)

---

[142] The modified *inflationary* version of the *Standard Cosmological Model*.
[143] Stephen Hawking & Leonard Mlodinow, *The Grand Design*. Bantam Press, 2011, p.165.

Some scientists also reject anthropic fine-tuning on the basis that this incredible expansion would inevitably have been very close to the critical rate determined by the initial cosmic energy density and was, therefore, an almost unavoidable natural consequence. However, this only puts the fine-tuning argument back one step, because, as Alister McGrath [144] points out, the initial cosmic energy density would itself have required a quite extraordinary degree of constraint to give rise to the universe as we know it.

Furthermore, is the fact of our existence on the planet enough on its own to validate the weak anthropic principle? Let's consider the situation where some blindfolded soldiers are to be executed by a firing squad. They hear the instruction, "Aim... ready ....fire!" But, although there are the sounds of shots, absolutely nothing further transpires - they're all OK. What can be the reason for this? Did the firing squad use blanks? Or did they aim to miss? Or were the guns perhaps in such poor condition that they didn't shoot straight? Whatever the reality, all are possible legitimate explanations for these guys' continued existence. Conversely, it doesn't seem sufficient for them to simply say "We're here because we're here!"

And what about the possibility of the multiverse? One might perhaps argue that if this exists and contains about $10^{10^{123}}$ universes, then only the one having the necessary fine-tuning could result in the potential for life – that is presumably our own by default. But is there a multiverse containing $10^{10^{123}}$ universes (subsequently discussed) and, if so, who or what created that?

Penrose himself considers the multiverse theory to be *worse than useless* as an explanation for the strong anthropic principle, instead preferring a hypothesis known as 'Conformal Cyclic Cosmology' (CCC) whereby the present Aeon, estimated at $13^1/_2$ billion years, is just the latest of a cyclical pattern of Aeons with their respective universes. Although Penrose provides associated theoretical analyses, this radical

---

[144] Alister McGrath, *A Fine-Tuned Universe.* Westminster John Knox Press, 2009, p.116

view is inevitably highly speculative and, again, would not solve the problem of how everything got started in the first place.

When it comes to Richard Dawkins, he, unsurprisingly, tells us his reasons for remaining an atheist. One of the principal ones relates to him actually playing the strong anthropic principle card by asserting that, however improbable it is for this universe and human beings to have been formed by accident or chance, it is still more probable than any associated ability to produce a Creator God or gods (theoretically the most advanced evolutionary product of them all). But, as John Lennox points out, the main monotheistic religions of Islam, Judaism, and Christianity all talk about the *uncreated God*, as the *uncaused first cause*. Created or evolved gods, Lennox rightly says, would be no gods at all.

It, therefore, seems that Dawkins cannot or will not think outside the box of evolution within a closed system, whereby nothing can get in and nothing can get out. Conversely, Christianity relates to an open system (sometimes referred to as an *open heaven*), where God reaches in and interacts with human beings. A rough but relevant analogy might be to imagine a huge painting created by some mega-artist, with many different figures, all of whom she somehow enables to live and think. The question is, can these figures find the transcendent artist within the painting? No, they can't; unless, that is, she makes herself known and actually enters the painting – as per the incarnation of Jesus Christ.

To close this particular discussion, it is probably worth giving a little more thought to the question of why certain scientists such as Roger Penrose seemingly direct all their efforts into searching for naturalistic explanations concerning the origin of the universe. Episode 1 of a BBC 4 series titled *Magic Numbers of Hannah Fry's Mysterious World of Maths* (first aired on October 10th 2018) gives us particular insight into this mindset. At the very start of this broadcast, Hannah, who is a British mathematician of some note and a very good presenter, makes the following statement, *"There is a mystery at the heart of our universe. A puzzle that so far no-one has been able to solve. If we can solve this mystery, it will have profound consequences for all of us. That mystery is* why mathematical rules and patterns seem to infiltrate pretty much everything in the world around us." She goes on to say, "Why does any of this matter. Well, maths underpins just about everything in our modern world. From computers and mobile phones to our understanding of human biology. The modern world wouldn't exist without mathematics.- maths is the underlying language of the universe, but how did it get there?" [145]

The last two phrases are particularly interesting because, although the first mirrors the thoughts of Kepler as mentioned earlier, the second, in stark contrast, clearly rules out the possibility of any transcendent being. This denial thus appears to delineate the starting point of worldviews held by some (or maybe many) atheistic scientists, and as such may perhaps best be viewed as representing an *absolute* statement. However, it might also be argued that this (seemingly) unwavering approach results in a kind of checkmate. To again quote the outstanding physicist, John Polkinghorne, *"From its own resources, science is unable to offer an adequate explanation of its impressive success."* [146] In other words, Polkinghorne regards the achievements of science as being too incredible and wonderful for its brilliant scientists to be the ultimate product of solely naturalistic processes.

Making a short detour into the world of Quantum Mechanics; a subject so weird and counterintuitive that Richard Feynman, an American Nobel Prize-winning theoretical physicist known for his pioneering work in this field, has written, *"...I think I can safely say that nobody understands quantum mechanics."* [147] By making this statement, it seems that Feynman is basically saying that although physicists can follow certain proven methods and related formulations to provide reliable results, nobody seems to *get* quantum mechanics at a *soulful* level.

---

[145] Hannah Fry, *Magic Numbers of Hannah Fry's Mysterious World of Maths,* BBC4 TV series, Episode 1, October 10th 2018.
[146] John Polkinghorne, *Theology In The Context Of Science.* Yale University Press, 2009, p.71.
[147] Richard Feynman, *The Character of Physical Law* (Cambridge, Mass.: MIT Press, 1965), p.129.

Certainly, no other theory in science has so many different ways of looking at it, resulting in a veritable *zoo* of interpretations. And these commonly involve philosophy, with questions such as, Do we have free will? or, Do things only become real when we look at them? The following discussion, inevitably representing only a tiny fraction of the unfolding picture of quantum mechanics, is primarily based on *The Quantum World*, produced by *New Scientist* [148] and *The Elegant Universe* by Brian Greene.[149]

By way of introduction, Newton's laws of motion are valid for the speeds and object sizes relevant to Earth and, apart from a required bit of tweaking concerning Mercury (using Einstein's theory of general relativity [1915]), can seemingly encompass planetary movement within the solar system where they represent a progression of earlier observational work by Kepler. Between them, Einstein's theories of general and special relativity [1905] deal with very large masses, such as stars and galaxies, and very high velocities (virtually up to the speed of light), with quantum theory dealing with the frantic and seemingly random movements of the *very small*. The latter range from sub-atomic particles, such as protons, neutrons, electrons, up-quarks, down-quarks, strange-quarks, muons, neutrinos and bosons, to molecules and large clusters of atoms.

General relativity and quantum mechanics are today considered to be the two foundational pillars of physics. However, although both have mathematical and, subject to certain constraints, experimental backing, they are, at their core, fundamentally incompatible. This has particular significance at the quantum level where general relativity provides increasingly nonsensical answers as the big bang is approached (*via* back-extrapolation). Nevertheless, most physicists believe that this incompatibility can ultimately be resolved, and considerable research has been, and is being, undertaken to determine how the universe behaves at its deepest level.

---

[148] New Scientist, *The Quantum World*. John Murray Learning, 2017.
[149] Brian Greene, *The Elegant Universe,* Vintage, 2000.

At the present time, however, much of the associated progress relates solely to mathematical calculations and cannot be verified experimentally. This is because even the most advanced detection system, the Large Hadron Collider, located on the Franco-Swiss border near Geneva, is limited to a distance scale of 10^{-20} metres, still a million, billion times bigger than that seemingly required to observe the expected quantum fluctuations of space and time,[150] including, if present, *quantum gravity*. To put this into more everyday language, Roger Penrose considers that for most relevant experimentation, particularly that relating to the earliest moments of the big bang, a collider the size of the solar system would be needed. [151]

Quantum theory was discovered, more or less by accident, in 1900 by the German physicist, Max Planck, when researching a seemingly unconnected problem in classical (approx. pre-20th century) physics. His specific findings revealed that, instead of the previous assumption that energy was always continuous, it actually came in distinct minuscule packages which he called *quanta*. This process could alternatively be termed *lumpy wave energy*, and a few years later Einstein extended Planck's theory to light with, in this case, the distinct minuscule packages being named *photons*.

Further work by the French physicist, Louis de Broglie, built on Einstein's photon equations and virtually proved, in his 1924 PhD thesis, that electron *particles* also behaved as *waves*.

This has now been confirmed by the results of numerous experiments; in particular, variations on Thomas Young's original (1801) *double-slit* experiment [152] which showed that, depending on whether or not detection apparatus was employed, sub-atomic photons and electrons exhibited both particulate and wavelike characteristics. This phenomenon, known as *wave-particle duality*, is at the heart of

---

[150] New Scientist, The Quantum World. John Murray Learning, 2017, p.160.
[151] Ibid, p.166.
[152] Brian Greene, *The Elegant Universe*. Vintage, 2000, pp.97-103 provides a full description of the double-slit experiment.

quantum theory. It is discussed below, after reference to two further foundational quantum components, *entanglement* and *uncertainty*.

The principle of entanglement concerns pairs or groups of sub-atomic or atomic particles, which upon collision can become so linked that, even if subsequently separated by vast distances, any changes made to one (e.g., electron energy level and spin) invariably and instantaneously affect the other– that is at apparent velocities far in excess of the speed of light. The explanation for this continues to be the subject of much debate among quantum physicists, although it appears that most now consider that actual information cannot be transferred at rates faster than the speed of light, thereby not violating Einstein's Theory of Special Relativity (this allows for the incredible expansion of the cosmos itself as the sole exception). So, a fairly bizarre concept and, not surprisingly, one that Einstein didn't like, calling entanglement theory "spooky action at a distance." He argued that the theory of quantum mechanics was incomplete, and that *hidden variables* acting at some deeper layer of reality might be responsible for its apparent weirdness.

However, the results of copious relevant experiments over the past decades have gone against Einstein's stance, with, for instance, the results of testing carried out (2008) on two entangled photons eighteen kilometres apart by the Swiss physicist, Nicolas Gisin, equating to the transference of information at approximately 100,000 times the speed of light. [153] Gisin and his team concluded that direct communications of this magnitude were simply not possible, although they also conceded that, thus far, they had been unable to come up with a rigorous alternative explanation for this *spooky action.*

A second connected example occurred at the Institute of Photonic Science (ICFO) in Barcelona where, in 2020, researchers reported a *world record* of 15 trillion[154] quantum entangled rubidium atoms.[155] This

---

[153] Nicolas Gisin, https://www.nature.com/articles/news.2008.1038
[154] A typical human cell is made up of approximately 100 trillion atoms.
[155] Live Science, https://www.livescience.com/physicists-entangle-15-trillion-hot-atoms.html

was achieved by firing a beam of polarised[156] light at a small glass tube filled with vapourised rubidium and inert nitrogen gas heated to 177°C. The collective state of this *cloud* of rubidium atoms, particularly its total spin, was then determined by measuring the rotation of the emerging light waves (on the other side of the tube).

Quantum physicists hope that this very promising outcome will come to represent a major breakthrough in the development of ultrasensitive sensors capable of measuring ripples in space-time and the detection of the evasive dark matter (Black holes? Neutron stars? et al), thought to permeate much of the universe. Furthermore, the 15 trillion entangled atoms are understood to represent approximately 100 times the previous record, with the fact that this condition was found to persist for at least a millisecond (a considerable duration in the atomic world) within a very hot environment indicating this quantum state to be less fragile than had hitherto been thought.

Finally, the fact that it was not possible to obtain information concerning the individual quantum states of (in this experiment) the multitudinous pairs of entangled atoms means that this particular research cannot be used to further the development of nascent technologies such as quantum computers.

As part of the emerging picture, Werner Heisenberg, a German theoretical physicist, introduced (1927) his *Uncertainty Principle*, a theory, which, albeit slightly modified, is still considered to be a fundamental component of quantum mechanics. Heisenberg said that, unlike in our *macro-world*, the *quantum world* limits the amount of information that can be gained from a specific physical system. Most significantly, position and momentum (directional velocity) of a particle in the quantum world cannot both be known in great detail – that is if you know precisely where the particle is, you can't know precisely where it's going, and if you know precisely where it's going, you can't know

---

[156] Polarized light has wave oscillations in one direction only, whereas the oscillations of unpolarized light, such as sunlight, are in random directions.

precisely where it is. This uncertainty is due in part to the higher energy light source required to accurately ascertain a particle's position inevitably causing changes in momentum; whereas a lower energy light source, although it may cause little disturbance, has a longer wave length resulting in an inability to precisely determine the particle's location.

Einstein was again unhappy with this theory and its basic nature - in direct opposition to the typically quantifiable data associated with classical physics - instead contesting that, despite appearance, an electron does still have both definite position and momentum. However, subsequent theoretical progress and experimentation have shown convincingly that Einstein was wrong.

Recent studies related to the above have led to the possibility that *uncertainty* and *entanglement* could be two sides of the same coin. If this is the case, quantum entanglement might provide a method of working around Heisenberg's Uncertainty Principle. Time will presumably tell.

At roughly the same time as Heisenberg's breakthrough, the understanding of *wave-particle duality* was significantly advanced by Erwin Schrodinger, an Austrian physicist. Schrodinger proposed that all quantum particles could be described in much the same way as ripples on the surface of a lake. He then succeeded in mathematically deriving an equation *(Schrodinger's Wave Equation)* that governed the shape and evolution of associated probability waves - termed *wave functions.* These functions, each containing information about a specific quantum system, are obtained by solving *Schrodinger's Wave Equation* in conjunction with the use of an operator known as the *Hamiltonian.* The German physicist, Max Born, was further able to demonstrate that the square of the related wave amplitude corresponds to the probability of measuring a particle at a given place, or having a given momentum, at a given time.

Employment of these functions thus indicates the likelihood of finding individual particles at specific locations within a fuzzy cloud of probabilities; some particles counter intuitively existing in two or more separate places at the same time, a property known as *quantum superposition*. This occurrence has been confirmed by double-slit light experiments where, analogous to water waves, the brightest areas on the phosphorescent screen behind the two open slits result from the coincidence of the wave peaks (or troughs) and the darkest where the peak from one slit coincides with the trough of the other (thereby cancelling each other out).

Unlike superposition, however, the existence of wave functions has not yet been confirmed. The reason generally given for this is that the very act of measurement causes instantaneous collapses of these functions, a characteristic known as *decoherence*. [157] [158] This means that the probabilistic configuration, including the indicated superposition, is eliminated as particles randomly pop up at single fixed positions - that is they become governed by the laws of classical physics. The inability to directly observe this process has resulted in different interpretations of quantum mechanics and Einstein even considered the probability concept to be absurd, eliciting his famed remark, *"God does not play dice with the universe."* [159]

Despite Einstein's strong objections, the work of Schrodinger and others, particularly Max Born, has been to progressively move quantum theory analyses away from the classical into the probabilistic field. Rigorous and precise mathematical formulation is maintained, but this relates to the probability rather than the calculated certainty of a particular outcome.

Although a number of scientists besides Einstein have, unsurprisingly, found it difficult to accept this state of affairs, the use of Schrodinger's

---

[157] Decoherence thus results in particulate behaviour, as per Newton's more intuitive *picture* of light.

[158] One way of visualising this basic mechanism, albeit perhaps somewhat simplistic, is to think of the 'heads' and 'tails' of a spinning coin as representing the 'superposition' of two quantum states, which then decoheres into a classical single state of just one exposed side when the coin falls into a stationary flat position.

[159] Albert Einstein, https://www.goodreads.com/quotes/2669-god-does-not-play-dice-with-the-universe.

wave functions in conjunction with pertinent experiments (such as the double-slit) has been found to give very accurate predictions time after time. For example, if the double-slit experiment is constrained to just single photons being repeatedly fired one by one at the two open slits, the pattern of the resultant particulate dots on the phosphorescent screen will gradually build up to be in accord with the shape of the relevant probability wave function – specifically, the squares of the wave amplitudes. This is quite extraordinary, with superposition and wavelike character thus apparently relating to each individual photon, considered to pass through both slits and subsequently interfere with itself. As previously, this mechanism breaks down when detection apparatus is employed.

The current record for superposition belongs to a team of research scientists from the universities of Vienna and Basel, who, in 2019, achieved this quantum state for hot complex molecules of up to two thousand atoms. [160]

As an alternative to probability wave functions, Richard Feynman (1948) formulated an approach known as the *sum-over-paths*. [161] For those people who believe we must *open our minds* to just about every possible eventuality, consideration of this viewpoint could be a useful training exercise. Feynman proposed that, not only did an electron pass through both slits of the double-slit apparatus, but, incredibly, arrived at the screen by taking every *possible* path simultaneously. He then demonstrated that he could assign a number to each path in such a way that their combined average agreed with both Schrodinger's wave-function approach and experimentation test results.

Furthermore, when it came to the macro-world, such as footballs, cars and human beings, he showed that all but one of the apparent infinity of paths cancelled out, leaving only the classical path with which we are all so familiar – that is the one defined by Newton's laws of motion.

---

[160] https://www.zmescience.com/science/physics/super-superposition-2000-atoms-in-two-places-at-once/
[161] Richard Feynman, https://faculty.washington.edu/seattle/physics541/2012-path-integrals/sum-over-paths.pdf.

All of that is pretty much unbelievable for an average-brained pleb like me but, as all football managers know, it's hard to argue against results. Much of the corroborative experimentation has additionally been undertaken subsequent to Einstein's death in 1955, and so this quote from Stephen Hawking is fair game, *"Einstein was confused, not the quantum theory."* [162]

As is evident from the foregoing, attempting to comprehend the counterintuitive principles relating to quantum mechanics is far from easy, with the inability to directly observe wave functions being particularly problematic. Indeed, despite the very positive contributions from Schrodinger, Born and others, there remains some doubt within the scientific community as to whether or not wave functions even exist as physical entities.

This is a quotation from *The Quantum World*, *"Quantum objects are described by wave functions that might or might not correspond to anything physical, and which exist in an abstract, multidimensional domain called Hilbert space."* [163] Even if they are actual physical entities (probably the majority view), the consensus of scientific opinion is that although a wave function associated with a single particle might be relatively robust, it is likely to collapse when exposed to interference from other bodies, such as adjacent atoms, and/or the effects of the surrounding environment.

This risk rises as the number of particles increases, with Brian Greene stating, *"But no matter how absurd nature is when examined on microscopic scales, things must conspire so that we recover the familiar prosaic happenings of the world experienced on everyday scales."* [164]

For example, the average human body contains very approximately seven billion, billion, billion (7×10^{27}) atoms plus much higher quantities of constituent sub-atomic particles and is, of course, subject to all sorts

---

[162] Stephen Hawking, *Lecture at the Amsterdam Symposium on Gravity, Black Holes, and String Theory.* June 21, 1997.
[163] New Scientist, The Quantum World. John Murray Learning, 2017. pp.149-150
[164] Brian Greene, *The Elegant Universe,* Vintage, 2000, p.111.

of environmental interference, such as gravity, heat, and vibration. Furthermore, biological life itself is thought likely to promote decoherence. The possibility that human beings could be affected in any meaningful way by un-collapsed wave functions accordingly seems extremely unlikely, if not ridiculous.

Not according to the American physicist, Hugh Everett, though. Writing in the late 1950s, Everett considered that, not only did wave functions exist as physical entities but also took exception to the separation of the quantum world from the everyday world, calling this a *monstrosity*. In a nutshell, Everett's method concerned the determination of what would happen *if the wave function did not collapse*. His associated seemingly correct, but *strictly theoretical,* mathematics indicated that the universe would split every time any measurement was undertaken or whenever any of us made a decision with multiple possible outcomes. He is accordingly considered to be the man who gave us the *multiverse*.

At the end of the day, quantum theory appears to be far from complete and although the existence of wave-particle duality and entanglement appear to be more or less *givens* at the infinitesimal scale, there is still considerable uncertainty in other related areas, particularly wave functions.

So where does all that leave us? Well, I suppose, pretty confused. But take heart, we are certainly not alone. The brilliant scientists working in this field are also rather confused and furthermore, as mentioned at the outset, often end up unavoidably invoking at least some philosophy. Again, quoting *The Quantum World*, "*Our understanding of the quantum world appears to be fundamentally flawed. If we take quantum theory at face value, either relativity, causality* (cause and effect), *free will or reality itself must be an illusion. But which is it?*"[165] Maybe an impossible question when you categorically discount a grand designer.

In the absence of this grand designer then, here are four possible interpretations, out of many, put forward in attempts to explain the counterintuitive world of quantum mechanics:

---

[165] New Scientist, *The Quantum World*. John Murray Learning, 2017, p.144.

Quantum mechanics is a developing and not yet complete science

Sir John Harvey Jones, a former chairman of ICI, once said something like, *"If you've got problems that you can't resolve, then you don't have enough facts."* The central feature of this viewpoint is that hidden variables are carrying missing information about quantum states. This knowledge might enable an acceptable *match-up* between quantum and relativity theories, and could perhaps even show that infinitesimal 'random' activity, rather than getting in the way, actually facilitates the order and regularity so evident in the world and the universe as a whole.

The Multiverse

A few choice examples from *The Quantum World*:

"The obvious implication of many worlds is that there are multiple copies of you, for instance – and that Elvis is still performing in Vegas in another universe." [166]

"For example, when Tegmark's (Max Tegmark, professor of physics at the Massachusetts Institute of Technology) *wife was in labour with Philip, their eldest son, he found himself hoping that everything would go well. Then he admonished himself. 'It was going to go well, and it was going to end in tragedy, in different parallel universes. So what did it mean for me to hope that it was going to go well?'"* [167]

From David Papineau, a philosopher of King's College, London, *"Say you put your money on a horse which you think is a very good bet. It turns out that it doesn't win, and you lose all your money. You think, 'I wish I hadn't done that.' But you brought benefits to your cousins in other universes where the horse won. You've just drawn the short straw in finding yourself in the universe where it lost. You didn't do anything wrong. There's no sense that the action you took earlier was a*

---

[166] Ibid. p.51.
[167] Ibid. p.59.

mistake."[168] Hardly a great argument to try out on your missus when you've arrived home after losing a packet at the racetrack.

"Every decision you make may spawn parallel universes where people are suffering because of your choice" [169] Really? Most of us have enough trouble coping with the hurt and suffering we have caused to others in just this one universe.

These infinite possible outcomes and scenarios are all examples of the difficulties posed to choice and free will, given that, in the multiverse, we are not stuck with a particular course of action because we're doing them all!

The universe could not exist in any meaningful sense until measured

This is based on the viewpoint that things only become real in a physical sense when observation and/or measurement cause the collapse of the wave functions so that particles and vastly larger bodies become fixed in our space-time framework. It's interesting to compare this view with Eastern thought, which commonly believes the visible universe to be, and to have always been, illusory– end of. In any event, who or what did all the observing and measuring to bring our universe into existence before humanity turned up?

The Universe is a simulation running on an advanced civilisation's supercomputer

This interpretation has been proposed by some scientists and philosophers, as per this quotation from *The Quantum World*, *"As outlandish as these multiverses might seem, at least they are allowed to be real. Philosopher Nick Bostrom at the University of Oxford has upped the ante by arguing that the universe we experience is just a simulation*

---

[168] Ibid. p.60.
[169] Ibid. p.58.

running on an advanced civilization's supercomputer. The idea is that a long-lived civilization will develop essentially unlimited computing power and may choose to run multiple 'ancestor simulations' that will soon outnumber natural universes, making it plausible that we are one of them." [170]

This is, therefore, *determinism*, whereby all events and human actions are controlled by external intelligence. We, accordingly, do not have individual free will and thus cannot be held morally responsible for our thoughts and actions. In other words, if this scenario were to be true, human beings would simply be players in a *cosmic puppet show*.

It is difficult to select a particular favourite from such an exotic and wide-ranging set of alternatives, although, no doubt unsurprisingly, my preference is either the first option or the fact that finite brains weighing about 3lbs, no matter how brilliant, simply cannot cope with issues of this nature. Some scientists might perhaps argue that it is our essentially classical brains that are the real problem, with all the apparent weirdness at the quantum level probably making sense if we had quantum brains. However, these classical brains, including those belonging to the founders of modern science, have certainly served us well enough in the past, with innumerable mathematical/physical propositions in the macro-world being duly confirmed by experimental data and experience.

What then can reasonably be concluded from the foregoing discussions and associated illustrations? Well, and this is surely the briefest of condensations, it seems that everything can ultimately come down to just two main points. Firstly, there are clearly strange goings-on at the infinitesimal level which defy the laws of classical physics, and, at the present time, are best explained by quantum theory. However, secondly, and this undoubtedly poses the greatest challenge to the more extreme interpretations of quantum mechanics, there appears to be no evidence to suggest that quantum states can survive for even a few nano-seconds outside of the infinitesimal arena. For instance, wave

---

[170] Ibid. p.53.

functions (assuming that they exist in the first place) will collapse way before the macro-level, with Richard Feynman's *sum-over-paths* reducing to the familiar single path of classical physics. So to repeat Brian Greene's very pertinent quotation, *"But no matter how absurd nature is when examined on microscopic scales, things must conspire so that we recover the familiar prosaic happenings of the world experienced on everyday scales."* [171]

Finally, it's intriguing to note that some adherents of the New Age movement are interested in the whole area of quantum mechanics, and one assumes that they consider it to fit well with their particular worldviews. More specifically, there appear to be no absolutes, anything is possible, nobody is accountable, and apparent facts relate to degrees of probability rather than certainty. However, as above, no matter how relevant this view might be at the infinitesimal scale, it simply does not cut it in the *big and bad* macro-world where every one of us, with all our different beliefs and theories, hang out.

Getting back to more familiar ground, in this case the continuation of the big bang theory by providing a few of the fundamental details. The modified and generally accepted, but still provisional, *inflationary* version of the Standard Cosmological Model commences at 10^{-43} seconds after the big bang (that is at *Planck time*),[172] when the calculated length of the universe was approximately 10^{-33} centimetres (that is the *Planck length)* with an associated temperature of 10^{32} K [173] (all units defined under footnotes).

---

[171] Brian Greene, *The Elegant Universe,* Vintage, 2000, p.111.

[172] The Planck time of 10^{-43} seconds is the smallest recognised unit of time, relating to how long it takes for light to travel the Planck length of approximately 10^{-33} cm (thought to be the initial size of the universe). Written out in full, it represents a tenth of a millionth of a millionth of a millionth of a millionth, of a millionth of a millionth of a millionth of a second. The pre-Planck era is considered to represent the miniscule period between the big bang and 10^{-43} seconds.

[173] K represents the *Kelvin scale,* commencing at the lowest temperature possible - *absolute zero* or minus 273 degrees Celsius (a surprisingly small negative, given the enormous range of positive temperatures).

These three numbers correspond to the point beyond which everything (particularly energy, density and temperature), tends to infinity, and the known laws of physics (most significantly, the gravitational framework of general relativity) break down. This feature, known as a *singularity*, is thought to be directly related to quantum fluctuations, which, in accordance with Heisenberg's uncertainty principle, become larger as the scale reduces, thereby destroying the *smoothness* and consistency associated with general relativity. Relevant scientific knowledge from the pre-Planck era is thus lacking; inevitably fostering questions such as, Did time start with the big bang/Was there something before? Does the concept of time even make any sense concerning this event?

Although these questions are, for the time being at least, unanswerable, Stephen Hawking has proposed a tenuous theory predicated on the existence of a fourth space dimension preceding that of time (*creating a no-boundary condition*) within the primordial universe ending at the Planck time. He then considers the question of "When did time begin?" to be analogous to attempting to find the *start point* of the *spherical Earth*.[174]

As touched on earlier, this topic has been the subject of much research, with particular endeavours being made towards the attainment of a complete and consistent theory for gravity. This is because, of the four fundamental forces,[175] only gravity, understood in conjunction with general relativity as above, cannot currently be described within a quantum framework. Indeed, some scientists believe that quantum gravity will turn out to be the *Holy Grail*, the one remaining *jigsaw piece* in the elusive quest for the *Theory of Everything* (ToE).

All endeavours thus far, constrained by the need to avoid a singularity in the pre-Planck era, are understood to have focussed on the very difficult task of merging general relativity and quantum mechanics. Of these, the

---

[174] Stephen Hawking & Leonard Mlodinow, *The Grand Design*. Bantam Press, 2011, pp.172-173.

[175] The four fundamental forces in ascending order of strength are gravity, the weak force (primarily radioactive decay), electromagnetism (includes visible light, X-rays and radio waves) and the strong force (holds the nuclei of atoms together).

leading contender and most well-known is M-theory, in turn based upon the earlier *superstring theory,* both with their predicted tiny and hidden extra dimensions.

However, despite the elegance of its extensively researched mathematics, M-Theory still appears to be far from complete, with some physicists doubting that it will ever constitute a realistic description of the physical universe. For instance, Roger Penrose has said that, in his estimation, M-Theory was "hardly science", [176] and John Lennox has described it in the following terms, *"A move to advance the cause of atheism by means of a highly speculative, untestable theory that is not within the zone of evidence-based science, and which, even if it were true, could not dislodge God in any case, is not exactly calculated to impress those of us whose faith in God is not speculative, but testable and well within the zone of evidence-based rational thought.*[177]

It would, of course, be of great assistance if the calculations and thought experiments of the scientists working in this field could be empirically tested. However, in keeping with the earlier reference to the Large Hadron Collider and, specifically, Roger Penrose's comments concerning its limitations, it seems inevitable that the great majority of future advances, at least in the short to medium term, will lie within the theoretical field. As previously, this undoubtedly has consequences for the detection of quantum gravity if present, with a workable and consistently applicable theoretical model presumably being the first objective.

In any event, the above limitations are not my main concern here. I'm more interested in what is apparently known in connection with the big bang than what is not. In particular, *The Elegant Universe* states that the matter making up absolutely everything (people, cars, houses, mountains, the Earth, the Solar System, and all the billions of galaxies with their cumulative trillions of stars and planets, plus ultramassive

---

[176] Premier Christian Radio, 'Unbelievable' with Justin Brierley, 25 September 2010.
[177] John Lennox, *God and Stephen Hawking – Whose Design Is It Anyway?* Lion Hudson plc, 2011, p.56.

black holes) was originally encapsulated by the primordial universe, an *ultramicroscopic point* (Planck-sized *nugget*) having the same ratio to the height of an average tree that an atom has to the observable universe. [178]

Can we actually believe this scenario, particularly in the light of science's current lack of knowledge concerning the big bang itself and the still only *provisional* theory associated with cosmic inflation? Both may change in the future of course, and it is further recognised that modern science has revealed certain counterintuitive facts of nature to be true. Nevertheless, my unchanged, or rather strengthened, conclusion is that the faith needed for a solely naturalistic model is far too great, whatever the future mathematics.

And talking of maths, I know from my own, obviously much simpler, calculations in geotechnical engineering and structures that it's comparatively easy if you've got a pretty good idea of what the final result *should* be, to achieve this by choosing or tweaking your assumptions and design parameters accordingly (shock horror!). This is something that Einstein did big-time when his theory of general relativity indicated the universe to be expanding with time, a view unacceptable to the vast majority of his fellow scientists who had completely bought in to the *static universe* model.

So to keep everyone happy and to sleep at night, Einstein introduced his (negative) *cosmological constant* - essentially a *fudge factor* to modify the associated field equations so that his theory was consistent with an essentially static universe. However, twelve years later (1929), observations by the American astronomer, Edwin Hubble, gave strong indications that the cosmos was indeed expanding, with current independent analysis implying a definite start point; a view not universally accepted until the mid-1960s, when the discovery of cosmic microwave background radiation (CMBR), seemingly left over from the primordial universe, provided additional strong evidence for the big bang.

---

[178] Brian Greene, *The Elegant Universe*. Vintage, 2000, pp. 82, 83, 130 & 358.

Following Hubble's work, Einstein soon revisited and changed his calculations back to the original form. He accordingly cited the introduction of the cosmological constant as the biggest blunder of his academic life. In actuality, the cosmological constant, now generally believed to have a positive value, has been a source of much consternation to physicists. [179] I wonder, could something similar have occurred during the development of the big bang theory? Maybe the adding of zeros by some overzealous theoretical physicists to make everything fit? Infinity rules OK! Just a thought.

And now for something completely different (Monty Python, 1969-74). Human beings – how much are we all worth in real terms? That is simply as individuals, not including any personal wealth we might have accumulated along the way. According to *blind evolution* (no grand designer) and the inevitable corollary that we are all primarily random accidents, this must come down to a question of the value of our constituent chemicals. For the *average* adult this is unlikely to be greater than £10, although it may be possible to up this slightly if the body can be split up into separate parts rather than being sold as a job lot.

When we, therefore, hear of some small child who has gone missing, we'll be rather bemused at any emotional distress on behalf of the parents. Sure, they may have lost a child, but proportionately low quantities of chemicals and hence very little capital. Only, if we attempted to voice opinions along these lines, we'd probably be termed pathologically insane and soon have a visit from people in white coats. No! - every human being is incredibly valuable and precious, and all

---

[179] After being assumed to be zero for a number of decades, a revised version of Einstein's cosmological constant was introduced in the late 1990s, generally being interpreted within quantum theory as the theoretical 'energy density of space' or 'vacuum energy.' However, there are monumental disparities between predicted and observed vacuum energies, with the former exceeding the latter by approximately 120 orders of magnitude or 10^{120}, and being called *"the worst theoretical prediction in the history of physics!"* The cosmological constant is also closely associated with 'dark energy', commonly thought to act as a type of anti-gravity – that is to be a major contributor to the accelerating expansion of the universe, as first indicated in 1998.

normal-thinking folks quite naturally expect every effort to be made to rescue people whose lives are in danger; even if, as is usually the case, they don't know them at all. Conversely, I'm not going to jump fully clothed into a river to save a bag of quality compost, even if it did cost £90 from Travis Perkins.

Human beings are certainly wonderfully made and indeed, having earlier stated my reservations concerning the concept of *irreducible complexity*, I need here to make a very important exception. This concerns the truly amazing self-replicating deoxyribonucleic acid or DNA, a *mega-molecule*, the origin of which will probably always be beyond a solely naturalistic explanation.

Francis Collins has said that he is *simply in awe* of DNA, the structure of which can be visualised as a twisted ladder formed by two sugar-phosphate sides and connecting *rungs* made up of different combinations of pairs of four nitrogenous bases denoted by the letters A, G, C & T. The nucleus of each human cell contains two *genomes* of 3.1 billion rungs/ base pairs, one from the father and one from the mother, spread out *in the correct order* over 23 paired chromosomes.

To illustrate the significance of this unbelievable accuracy, he summarises his teams' eventual discovery of the reason behind many cystic fibrosis cases as follows, *".....showing unequivocally that a deletion of just three letters of the DNA code (CCT, to be exact) in the protein-coding part of a previously unknown gene was the cause of cystic fibrosis in the majority of patients."* [180]

Our body cells, with their nuclei-based DNA, are estimated to total very approximately 70 trillion (70×10^{12}); each *"carrying out almost as many unique functions as all the manufacturing activities of man on Earth."* [181] That is again absolutely mind-blowing, as is the fact that if the total amount of DNA within a human body could be stretched out as a single

---

[180] Francis Collins, *The Language Of God*: Free Press, Simon & Schuster, plc, 2006, p.115.
[181] Michael Denton, *Evolution: A Theory in Crisis.* Burnett Books, 1985, p.328.

linear thread, it would encircle the world $2^{1}/_{2}$ million times or extend to the sun and back 300 times.

How on earth could the incredible precision and capability of DNA have come about through an entirely naturalistic process? If we see even a four-letter word scrawled on a scrap of paper, we instinctively argue upwards to intelligence and not downwards to *chance and necessity*.

The following three citations further demonstrate the astounding nature and capabilities of DNA:

"DNA houses an amazing amount of genetic information. For example, all the data needed to specify the design of a human being, including such features as hair, skin, eyes and height, and to determine the arrangement of over 200 bones, 600 muscles, 10,000 auditory nerve fibres, two million optic nerve fibres, 100 billion brain nerve cells and 400 billion feet of blood vessels and capillaries is packed into a unit weighing less than a few thousand-millionths of a gram,' [182] [183]

"……..and it has been shown that one chromosome may contain the information equivalent to 500 million words. At 400 words to a page, it would take 5,435 books, each 230 pages long, to record the information contained in a single chromosome, and a library of 250,000 such books to store all the information secreted in the forty-six chromosomes in a single human egg………. As if that were not amazing enough, all this information is encoded in a 'language' that has only four 'letters' and whose dictionary contains only sixty-four three-letter words." [184] To again refer to Francis Collins, DNA is truly awesome.

---

[182] A thousand-millionth of a gram is known as a 'nanogram (ng)'. If the commonly assumed average value of 1ng mass per body cell is adopted for a 70kg human being, then the result is a total of 70 trillion, as above – a reasonable approximation, given that the results from various methods of calculation show appreciable divergence.

[183] T. S. Kuhn, *The Structure of Scientific Revolutions, 2ⁿᵈ Edition.* University of Chicago Press, 1970, p.69.

[184] John Blanchard, *Does God Believe in Atheists?* 2003, Evangelical Press, pp.295-296.

"...but it is worth noting here that DNA can make copies of itself only with the help of specific enzymes that in turn can be produced only by the controlling DNA molecule. In other words, as each is dependent on the other, both must be present before any copy can be made. Nobody has yet come up with a 'natural' (that is, atheistic) picture of how this could happen." [185]

In conclusion, the DNA molecule contains colossal and incredibly specific encoded information – that is a vast library of software instructions directing and detailing not only the formation of human beings but every other living thing on the planet. Bill Gates, the co-founder of Microsoft, once said that, *"DNA is like a computer software program, but far, far more advanced than any software ever created."* [186] Stuff like that simply does not fall from the sky, intelligence has to be involved. God is God of the *micro* as well as the *macro*.

As a brief addendum, a quote from the internationally known apologist and author, John Blanchard, *"A cell consists of thousands of proteins, each one made up of chains of hundreds of amino acids organised in a very precise sequence"* and, *"Yet Francis Crick admits that the probability of getting even 'one' protein by chance would be one in 10^{260} and calls this number 'quite beyond our everyday comprehension'."* [187]

And what about our amazing human brains? Atheistic science would have it that these function solely by naturalistic procedures, utilising 100 billion nerve cells (neurons) that firstly gather and then transmit information throughout the nervous system by means of electrochemical processes. Thus if we are *in luuuv*, it's just a whole bunch of the right types of these processes firing up. But this *myopic explanation* is not difficult to refute. For example, it's no problem to see the sound-waves resulting from a piece of music if we have appropriate equipment, but looking at these will not cause us to become emotional over a very sentimental song - it has to be heard.

---

[185] John Blanchard, *Is God Past His Sell-By Date?* Evangelical Press, 2002, p.92.
[186] Bill Gates, *Goodreads*. https://www.goodreads.com/quotes/336336-dna-is-like-a-computer- program-
[187] John Blanchard, *Is God Past His Sell-By Date?* Evangelical Press, 2002, p. 103.

Visual sound-waves could thus be viewed as an analogy for the brain's physical processes, and the hearing response as an analogy for what moves our minds/souls. Also, if you think your thoughts are due primarily to fairly random electrochemical processes, why would you believe them? Indeed, why would you believe that they are correct in telling you that your thoughts are due primarily to fairly random electrochemical processes?

C.S. Lewis, as usual, says it best, "*Supposing there was no intelligence behind the universe, no creative mind. In that case, nobody designed my brain for the purpose of thinking. It is merely that when the atoms inside my skull happen, for physical or chemical reasons, to arrange themselves in a certain way, this gives me, as a by-product, the sensation I call thought. But, if so, how can I trust my own thinking to be true? It's like upsetting a milk jug and hoping that the way it splashes itself will give you a map of London. But if I can't trust my own thinking, of course I can't trust the arguments leading to Atheism, and therefore have no reason to be an Atheist, or anything else. Unless I believe in God, I cannot believe in thought: so I can never use thought to disbelieve in God.*" [188]

Charles Darwin himself was troubled by a fairly similar type of thinking, confessing, "*With me the horrid doubt always arises whether the convictions of man's mind, which has been developed from the mind of the lower animals are of any value or at all trustworthy.*" Would any one trust in the convictions of a monkey's mind, if there are any convictions in such a mind?" [189]

So what exactly is naturalistic science's take on the great importance virtually all of us put on human life and its seemingly inestimable value – what's their story? Well, to recap, once upon a time (if that word means anything) there was an infinitesimal point, so minute that a single atom would be gargantuan by comparison. Where this tiny feature came

---

[188] C. S. Lewis, Goodreads, https://www.goodreads.com/quotes/598950-supposing-there-was-no-intelligence-behind-the-universe-no-creative

[189] Charles Darwin, Letter to William Graham, 3rd July 1881. Goodreads. https://www.goodreads.com/ quotes/344552-but-then-with-me-the-horrid-doubt-always-arises-

from, no-one knows. Did it represent the remnant of a previously collapsed universe or universes, or was it brand new approximately 13½ billion years ago? The thing is that although the point was absurdly small, it had a vast amount of energy – apparently in the form of immense density and colossal temperature.

Then one day (if that word means anything) the volatile point erupted, an event that can be summarised by two astounding facts. Firstly, the point contained sufficient energy to eventually create the entire known universe and, secondly, the expelled material was instantaneously governed by incredibly fine-tuned laws that, amongst other things, paved the way for carbon-based biological life on planet Earth. The probability of this scenario occurring by chance or accident has accordingly been calculated as less than 1 part in $10^{10^{123}}$, a seriously insane number so large that to write it out in full would require a zero to be put on every atom of approximately 10^{113} universes of essentially the same size as our own (see Talking Big Numbers).

A brief *time out* in case further clarification is required. The above probability is not dealing with the actual origin of biological life on the early Earth, but simply the chance existence of both a sufficiently stable universe and the presence of the required core elements of carbon, nitrogen, oxygen and hydrogen. The subsequent probability of these elements then being converted to the necessary amino acids and related proteins to eventually produce simple cell-based life by solely naturalistic means, an extension of Blanchard and Crick's comments, has been calculated by Robert Shapiro, a former professor emeritus of chemistry at New York University and an atheist, as less than 1 part in $10^{100,000,000,000}$.[190]

So massively smaller than the *notorious* $10^{10^{123}}$, although to write out the associated one hundred thousand million zeros at one per second would still require 3,171 years. It accordingly follows that there is a truly

---

[190] Robert Shapiro, *Origins, a Skeptic's Guide to the Creation of Life on Earth*. Summit Books,1986, p.128.

vast and almost inconceivable chasm between the most highly ordered non-biological system and a living cell. Finally, for anyone overdosing on zeros, I believe treatment is still available under the NHS.

In any event, primitive life, probably single-celled micro-organisms - let's say *germs*, turned up on planet Earth. These germs then grew up by utilising a biological process called *evolution*, without assistance from any kind of external intelligence. In essence, this *blind evolution* constitutes initial random mutations of DNA, the origin of which is unknown, followed by natural selection or (*selfish*) *survival of the fittest*. So hardly a system to inspire hope for the future. Yet these germs all *done good*; indeed, unbelievably good, as they finally matured into human beings having attributes including love, joy, goodness, faithfulness, compassion, empathy, sympathy, with feelings and emotions that enabled them to appreciate beauty, fine music, good food etc. Furthermore, these beings had a strong sense of justice, with even little children being aware of fairness and the concepts of right and wrong. And, to top it all, they had incredible brains, with perhaps the scientists being the brainiest of the lot. What a story; how totally spiffing and fantastic! It certainly makes the Brothers Grimm's tale of the transformation of a frog into a handsome prince look decidedly ordinary (at best).

Finally, what is the ultimate *why* question for those scientists of an atheistic disposition? Well, the popular view seems to be "Why is there something rather than nothing?"[191] which, of course, corresponds to the previously discussed ultimate *how* question of "How did the universe come about?" To Stephen Hawking, the answer was gravity. In *The Grand Design*, a book he co-authored with Leonard Mlodinow in 2010, we find the statement, *"Because there is a law like gravity, the*

---

[191] This might also be considered as the ultimate metaphysical question, the boundary between physics and philosophy being somewhat blurred.

universe can and will create itself from nothing...." [192]

This statement undoubtedly raises many questions, but I'm going to limit myself to just four.

The first and most obvious is "Who or what created gravity?" and secondly, Why does Hawking cite the law of gravity when, as previously explained, laws themselves can create or cause nothing? As a second *for instance*, I know that if I have £500 in my bank account and then put in a further £500, I'll have a total of £1,000. But knowing this fact will make absolutely no difference to my bank balance (unfortunately). Action in the form of paying money in is needed before the laws of basic arithmetic can come into play.

Thirdly, Hawking says that the universe can and will create itself. That has to be a bit weird; X might be able to create Y, but X creating X? – c'mon, that's like saying I had to pre-date myself first so that I could create myself later.

Fourthly, Hawking uses the little phrase, *from nothing*. That, of course, makes no sense if we're thinking of the familiar philosophical *nothing*. However, this relates to something rather different, such as a quantum vacuum (e.g., *empty* space) considered to be occupied by quantum energy fields (e.g., electromagnetism and, possibly, gravity) that are subject to random, localised fluctuations as *virtual particles* and *anti-particles* pop into and out of existence– clearly not *nothing* then. So in an attempt to make it all fit, Hawking, and others like him, have had to re-define the word *nothing*.

The prominent American astrophysicist and neo-atheist, Lawrence Krauss, has also contributed to this line of reasoning by saying, *"Because something is physical, nothing must be physical - especially if you define it as the absence of something."* [193] Krause may be an incredibly

---

[192] Stephen Hawking & Leonard Mlodinow, *The Grand Design*. Bantam Press, 2011, p.227.

intelligent guy, but that looks like nonsense to me. Maybe a *Graham Martin* from a parallel universe would be able to provide a bit more insight. Try the third to the left of the one where I won all my Olympic gold medals and scored the winning goal in three World Cup finals.

Richard Feynman once said, "*I believe that a scientist looking at non-scientific problems is just as dumb as the next guy...*" [194] and I reckon that more or less brings us round full circle. Science is a wonderful subject which has, and always will, involve(d) some of the greatest minds on the planet; we certainly need them. However, despite their great specialist knowledge and often assumed authority, when this extends into areas beyond their expertise (such as philosophy) they might be talking nonsense.

It seems fitting to end this chapter with a secular account of what happens when you die, written by Aaron Freeman, an American journalist, author, comedian, cartoonist, and blogger. I presume it's a send-up, but it doesn't matter either way.

"You want a physicist to speak at your funeral. You want the physicist to talk to your grieving family about the conservation of energy, so they will understand that your energy has not died. You want the physicist to remind your sobbing mother about the first law of thermodynamics; that no energy gets created in the universe, and none is destroyed. You want your mother to know that all your energy, every vibration, every Btu of heat, every wave of every particle that was her beloved child remains with her in this world. You want the physicist to tell your weeping father that amid energies of the cosmos, you gave as good as you got.

And at one point you'd hope that the physicist would step down from the pulpit and walk to your brokenhearted spouse there in the pew and tell her that all the photons that ever bounced off your face, all the particles whose paths were interrupted by your smile, by the touch of your hair,

---

[193] Lawrence Krauss, www.christiantoday.com/article/john.lennox.do.not.be.silent.about.your.faith/41399.htm.
[194] Richard Feynman, *Goodreads*. https://www.goodreads.com/quotes/78265-i-believe-that-a-scientist. looking-at-nonscientific-problems-is

hundreds of trillions of particles, have raced off like children, their ways forever changed by you. And as your widow rocks in the arms of a loving family, may the physicist let her know that all the photons that bounced from you were gathered in the particle detectors that are her eyes, that those photons created within her constellations of electromagnetically charged neurons whose energy will go on forever.

And the physicist will remind the congregation of how much of all our energy is given off as heat. There may be a few fanning themselves with their programs as he says it. And he will tell them that the warmth that flowed through you in life is still here, still part of all that we are, even as we who mourn continue the heat of our own lives.

And you'll want the physicist to explain to those who loved you that they need not have faith; indeed, they should not have faith. Let them know that they can measure, that scientists have measured precisely the conservation of energy and found it accurate, verifiable and consistent across space and time. You can hope your family will examine the evidence and satisfy themselves that the science is sound and that they'll be comforted to know your energy's still around. According to the law of the conservation of energy, not a bit of you is gone; you're just less orderly. Amen." [195]

Whatever Aaron Freeman's main reasons for writing this piece, it certainly serves very well as a pop at a solely atheistic and naturalistic perspective, which is unwrapped and starkly laid bare. Is this all the expectation and sustenance that science has to ultimately offer us? Do we really prefer a future devoid of all hope over Christ's amazing offer of eternal life involving continued and transformed/perfected individual conscious existences? Conclusion – we are not made for atheism.

---

[195] Aaron Freeman, *Goodreads*. https://www.goodreads.com/quotes/791982-you-want-a-physicist-to- speak-at-your-funeral

CHAPTER EIGHT

Eastern Spirituality, Islam, Judaism - Reflections, Comparisons & Questions

I had considered that, despite fairly wide-ranging relevant reading including the Quran, my knowledge was still insufficient to do justice to a topic as vast and far-reaching as this. However, upon reflection, I realised that I probably knew enough to do *broad-brush*, and hopefully achieve my main objective of drawing out some of the principal differences between the above worldviews, particularly as they relate to Christianity. This self-imposed limitation is also appropriate, given the great diversity of Eastern spirituality and resultant nigh on impossibility of any detailed neat and consistent packaging - even allowing for the fact that related discussions are usually restricted to Pantheistic Monism and Zen Buddhism, the forms most popular in the West.

To make it clear from the start, the overall aim of this chapter is not to put Christianity on some sort of pedestal from where it imperiously looks down on all other worldviews, but is rather an attempt to view the chosen selection through their own particular lens as far as this is possible and then briefly describe and highlight certain salient distinctions. In other words, the following discussions are *beliefs-oriented*, rather than being concerned with specific details of peoples' ethnicity and cultural backgrounds. These are irrelevant to true Christianity, apart from hopefully influencing and ensuring that the gospel message is imparted in an appropriate and sensitive manner.

As noted previously, there are real pressures within current Western societies for people to adopt the surely very *reasonable* and *mature* position whereby all religions and worldviews are deemed to ultimately lead to one common destination. In actuality, it appears fairly usual for various individuals, right up to government cabinet level, while of course rightly condemning any form of terrorism or discrimination, to assert that, say, Islam and Christianity are two great religions and basically *peas from the same pod*. So why are government ministers saying that? Is it because their own investigations, the main results of which they are quite happy to discuss or summarise, have revealed the similarities between the two faiths to far outweigh any dissimilarities or are they automatically going down the Postmodern and PC road? One strongly suspects the latter, but we shall see.

It is obvious, from even a cursory study, that the spiritual fervour of certain parts of the world, particularly the East and Middle-East, outstrips the overall fairly lukewarm nature of Christianity found in the West. Indeed, this observation is also valid when it comes to previous Western believers. For example, the great 16th century German reformer, Martin Luther, would always start the day with at least two hours of prayer, whereas Christians in our culture today, almost inevitably affected by the overriding spiritual apathy, can easily become slack and a bit woolly.

This contrast is particularly illustrated by Sundar Singh who, primarily due to his culture and background, could meditate for long periods and writes about this continuing for a whole month while sitting on a rock in India. However, when he visited Western nations such as Great Britain and the USA in the 1920s, he said that the much more materialistic and less spiritual natures of these countries meant that even he found meditation difficult. What would he say *now*?

It's clear that various teachings relating to Eastern worldviews have found their way to the West and had an appreciable effect on our societies – typically as evidenced in New Age thought. However, New Age shows obvious differences to much Eastern spirituality, most significantly in its emphasis on the prime importance of the individual and the linked belief that the visible universe has physical substance rather than being illusory.

Indeed, some Eastern purists consider that these and other differences (such as the interpretation of *karma* – see below) represent an unacceptable compromising of their beliefs to fit the preferences, desires and capabilities of Western peoples. Thus, while many adherents of both New Age and Eastern spirituality search for self-realisation, often utilising the practices of yoga and meditation (sometimes also chanting or silently repeating a specific mantra, such as the *eternal* and intellectually contentless word *OM*), ultimate states, as concluded below, are perceived as being very different.

Other things to note are that Eastern culture is primarily society and extended family-based compared to the prevailing individualistic nature of the West and that certain religions, particularly Hinduism, come down to pluralism, where the collective wisdom of sages and seers normally has priority over the teachings of one specific leader. It's accordingly not difficult to appreciate, given the extreme resultant diversity, why Hindus often champion the belief that all roads eventually lead to Ultimate Reality/God; something made easier by the typical Eastern view that time is cyclical and fundamentally unreal, and history is therefore unimportant. Stories rather than claimed historical truths are thus generally more interesting and palatable to the Eastern mind.

Moving on to a consideration of the two Eastern worldviews most influential in the West, *Pantheistic Monism*, as particularly relevant to the Hindu school of *Advaita Vedanta* (originated circa 6th century AD), and Zen Buddhism.

The first of these can easily be defined simply from its name; *Pan* – all; *theistic* – god or gods; *Monism* – the same stuff, with no distinctions between anything, including mind and matter. So putting it all together, absolutely everything, including the soul at its deepest level of existence (designated *Atman* or *true self*), is one and the same and also the essence of *Brahman*, the *soul of the cosmos* or *all-soul* or *the One*. Thus, *Atman is Brahman* or *thou art that*; the principle of monism also excluding personality, which involves a *thinker* and a *thing thought* and is therefore dualistic.

More expansively, one's *oneness* with Brahman/the soul of the cosmos invokes the principle of non-duality as the true self is understood to pass beyond personality, consciousness, knowledge, good and evil, language and time, becoming lost in the *undifferentiated One* - rather like a water-drop losing its individuality when it falls into a bucket of water. This is known as *Moksha*, as described below.

The above *pecking order* is intuitively foreign to most of us in the West. How can monism top the more complex dualism and how can the impersonal be superior to the more complicated personal? Surely personality requires the greater intelligence.

The following quotation from Tim Keller, although not specifically connected to this question, does nonetheless provide us with some general insight into the differences between Western thinking and Pantheistic Monism. According to Western thought, he says, *"This object A is not that object B. That's what our senses (and science and logic) tell us. While one person suffers losses, another person has plenty. But this is a deceptive appearance called 'maya'. There is not only no evil but no good, no individuals, no material world. Everything is actually part of the One, the All-Soul, the Absolute Spirit. Nothing is outside of it. Ultimately we cannot lose anything. We are part of everything. The ultimate truth is 'Tat tvam asi' – 'Thou art that'."* [196]

Indeed, the differences between Pantheistic Monism and New Age spirituality are probably best summarised as follows: In the former, Atman is BRAHMAN and, in the latter, ATMAN is Brahman. In other words, contrary to the water-drop analogy relevant to the purist Eastern view, self-realisation or cosmic consciousness in New Age commonly manifests in the belief of one's unlimited potential and ability as certain individuals (e.g., Shirley MacLaine and David Spangler) perceive themselves to be members of a new species and even 'gods' in control of creation. A contrast then between the metaphysical union of the East,

---

[196] Timothy Keller, *Walking With God Through Pain & Suffering*. Hodder & Stoughton, 2015, p.40.

whereby one can only *'know'* oneness with everything by *becoming it*, and the rationality common in the West.

Two concepts intrinsic to Pantheistic Monism, and indeed most Eastern spirituality, are *karma* and *reincarnation*. *Karma* (from *action, work*) drives the seemingly endless cycle of suffering and rebirth (reincarnation) for each soul. Good or bad intents and deeds produce seeds that mature in subsequent rebirths as either *good karma* or *bad karma*. The ultimate aim of all life is *Moksha*, a summary Sanskrit word defined by *The World's Religions* as, *"Liberation from the cycle of birth, death and rebirth."* [197] Within Pantheistic Monism, Moksha is achieved, as above, through one's oneness with Brahman/the soul of the cosmos.

Karma puzzles me. I would certainly like to understand how to view the formidable paradox between the stated absence of good and evil, and the fact that a soul's karma depends solely on moral intent and behaviour during present and past earthly existences (temporary individual embodiments of Atman known as 'jiva'). This refusal to deny morality inevitably fuels the caste system under which the *low-born* are faced with the futility of a life weighed down by karmic debt and no prospect of freedom. Furthermore, the principle of karma demands that every soul experience suffering for his/her past sins, so there is no benefit to be had in alleviating this pain. The soul helped in this way will have to suffer later. There is accordingly, no agape/unconditional love, nor would any such love be in the interest of the receiver. Good deeds are done primarily to attain *Moksha* and are, therefore, a self-helping way of life.

Nevertheless, it seems reasonable to accept something akin to karma during our present lives here on planet Earth. Our actions have consequences, which may well come back to *bite us* later on in life. However, the traditional linking of karma and reincarnation can easily become a very dangerous concept. For example, Shirley MacLaine has in recent years caused widespread outrage by suggesting that the six

---

[197] *The World's Religions, A Lion Handbook.* Lion Publishing plc, 1994, p.435.

million Jews and others systematically murdered in Hitler's concentration camps in the 1940s were *balancing their karma* for crimes committed in past lives. And Glenn Hoddle lost his job as England football manager in 1999 after an interview with the Times Newspaper, *"You and I have been physically given two hands and two legs and half-decent brains. Some people have not been born like that for a reason. The karma is working from another lifetime. I have nothing to hide about that. It is not only people with disabilities. What you sow, you have to reap.*[198] Hoddle subsequently insisted that he had been misunderstood but, in any event, this episode again demonstrates the potential problems associated with this teaching.

It is illuminating to compare the born-again and reincarnation experiences of Christianity and Pantheistic Monism. In the former, spiritual rebirth occurs and is knowingly experienced within our present earthly life. And we go on, as essentially the same persons, into conscious eternal life. In the latter, the individual person (jiva) is generally considered to not survive physical death but rather the impersonal and indestructible Atman is reincarnated as another being, dependent upon good or bad karma, a repetitive process unto Moksha. This concept is not normally problematic in the East where little credence is given to the person/individual, typically deemed to be illusory; contrary to the West, where the vast majority seem to believe that reincarnation involves a continuation of personhood.

Taking a very brief look beyond Advaita Vedanta, attention is drawn to another school of Hinduism, Dvaita Vedanta, which views Brahman *as Ultimate Reality/God,* a being who is sovereign over all his creation and thus superior to, and separate from, individual souls. This is dualism as opposed to monism, and is accordingly closer to Christianity than Pantheistic Monism. Brahman is here considered to be represented in three forms of 'God personalised', each corresponding to a distinct

---

[198] Glenn Hoddle, *The Times Interview.* London, January 1999.
https://www.independent.co.uk/news/pressure-is-on-england-coach-hoddle-to-quit-for-his-sins-1077311.html

cosmic function - *Brahma* (Creator), *Vishnu* (Preserver) and *Shiva* (destroyer), collectively known as *Trimurti* (means three forms). This is evidently very different to the Christian Trinity, where God is a single transcendent being comprising three co-equal, co-eternal, and intercommunicating persons.

The Trimurti are followed by more than 33 million demi-gods allegedly appointed by *Krishna* (one of ten avatars/incarnations of Vishnu) to oversee different parts of the physical universe, thereby indicating that it is not illusory.

Moksha is again relevant to Dvaita Vedanta, and, in this instance, is commonly believed to be achieved when the love and adoration of Brahman/Ultimate Reality are sufficient to remove the weight of Karma that requires the self to be reborn.

Due to the prevailing view that all roads eventually lead to Ultimate Reality/God, as touched on earlier, *deistic* forms of Hinduism do not appear to exclude adherents to the Pantheistic Monism of Advaita Vedanta. Indeed, the majority of Hindus worship both local and global gods, privately and during festivals, and engage in various required rituals and duties. Bathing in the *sacred* River Ganges, the symbol of life without end, is also relevant to most forms of Hinduism; many Hindus believing that this act *washes away sins* [199] and that if a dead person's ashes are extracted from the funeral pyre and laid in the Ganges at Varanasi (Eastern India), they will escape the cycle of birth, death and rebirth and instantly attain Moksha.

Buddhism arose out of Hinduism (particularly in the 6th and 5th centuries BC), due principally to the life and teachings of Siddharta Gautama (*The*

---

[199] The *'washing away of sins'* by bathing in the Ganges is broadly consistent with certain truths or rituals in various religions; sign-posting the way to Ultimate Reality and the 'Big Picture' of Jesus Christ. There is, nevertheless, a significant difference between this act and baptism in true Christianity, where the latter external action simply symbolises and summarily interprets what has already taken place internally at the time of conversion.

Buddha) born as a prince in Northern India in about 560 BC. Buddhism and the very much later (circa 6th century AD) Far-Eastern *Zen Buddhism* share many common features with Hinduism, such as karma and reincarnation, although there is no related caste system. Unlike Pantheist Monism, however, where the true self's *oneness* with Brahman/the soul of the cosmos could be said to represent ultimate enlightenment, the definitive goal of Zen Buddhists is the achievement of a state wherein they can *see* their original mind or *face before they were born* – that is without the intervention of the intellect.

Running in tandem with this is the belief that there is no such thing as a *self* in any individual being or indeed any essence in anything – that is, Zen Buddhism considers there to be no nameable identity at the core of each person and thus typically uses the terms *not-soul* or *non-self* (*an-atman*). The related philosophy is based on the *Four Noble Truths*, whereby (i) all life is suffering, (ii) the cause of suffering is desire or craving, (iii) suffering ends only when craving is extinguished, and (iv) this can be achieved by following the *Eightfold Path* to enlightenment.

The Eightfold Path is an all-embracing approach to life – right attitudes, intentions, speech, conduct, occupation, effort, mindfulness, and meditation. There is accordingly a very strong emphasis on living a *balanced life*, where simplicity and service to others are deemed to be more important than extreme disciplines such as asceticism and deprivation. Craving and pain in suffering are considered to be based on the illusion that we are individual selves or persons.

Zen Buddhism places great importance on meditation and intuition, as summarised by these quotations from *The World's Religions*, "*Central to....Japanese Zen is the practice of meditation according to strict rules*" [200] and "*Common to both movements* (branches of Zen), *however, is a clear opposition to intellectualism and the supremacy of reason. Concern with teaching is rejected. Zen is entirely intuitive.*" [201]

---

[200] *World's Religions, A Lion Handbook*. Lion Publishing plc, 1994, pp. 237 & 238.
[201] Ibid. p.238.

It is not surprising that Zen Buddhism is relatively popular in the West, perhaps particularly finding willing partners among those raised in the no plausibility structure societies of recent times. It seemingly represents a reasonable *middle road* and who could fault the admirable objectives of the Eightfold Path?

Nevertheless, the first three of the Four Noble Truths can surely only be understood as being very negative, and Zen Buddhism accordingly agrees with Stoicism (and Torquay United supporters) in maintaining that it's a bad thing to live in hope, which it typically considers to be *a killer.* Contrast this with the promises of Christ such as, *"I have come that they may have life, and have it in all its fullness."* (John 10:10) And, *"I have told you this so that my joy may be in you and that your joy may be complete."* (John 15:11) Specifically, an increasing love for Christ rather than necessarily extinguishing attachments to earthly things (see below) opens the way for personal transformation.

Final reality or final enlightenment in Zen Buddhism is accordingly not related to Brahman or some other 'ultimate' but rather to the 'Void', a concept that seems particularly difficult to understand properly, at least for Westerners. Hopefully, this description by James Sire will be of some help, *"Zen Buddhist monism holds that final reality is the Void. Final reality is nothing that can be named or grasped. To say it is nothing is incorrect, but to say that it is something is equally incorrect. That would degrade its essence by reducing it to a thing among things. The Hindu One is still a thing among things, though it is the chief among things. The Void is not a thing at all. It is instead the origin of every thing."* [202]

The void then corresponds to not-soul/non-self plus emptiness of the mind, so that it is also *no-mind*. Illusory thoughts and experiences, attachments and desires, together with the sense of self are, therefore, left behind as increasing *letting go* results in a natural stillness and quiet, freedom and happiness. This also marks the extinguishing of the fires that cause rebirth and suffering – the ultimate state known as *nirvana*.

---

[202] James Sire, *The Universe Next Door.* InterVarsity Press, U.S.A., 2004, p.158.

That almost completes my sojourn into Eastern spirituality, particularly as it is relevant to those of us in the West. As stated at the outset, the great diversity of beliefs means that no neat packaging is possible; particularly as so many of life's experiences are routinely considered to be illusional, and attributes such as reasoning, rationality, logic and resultant objective truths thus seem unimportant.

This viewpoint again raises serious difficulties for Westerners. Can all of these attributes, which Augustine of Hippo considered to represent the height of human nature and the teachings of Aristotle and the Stoics all rely upon, be simply overridden and disregarded? And yet it appears that the vast majority of Eastern indigenous populations do indeed believe that almost all spiritual knowledge should be solely *experience-based* and thus have little incentive to challenge associated incongruities such as the absence of good and evil versus behaviour-related karma.

Whether the East's many outstanding scientists and medical practitioners also take this view is uncertain, although it seems likely that at least some, with their academic and logically trained minds, must struggle to satisfactorily compartmentalise the inevitable conflicts.

Eastern culture, as previously highlighted, is also more spiritually orientated than in the West, and the dedication and discipline of followers of their religions and worldviews would put many Western Christians and others to shame. It is, however, difficult to relate these great efforts to anything other than mankind's side of the universal bridge – that is the associated experiences, teachings, rituals and duties seemingly correspond to *human works*, rather than to the encountering of God's grace, as occurs within genuine Christianity.

To summarise, of the two Eastern worldviews most influential in the West, purist Pantheistic Monism is predicated on the belief that Moksha (sometimes viewed as *ultimate enlightenment*) can only be attained by the true self or Atman becoming *one with all* - that is a metaphysical union with the One (Brahman). Zen Buddhism, which is not connected to any *ultimate*, stands on the belief that nirvana results primarily from *intuitive understanding/enlightenment* linked to a meditative search *within* rather than any outward pursuit of intellectual and rational answers, deemed to lead to deception and delusion.

Finally, the following bullet points provide further insights into the differences between Eastern spirituality and Christianity:

- Brahman of Eastern Spirituality is shrouded in much mysticism and mystery; characteristics that are also present within the Christian faith. Christianity is, however, founded on authentic revelation from beyond this *hazy veil*, meaning that believers may know something of God's true character and experience fruitful and ongoing reciprocal relationships. As previously, *"The idea of revelation expresses the basic Christian belief that we need to be told what God is like."* [203]

- Meditation is a feature of both, although, unlike the emptying of the mind general to the East, Christians focus their attention on the biblical Scriptures and, particularly, Jesus Christ, the *Prince of Peace*, (Isaiah 9:6b) as communion with God is sought. This latter process may reasonably be compared to tuning a radio to a specific bandwidth so that believers may reliably *hear* God's voice – He then is the *broadcaster* (proactive) and, we, the receivers (responsive).

- Those of a purist Eastern disposition generally deny the existence of individual identity, whereas an authentic Christian walk will lead to believers actually finding their *true* identities in Christ. Quoting from the Apostle Paul's letter to the Ephesians and The Message version of the Bible, *"It's in Christ that we find out who we are and what we are living for."* (Ephesians 1:11 MSG) This is because God who created, or we could say *invented,* human beings knows us through and through and is, therefore, in a far better position to direct our lives than we are. In other words, when an inventor comes up with

---

[203] Alister McGrath, also citing Eberhard Jungel. *Christian Theology – An Introduction.* John Wiley & Sons Ltd, 2017, p.136.

some type of invention, who knows its purpose better, the inventor or the invention?

- Although varying in specifics, Eastern views on final destinies seem to point towards states close to oblivion, whereas Christ promises eternal life involving transformed /perfected and joyful individual conscious existences.

Switching focus to the Monotheistic (*Mono* - one; *theistic* – God) religions of Islam and Judaism, including, where possible, comparisons with the Christian faith. Unlike most Eastern teachings all three believe God to possess personality, the visible universe to be physical and that, as created beings, no matter how intelligent, men and women are responsible to their Creator for the lives they lead. Furthermore, in contrast to many Eastern religions, the Quran and the Bible forbid the use of idols in both direct and indirect (as aids) forms of reverence and worship. It thus seems safe to conclude, even before description and discussion, that both Islam and Judaism are closer to Christianity than Pantheistic Monism and Zen Buddhism.

As with Eastern worldviews, *Islam* is very diverse, with many different *denominations* and associated sub-branches. Of these, the largest and best-known groups are the Sunnis and Shi'ites, representing roughly 85% and 10% respectively of the total adherents and originating from the different views concerning the correct succession to Muhammad, the founder of Islam (means *submission to the will of God*).

Scholarship is undoubtedly very important to certain schools of Islamic belief, and there is sometimes the accompanying insistence that this must relate solely to the Arabic language as spoken by Muhammad. It is, however, unclear as to how much of this scholarship extends beyond the Islamic scriptures. These are generally taken to be, firstly, the Quran (means *recitation*), the holy book of the Islamic faith and, secondly, the Hadith, a large collection of writings recording the purported sayings and traditions of Muhammad, revered and received as a major source of religious law and moral guidance. It is difficult, due to variations between different Islamic traditions, to create an accurate portrayal of

Muhammad, but the following outline account does appear to be in general alignment with the accepted consensus.

Muhammad (means *Praised*), lived between approximately AD 570 and 632, with Muslims (means *one who submits*) considering him to be the last and greatest of a series of prophets such as Adam, Abraham, Moses and Jesus. Muhammad was born in the Arabian town of Mecca where, having been orphaned at the age of six, he was brought up by close relatives. Mecca at that time was a hub of religious activity, with worship being centred on a large cube-shaped stone building, the *Ka'aba*, which was also known as the *House of Allah* (*The God*). However, although recognising Allah, the Arabs during Muhammad's youth seem to have been as much attached to other deities, with the Ka'aba being full of the images of various gods and goddesses. The culture of his homeland was, therefore, polytheistic (many gods).

At about the age of twenty five, Muhammad married a wealthy widow, Khadijeh, some fifteen years his senior and through whom he fathered two sons (both died in infancy) and four daughters. In addition to love and wealth, Khadijeh gave him an influential position in Meccan society, and he apparently remained faithful to her until she died some twenty five years later in about AD 620. Nevertheless, at the time of his death, a further twelve years on, Muhammad had acquired at least ten wives and two concubines.

Muhammad had various encounters with both Jews and Christians, whose belief in one God appears to have been primarily responsible for challenging the polytheism of his background and also resulted in him gaining some understanding, albeit rather mixed, of the two faiths. He seems to have been a sensitive and deep-thinking person, a man who would sometimes retreat into a cave for meditation. During one of these times, when he is understood to have been about forty years old and in the month of Ramadan, the angel Gabriel is said to have appeared to him instructing that he recite what he heard.

Similar episodes purportedly occurred on a number of subsequent occasions over a period of about twenty years, although the mode of transmission seems to have varied between Gabriel himself, Gabriel's voice only, and a bell through which angelic words were conveyed to him. It is also understood that during these times Muhammad would sometimes fall to the ground foaming at the mouth, and he initially considered that the source might be the *Jinni* (thought to have been intelligent spirits of lower rank than the angels, who were able to possess humans). However, over time, he came to believe that he was indeed hearing the very *Word of God* and that he was both a prophet and the only *reciter*. Although Muhammad was almost certainly illiterate, most Muslim scholars believe that many of his recitations were written down during his lifetime. Following his death, these were collected and incorporated in the Quran.

Two other incidents in Muhammad's life are also worthy of inclusion. The first concerns his alleged *night journey* in about AD 621, an episode that is briefly described in the Quran, with other details being found in the Hadith. There are various accounts of this journey but in essence it is understood to have comprised two phases, the *Isra* from Mecca to Jerusalem on the back of Buraq, a heavenly stallion in Islamic mythology, and the *Mi'raj* from Jerusalem to heaven accompanied by the angel Gabriel. There are different views concerning whether this journey was physical and/or spiritual with at least one tradition, apparently based on the witness of his wife, Aisha, maintaining that he never left his bed.

The second event occurred the following year when, after enduring mounting local resistance and aggression because of his brave stance on worshipping only the one God, Allah, Muhammad and his followers moved from Mecca to Yathrib some 200 miles to the north (now Medina - *The City of The Prophet*). This migration is known as the *Hijrah* and is the recognised start date of Islam. Today in Muslim lands, all letters, newspapers, documents etc. are dated from AD 622.

It seems evident that Muhammad was a very courageous man with great abilities, particularly leadership, who achieved remarkable successes by overcoming seemingly insurmountable difficulties. By the end of his life he had succeeded in uniting the whole of Arabia, including hitherto warring tribes, and completely transformed religion from polytheism to monotheism (under the sovereignty of Allah). Although these accomplishments required the use of considerable force, they are nonetheless still very impressive, particularly given the overall timeframe of about 20 years.

There are differing opinions when it comes to the quality and status of the Quran, a compilation containing more than a few indications of fallible human authorship and, particularly, various mistakes and misunderstandings of the Bible (referred to below). Nevertheless, it would appear that most consider it to represent an impressive literary accomplishment, and there seems to be general agreement concerning its portrayal of Muhammad as, in many ways, an outstanding man whose appreciable influence on human history should not be underestimated. A further related point, which seems to have largely gone under the radar in the West, is how much Islam has contributed to the human race - particularly in mathematics, medicine and architecture during its *Golden Age* between the 9th and 14th centuries. Indeed, Islam is understood to have greatly influenced the rise of European science during the Renaissance, which began in Italy during the latter century.

The Bible and Christianity as a whole have been subjected to extensive critique and associated attacks over the past 250 years or so. And rightly so; any religion or worldview that claims to speak on behalf of God should expect, and probably even welcome, very thorough investigation. If something is true, then why should there be any need to be defensive? And if it is not true, then a debt of gratitude is owed to those responsible for *opening our eyes.*

A similar attitude does not, however, appear to be forthcoming from Islamic leaders and spokespersons, with the general impression being one of wariness concerning comprehensive examination and debate. In other words, there seem to be several, if not many, *no-go* areas with, unlike in true Christianity, most Muslims being actively discouraged from voicing theological questions and any related difficulties. The following discussion is therefore intended to highlight and compare a number of the tenets behind the two faiths, including several of the more problematic doctrines pertinent to Islam.

As per the Christians, Muslims believe there to be one God who is the Creator and sustainer of all things. Both also assert this transcendent God to be all-powerful, all-knowing and all-present; having the right, as their Creator, to judge all human beings on how they have behaved and conducted themselves during their lives here on Earth. Furthermore, although both the Christian and Islamic scriptures refer to the Creator by one principal name (Yhwh/Yahweh/Jehovah and Allah respectively), they also include many related praiseworthy titles and designations. Indeed, the Hadith indicates 99 such, including The *One*, The *Real*, The *Eternal*, The *Light*, The *Self-Sustaining*, The *Compassionate*, The *Merciful*, and The *Glorious*. So very positive and familiar stuff, as all of these titles are also relevant to the God of Christianity.

However, if we dig a bit deeper, some very important differences begin to emerge. Perhaps most significantly, although the Quran teaches that God is nearer to man than a man's jugular vein, presumably meaning that Allah has full knowledge of a man's thoughts, his sheer transcendence means that there is little chance of this process being reciprocated so that he may be known in any real sense by human beings. Despite the above titles, Islam says nothing about his essence, no intimate disclosure of any inner feelings and emotions. He is simply much too exalted to speak directly to men and women, who are all too aware that nothing happens outside of his predestined and infallible will. Allah is therefore perceived as a sovereign being who reigns supreme and does as he pleases. So in this very important respect, he is a remote god who cannot be questioned by mere mortals. Believers can, therefore, only be obedient and submit to his commands, as specifically revealed in the Quran and Hadith.[204]

In contrast, when we turn our attention to the God of Christianity, we discover that, although He is indeed absolutely and wonderfully

---

[204] A significant minority of Muslims practise the essentially mystical approach of Sufism and are known as *Sufis*. These adherents are extremely devout and do indeed long and search for intimate relationships with the divine. However, the Islamic religion generally seems unaware of any such need and is therefore unable to offer a solution.

transcendent, He is also immanent and can be known personally and intimately as He abides within believers through His Holy Spirit. Even then, as infinitely simpler beings, we can inevitably only comprehend a fraction of His ineffable (beyond description) nature and staggering profundity (presumably in like fashion to the *Charlie Cat* analogy).

So the God of the Bible is relational with His followers, at times allowing them to struggle and 'wrestle' with Him concerning things they dislike and do not agree with – e.g., Abraham, Jacob and some of the psalmists in the OT and the Apostle Paul in the NT. These struggles of course vary, but are not necessarily of a selfish or arm-twisting nature, quite often simply representing endeavours to persuade God to demonstrate His revealed character of love, compassion, mercy and justice. Not that He is reluctant to do this in the first place, but knows that interchanges of this nature will lead to heightened degrees of intimacy and human confidence. Indeed, contrary to the experiences of most Muslims and somewhat ironically, today's Western Christians can sometimes be guilty of concentrating on intimacy to the detriment of the awe and wonder very properly due to God.

The intimacy and *know-ability* of God are primarily due to two attributes, neither of which are included within the 99 titles and designations relating to Allah. The first of these is that God is not only loving but is, in actuality, love itself; resulting in a constant reaching out to all humankind as He seeks relationship. God is accordingly the proactive one in this process - not human beings, who are simply called to respond. Love is, therefore, the central essence of God, whose triune nature is consistent with this always having been the case.

Conversely, it is difficult to envisage how Allah, as a strictly monotheistic entity, could have been capable of anything beyond narcissism (self-love) prior to the creation of cognitive beings. And is this marked contrast supported by the relevant teachings of these faiths? The short answer is "Yes." The Bible mentions the word *love* (or loves/loved) on many more occasions than the Quran, including a total of 27 times in just 15 verses of the Apostle John's first letter. Furthermore, God's unconditional love for all human beings (Matthew 5: 44-45) is not mirrored by Allah, whose conditional love is dependent upon performance and obedience.

The second, and possibly even more important, attribute of God is that He can be known as *Father*, *Papa*, *dad* or even *daddy*, something that is not the case for Allah. There is a very powerful book called, *I dared to call him Father*, written by Bilquis Sheikh,[205] a high-born Muslim lady from Pakistan, that recounts her amazing spiritual journey leading up to and following her conversion to Christ.

Muslims do not know God as the personification of unconditional love and the perfect Father who, above all else, loves them dearly and longs for personal relationships, having already done everything on their behalf to make this possible both in the present life and following physical death. Indeed, some Islamic believers would consider certainty at this level to be very presumptive and, possibly, even bordering on blasphemy. Unless they are martyred (wherein all sorts of sexual treats await - men only!), Islam provides no certainty regarding the future destiny of adherents. Everything depends on them and how they have lived their lives.

So, as per Eastern religion, Islam is based on *human works*, whereby men and women attempt to build the bridge to Allah/God from their side of the great divide - again, no God-given grace is readily available. Devout Muslims accordingly live out the best lives that they possibly can, principally by attempting to obey the almost countless commands/rules regulating every aspect of life contained within the Quran and Hadith, and, most importantly, adhering to the included five pillars of Islam (see below). They hope that, come the day of judgement, their good deeds will be heavier than the bad and *tip the balance* in favour of paradise rather than the fires of hell. Some might also hope that, even if the balance tips the wrong way, the compassion and mercy of Allah might come to their aid, but know that this can in no way be relied upon.

---

[205] Bilquis Sheikh (with Richard Schneider), *I dared to call him Father*. Chosen Books Publishing Co. Ltd.,1981.

> **The Five Pillars of Islam**
>
> **Shahada:** sincerely reciting the Muslim Testimony of faith
>
> **Salat:** performing ritual prayers correctly five times each day.
>
> **Zakat:** paying an alms (or charity) tax to benefit the poor and the needy.
>
> **Sawm:** fasting during the month of Ramadan.
>
> **Hajj:** a pilgrimage to Mecca at least once in their lifetime.

Another very important difference between Islam and Christianity is that the former says nothing about humankind being made in the spiritual image of Allah. The God of the Bible thus seems in some ways to be surprisingly *human* – not due to Him being like us, but due to us being like Him! (albeit very imperfectly). Because of this, Christ could take on human nature and sinful human beings could potentially respond to the Holy Spirit and the message of the gospel. All individuals are accordingly precious to God, with their lives being highly valued and treasured. The fact that Islam has generally failed to comprehend this truth appears to have sometimes led to certain groups placing more importance on family honour than the lives of their own flesh and blood.

Islam's terms of admission are the simplest of all. It is the easiest religion in the world for non-Muslims to join. All that's required is the purposeful recital, in the presence of at least one witness, of the one-sentence Testimony of Faith (*Shahada*) – *There is no god but Allah and Muhammad is the messenger of God.* There seem to be no *born-again* experiences, with most Muslims apparently viewing their faith as simply relating to being born into a particular nation/culture; something that many assume is also the case for Christians born in the West. Cultural Christianity can, of course, be inherited but, again, is only a very poor reflection of true Christianity.

The Islamic scriptures contain very little geographical or historical narrative, concentrating instead on instructions concerning how to live and warnings against different beliefs. This means that corroboratory archaeological evidence is all but absent. The Bible, on the other hand, is overflowing with such narrative – that is real people and real events, grounded in real history, real geography and real time. Many associated books have accordingly been published and various biblical archaeological societies established. One specific example of how knowledge of biblical narrative can come up trumps occurred in World War 1 when British forces under the command of General Allenby confronted the Turks at a town named Michmash. Before actual engagement, a brigade major remembered that the Bible referred to a town of the same name and, upon finding the appropriate verses (1 Samuel 13:23 & 14:4-5), discovered that it could be accessed by a secret path. A subsequent investigation revealed that this path, dating back some 3,000 years, was still in existence and the British used it to out-manoeuver the Turks and take control of the town.[206]

No comparison between Islam and Christianity would be complete without direct reference to their two principal characters, Muhammad and Jesus Christ; presented below as a series of summary bullet points:

- ❖ Islam deems Muhammad to be the final and greatest prophet/messenger from God, but Muslims would be horrified by any suggestion that he might in some way be equal to Allah himself. Conversely, the Bible presents Jesus Christ as the Son of God and co-equal with God from eternity; a being through whom everything was created but, incredibly, temporarily made lower than the angels (the *God-man*). All of this is categorically denied by Muslims and indeed, as per several other religions, Islam considers the idea of God appearing in human form to be offensive.

---

[206] https://en.wikipedia.org/wiki/Edmund_Allenby,_1st_Viscount_Allenby

- The Quran, therefore, does not accept the Christian Trinity, and even warns and admonishes its readers concerning the negative repercussions of harbouring such an image. It is interesting that the angel Gabriel who allegedly gave this message to Muhammad, *"...Allah is only One Allah. Far is it removed from His Transcendent Majesty that He should have a son."* (Quran – Surah 4:171b) is purported to be the same angel Gabriel that told Mary she would give birth to the Son of God (*Immanuel - God with us*) called Jesus (*the Lord saves*). There is also some confusion here, as it seems that Muhammad was under the misapprehension that the Christian Trinity comprised God as father, Mary as mother and Jesus as their son (probably picked up from local Syrian churches who called Mary the *mother of God*).

- It accordingly follows from the above that, although Muslims believe Jesus to have been born of a virgin, they cannot accept the biblical claim that He *chose* to take on a human form, having existed from all eternity. No such claims are made for Muhammad, who is considered to have had no previous existence and be the result of normal human conception and birth.

- Although refusing to accept Jesus Christ's divine ontology, many Muslims seemingly still consider Him to be a great prophet or apostle, second only to Muhammad, and thus worthy of their respect and perhaps even love – an obvious improvement on the attitudes of many present-day Westerners.

- The Islamic scriptures accept that Muhammad, although greatly revered and considered to be the principal (if not sole) source of spiritual guidance, was still only a man in need of forgiveness, whereas they agree with the Bible in confirming that Jesus Christ was indeed sinless.

- Unlike Jesus, whose miraculous powers they recognise, the Islamic scriptures attribute none to Muhammad with many Muslims today believing that the Quran itself is his *miracle*. This disparity is, of course, consistent with the infinite chasm between Muhammad as a created human being and Jesus as the uncreated Son of God. As a former civil engineer steeped in analytical thinking, I consider it to be very logical for Jesus Christ to have total control over His creation and express this through miraculous signs.

- It seems clear from the early parts of the Quran that Muhammad initially had a high regard for the contemporary Jews and Christians, whom he referred to as *People of the Book*. However, the rejection of his claims to be their final prophet or apostle (no prophecies similar to those pointing to Christ), resulted in him becoming increasingly hostile, claiming that the biblical Scriptures had been corrupted and, in particular, all references to him, deleted. It is very important to understand that, although this view is presented as *unquestionable fact* to all Muslims from their infancy upwards, there is not a shred of supporting evidence, scholarly or otherwise, to back it up. The Scriptures that make up the current Bible were originally completed centuries before Muhammad came on the scene, with nothing to suggest that they contained significant differences to modern-day versions (see appendix). In particular, Codex Vaticanus (virtually the complete Bible) and Codex Sinaiticus (almost all of the NT and over 50% of the OT), circa AD 300/325 and AD 330/360 respectively, make absolutely no mention of Muhammad. These actual manuscripts, written over two hundred years before he was born, can be viewed in the Vatican and British Museums.

- Islam asserts that Jesus Christ Himself was not crucified but whisked up to (an inferior) heaven by God and a look-alike put on the cross instead. It is not altogether clear how the Islamic scriptures, written some 600 years after the event and in a region remote from Palestine, came up with this idea, although it may relate to a migration of the heretical teaching of Docetism (Jesus only appeared to have a physical body, being instead of celestial/spiritual substance), itself linked with 2nd to 4th century Gnosticism. This alternative rendering is hardly a scholarly interpretation, especially when compared with the traditional early accounts (again, see appendix) confirming that Jesus Christ was indeed subjected to bodily crucifixion – that is as recorded by the NT writers (1st century) and the renowned Jewish and Roman historians, Josephus (1st century) and Tacitus (died circa AD 120), all writing from within the Roman Empire. Yet this Islamic fabricated version is again taught as unquestionable fact to all Muslims from their infancy upwards.

- ❖ Even if we allow Muhammad's journey (spiritual or otherwise) from his home on Earth to heaven, it would still have been in the opposite direction from Christ's visit to Earth from His *home* in heaven.

- ❖ Muhammad is still in his tomb. Whether Christ's tomb is or is not in the Church of the Holy Sepulchre in Jerusalem, and quite frankly I'm not that fussed, the overwhelming truth is that Jesus' remains are not in it.

To summarise, the Islamic religion of 'submission' stands in stark contrast to the 'good news' of Christianity. Although Allah has given laws and issued warnings concerning failures to keep them, unlike the Fatherhood and loving essence of the God of Christianity, his inherent character is not disclosed to men and woman. Furthermore, only believers that are martyred for their faith can have any confidence concerning their ultimate destiny, and Muslims are certainly not offered any rescue plan that Allah has personally won for them. There is also no idea of him actually living within and in intimate partnership with human beings, as per the loving and transforming Spirit of Christ. It is, therefore, the will of Allah rather than relationships that reigns supreme.

Again, unlike Christianity, there appear to be few, if any, external corroborative tests that can be applied to Islam. We thus seem to be left in a kind of circular self-authentication, whereby the Quran says that Muhammad is the prophet of God and he says that the Quran is the Word of God – *fideism*.

I guess that the answer to the question posed at the start of this chapter concerning whether people right up to government cabinet level are correct in believing Islam and Christianity are *peas from the same pod* is now self-evident. My opinions and conclusions are not, of course, meant to represent any defamation of Muslim believers themselves, whose sincerity for their faith is often both impressive and humbling.

Similar to other religions, *Judaism* comprises various groups and sub-groups with, in this case, *Orthodox*, *Conservative*, and *Reform* representing the three major divisions. However, although reference is made to modern Judaism within this section, the main emphasis is on the OT teachings and practices. This is because it's through reading the OT or the Jewish Tanakh, for all intents and purposes the same Scriptures, that the relationship between Judaism and Christianity can best be examined and understood. In particular, many prophecies point very clearly to Jesus Christ, together with other areas of significant cross-over/fulfilment. Indeed, without these connections and resultant continuity between the OT and NT, Christianity would probably have progressed no further than a comparatively minor sect, either outlawed or on the periphery of Judaism. As noted earlier, this close association is in direct contrast to the claimed affinity between Islam and Judaism/Christianity, where there is no evidence for any such homogeneity.

There are accordingly many interwoven common strands between Judaism and Christianity, with the former having played the fundamental role of *parent* to the latter. Both Jews and Christians thus worship Yahweh (as per the OT/Tanakh), with the crux of their differences relating to the ontology or essential nature of Jesus Christ (as already discussed in some depth and considered further below). It is additionally of relevance to point out that the Jews or, more correctly, the antecedent Hebrews, are generally credited as being the first people to gift monotheism to the world.

Prior to this, polytheism, whereby peoples of particular areas or tribes subjected themselves to and worshipped the local *gods*, seems to have been a universal practice. We are thus on *Holy Ground* when considering Judaism and all Christians should be very thankful for the Jewish nation, whose very existence has enabled their participation in a wonderful inheritance. I know that I feel a real affinity with Jewish people, something that has increased during my necessary research.

Before exploring the Jewish faith and its interrelations with Christianity, it is necessary to address two very important aspects, the first of which concerns confession. Specifically, the clear consensus of historians is that, overall, the perception and treatment of the Jews by Christians, dating back to at least the time of Origen, a 3rd century Christian scholar and theologian, have been truly awful - something for which we should rightly all feel very ashamed.

And in this case, we certainly can't hide behind the fact that the high-profile individuals involved were not true Christians. Origen certainly was, as were other pioneers of the faith, such as Augustine of Hippo, Thomas Aquinas and Martin Luther. Indeed, after an exemplary attitude towards the Jews in the earlier years when many of his thoughts were penned, the final decade of Luther's life, dogged by miserable physical and mental health, represented a period in which his writings towards this race became increasingly malevolent. Some four hundred years later, Adolph Hitler and his cronies, who of course had no interest in Luther's earlier positive work, used these later toxic writings in an attempt to justify some of the Third Reich's hideous ideas and subsequent atrocities – what an appalling legacy!

Furthermore, although a significant minority of German Christians, sometimes assisted by fellow believers from other European countries, did reach out to help persecuted Jews during World War II, often at huge risks and costs to themselves, the majority seem to have *gone missing*.

So why has there been this persecution and abandonment of Jews by Christians and others? Historically, the principal reason seems to be the charge of *deicide*, whereby all Jews were held responsible for the killing of the Son of God; considered to be the same essence as God the Father and the Holy Spirit. Even now, in UK 2020, anti-Semitism is still with us (e.g., allegedly within the Labour Party), although, thankfully, there appears to be no particular evidence for its existence within the Christian Church. Anti-Semitism is abhorrent and indefensible. Jesus Christ paid the price for the sins of the whole world, not only those of the Jewish nation. And even then, we need to differentiate between the terrible actions of the religious leaders at the time rather than the ordinary Jews, some of whom undoubtedly believed in Christ as their Messiah. There is accordingly absolutely no justification for pointing the finger of blame at the Jewish nation for Christ's death; as previously concluded, the responsibility rests with humankind as a whole.

The second aspect, as has already been noted in connection with OT prophecy, concerns the fact that most Jewish people, living or dead, have not embraced Jesus Christ as their Messiah. Thus, although much evidence has already been put forward for this fundamental Christian truth, it still seems rather presumptuous to disagree with certain features of Judaism without some additional groundwork.

Perhaps the first thing that needs to be said in this respect is that Jesus Christ was a Jew, as were all the first Christians. In actuality, the NT records that shortly after the crucifixion and resurrection of Jesus, *"The number of disciples in Jerusalem increased rapidly, and a large number of priests became obedient to the faith."* (Acts 6:7)

This situation did not, however, last for long, apparently fizzling out during the diaspora that followed on from the destruction of Jerusalem by the Romans in AD 70. Nevertheless, the status quo was still long enough for probably the most important conversion in the whole history of the Christian faith to take place - that is, as previously, *Saul of Tarsus*/Apostle Paul.

Most of us are familiar with the phrase, the footballer's footballer; well Saul was *the Jew's Jew*. This is what he says about himself in his Jewish CV, via a letter to the Philippians, *"If anyone else thinks he has reasons to put confidence in the flesh, I have more: circumcised on the eighth day (see subsequently), of the people of Israel, of the tribe of Benjamin, a Hebrew of Hebrews; in regard to the Law, a Pharisee; as for zeal, persecuting the church; as for legalistic righteousness, faultless."* (Philippians 3:4-6)

Yet he goes on, *"But whatever was to my profit I now consider loss for the sake of Christ. What is more, I consider everything a loss compared to the surpassing greatness of knowing Christ Jesus my Lord, for whose sake I have lost all things. I consider them rubbish, that I may gain Christ and be found in Him, not having a righteousness of my own that comes from the Law, but that which is through faith in Christ – the righteousness that comes from God and is by faith."* (Philippians 3:7-9) That is a pretty dramatic turnaround, and so very important to notice the major emphasis he puts on <u>knowing</u> Christ Jesus my Lord.

It is often not recognised, but some Jews today, estimated to be approximately one million worldwide, do acknowledge Jesus Christ, or rather *Yeshua*, as their Messiah. These believers are known as *Messianic Jews*, people who consider that they can be both Jewish and Christian. This is well illustrated in a quotation from a book by Corrie ten Boom, a Dutch Christian lady who protected and helped Jews in the 2nd World War, resulting in both her and other family members experiencing the horrors of Nazi concentration camps (where her sister and father died).

It is 1941, and Corrie is talking about a Jewish friend nicknamed *The Bulldog*, "*The Bulldog's chief delight at the Beje* (Corrie's home), *after talking with Father, were the tomes of Jewish theology now housed in Tante Jan's big mahogany case. For he had become a Christian forty years earlier, without ceasing in the least to be a loyal Jew. 'A completed Jew!' he would tell us smilingly. 'A follower of the one perfect Jew'."* [207]

Many messianic books and sundry works have accordingly been written, with *Jesus was a Jew* [208] and various articles by Dr Arnold Fruchtenbaum, an acclaimed Jewish messianic scholar, sourcing some of the following discussions. It is also particularly relevant that the newborn Church very much emphasised its Jewish roots and the question of belonging related more to whether Gentiles, rather than Jews, could become Christians. More than a few messianic Jews, while recognising that the NT extends significantly beyond Judaism, have thus been surprised to discover the inherent 'Jewishness' of much of its contents.

As highlighted earlier, there is continuity across both the OT and NT, or, as the 4th/5th century theologian, Augustine of Hippo, put it, *"The New Testament lies hidden in the Old, and the Old Testament is unveiled in the New."* [209] This is something corroborated by a feature known as *intertextuality*, whereby, from the numerous back-references, the NT could almost be viewed as one long commentary on the OT Psalms. This is, therefore, a remarkable characteristic, again pointing to the consistency and integrated nature of the Bible.

The final bit of groundwork for justifying what is to come is, in my opinion, the most important. It concerns how the understanding of certain messianic prophecies has changed within Judaism over time. In particular, some OT prophets referred to the Messiah as a conquering king and others to a Messiah who, as a suffering servant, was to die a substitutionary death for the sins of the people. It's not altogether clear how the ancient religious teachers viewed these two seemingly contradictory portraits, although at some stage (certainly by the first few centuries of the 1st millennium AD) the conclusion was reached that

---

[207] Corrie Ten Boom (with John and Elizabeth Sherrill), *The Hiding Place*. Hodder and Stoughton, 1976, p.73.
[208] Arnold Fruchtenbaum. *Jesus Was A Jew*. Aries Ministries Press, 1995.
[209] Augustine of Hippo, as cited by Alister McGrath, *Christian Theology – An Introduction, Sixth Edition*. John Wiley & Sons Ltd, 2017. p.116.

there were, in fact, two different Messiahs - the conquering king being the *Son of David* and the suffering servant, the *Son of Joseph*. In any event, probably strongly influenced by their repeated captivity under different nations, virtually all Jews at the time of Christ were desperately looking solely to the conquering king Messiah, the Son of David, who would free them from the tyranny of the Roman Empire.

So they had in mind the following prophecy, as previously quoted, *"For to us a child is born, to us a son is given, and the government will be on His shoulders. And He will be called Wonderful Counsellor, Mighty God, Everlasting Father, Prince of Peace. Of the greatness of His government and peace there will be no end. He will reign on David's throne and over His kingdom, establishing and upholding it with justice and righteousness from that time on and forever. The zeal of the LORD Almighty will accomplish this."* (Isaiah 9:6-7)

Nothing much seems to have changed over time concerning the Son of David Messiah. However, in the 11th century AD a rabbi known as *Rashi*, possibly to counteract Christian claims that Jesus Christ was the suffering servant (Son of Joseph) Messiah spoken of in Isaiah 53 ($8^{th}/7^{th}$ century BC), advanced the argument that the whole passage spoke instead of the nation of Israel. Although this interpretation initially met with strong opposition, it became the accepted Jewish position by at least the start of the 19th century. The Christian explanation is, and has always been, that rather than two different Messiahs, the OT speaks of a single Messiah coming first as a *suffering servant* as a ransom for sin and then second, as a *conquering king* who will establish the kingdom of God bringing great joy, peace and justice.

Because of its crucial importance to this specific discussion, the following quotation represents the entire Isaiah 53 prophecy, prefaced by the final three verses of the previous chapter and annotated as appropriate,

"See, my servant will act wisely; [Christ's wisdom leaves human wisdom for dead]

He will be raised and lifted up and highly exalted. [Christ's triumphant and glorious final destiny]
Just as there were many who were appalled at Him –
His appearance was so disfigured
beyond that of any man
and His form marred beyond human likeness - ['bang-on' - see related description in chapter six]
so will He sprinkle [cleanse] *many nations,*
and kings will shut their mouths because of Him. [Jesus Christ is described as 'King of kings and Lord of Lords'] *For what they were not told, they will see, and what they have not heard,*
they will understand. [probable reference to the spreading of the gospel among Gentile nations]

Who has believed our message and to whom has the arm of the Lord [denotes power] *been revealed?*
He grew up before Him like a tender shoot, [humble beginnings and gentleness personified]
and like a root out of dry ground. [surrounded by the unfavourable 'soil' of man's sin]
He had no beauty or majesty to attract us to Him, [God in essence, but no trappings of human royalty]
nothing in His appearance that we should desire Him. [smashed up, flogged and crucified]
He was despised and rejected by men, [He certainly was - for most of His life]
a man of sorrows, and familiar with suffering. Like one from whom men hide their faces [probable reference to God]
He was despised, and we esteemed Him not. [surrounded by persecutors and naysayers]

Surely He took up our infirmities and carried our sorrows, [He died for us]
yet we considered Him stricken by God, smitten by Him, and afflicted. [crucifixion – hanging on a 'tree' seen as a curse]
But He was pierced for our transgressions, [crucifixion nails + spear in His side]

He was crushed for our iniquities;
the punishment that brought us peace was upon Him,
and by His wounds [or 'stripes' – from flogging] *we are healed.* [forgiven and redeemed]
We all, like sheep, have gone astray, each of us has turned to his own way; [I certainly have!] *and the Lord has laid on Him the iniquity of us all.* [again, He died for us]

He was oppressed and afflicted, yet He did not open His mouth;
He was led like a lamb to the slaughter, [the *'Lamb of God'*, as per the Passover – subsequently explained]
and as a sheep before her shearers is silent,
so He did not open His mouth. [very little said in His various trials, and offered no defence]
By oppression and judgment He was taken away. [He was given an unfair trial]
And who can speak of His descendants?
For He was cut off from the land of the living;
for the transgression of my people [all our sins were put onto Him] *He was stricken* [substitutionary punishment - as above]
He was assigned a grave with the wicked, [the thieves on the adjacent crosses],
and with the rich in His death, [tomb of Joseph of Arimathea - a rich bloke]
though He had done no violence,
nor was any deceit in His mouth. [He was Plato's 'just man']

Yet it was the LORD's will to crush Him and cause Him to suffer, [a predetermined rescue plan]
and though the LORD makes His life a guilt offering, [for our sin]
He will see His offspring and prolong His days, [resurrection, an indestructible life, and innumerable followers]
and the will of the LORD will prosper in His hand.
After the suffering of His soul,
He will see the light of life and be satisfied; [resurrection]
by His knowledge my righteous servant will justify many,

and He will bear their iniquities.

Therefore I will give Him a portion among the great, [see final para. of One Solitary Life]
and He will divide the spoils with the strong, [redeemed sinners]
because He poured out His life unto death, [sacrificially on the cross]
and was numbered with the transgressors. [the thieves and the rest of us]
For He bore the sin of many, [everyone]
and made intercession for the transgressors." [we need to repent to receive this free gift]
(Isaiah 52:13-53:12)

It certainly seems very clear that this prophecy is speaking of Jesus Christ as the *Son of Joseph Messiah* but, in any event, it surely cannot be interpreted as referring to a nation. I don't know exactly how today's rabbis treat this passage, but strongly suspect that it is generally ignored. This then allows a concentration on the *Son of David Messiah* who, as he is to bring (universal) joy, peace and justice, has obviously not yet come; the upshot being that the claims of Jesus Christ as the Jewish Messiah can be considered as false.

Many Jews are also angered by Christian insistence that Jesus is the Son of God, which they deem to be blasphemy. But, as has already been highlighted, Christ was not a human being aspiring to be God, but God Himself voluntarily taking on the role of manhood. The triune nature of God is therefore rejected. That said, some of today's Jews, while not of a messianic persuasion, have nevertheless much warmth towards Jesus who they regard as a great Jewish moralist, teacher and prophet.

Before going any further it may be useful to include some background information, and thus the following represents a very brief historical outline of Israel, God's sovereignly chosen nation. Abraham, who lived in approximately 2,000 BC and was the first person to be identified as *Hebrew*, had various grandsons, one of whom, Jacob, later came to be known as *Israel*. Jacob's twelve sons were the ancestors of the original twelve tribes of Israel. All of these people, including Jacob's father, Isaac, are known as *The Patriarchs*.

Following a period of about 400 years in Egypt, the latter part of which was spent as cruelly treated slaves, the Israelites were finally delivered out of this country by Moses; an exodus involving the parting of the Red Sea or *Sea of Reeds* and the drowning of the pursuing Egyptian army. This event is regarded as the foundational experience of Israel's entire history, and is thus still commemorated today (getting on for 3,500 years later).

The people that came out from Egypt comprised a combination of the majority tribal Israelites and a substantial minority of hangers-on (mainly of mixed heritage); sometimes referred to as 'the rabble' and seemingly having a disproportionately negative effect on the assembly as a whole. Many individuals also retained a limited and primitive slave mentality. So a 'challenging multitude' hardly covers it! In actuality, although progress was made during the following forty years in the Sinai Desert, it wasn't until they eventually entered the Promised Land of Canaan under Joshua that the Israelite nation began to take shape.

This process took centuries, peaking during the reigns of King David and his son, King Solomon, in the 10th century BC – the *Golden Age of Israel*. The nation then split following the death of Solomon, with the northern ten tribes continuing to be known as Israel, and the Benjamite tribe being absorbed into the southern kingdom of Judah (the *Jews*). Both kingdoms were subsequently conquered and taken into temporary exile by the Assyrians (circa 721 BC) and Babylonians (early 6th century BC) respectively, with the former also importing foreigners into Israel as colonists. This action and the resultant fairly widespread interbreeding, plus general confusion concerning the details of returning exiles, led to the northern ten tribes losing their basic identity, with the largest recognised group relating to Samaria and being known as Samaritans.

No similar loss of identity appears to have taken place for the Jews of the southern kingdom who were repatriated in conjunction with an approved foreign edict, and looked down upon and hated their *impure and inferior* Samaritan cousins. By at least the time of Christ, the Samaritans were a despised and economically depressed people with little influence over the country as a whole. As might be expected, Jesus completely bucked the general trend and went out of His way to befriend Samaritans – e.g., His parable of 'The Good Samaritan', as referred to previously.

There are, of course, very appreciable cultural differences between ancient Israel and the 21st century West, a circumstance resulting in certain correlation difficulties which, although not insurmountable, are best understood when the whole subject of context is kept in mind. In particular, it's again important to appreciate that God was endeavouring to shape and form relationships with an uncoordinated and essentially mongrel assembly of people, some of whom were undoubtedly stubborn and headstrong. His just and righteous judgments were thus always based solely on their behaviour, an approach that, from time to time, had to be extended to deal with the conduct of neighbouring nations.

The most significant characteristic of Judaism is that it is a religion built on covenants (agreements) with the monotheistic Creator God, *Yahweh*. Unlike today's norm, however, covenants in the Ancient Near East (ANE) were generally un-negotiated treaties where the king of a stronger nation typically declared a beneficial service (e.g., protection) on behalf of a subordinate nation (the *Vassal State*). They, in turn, agreed to fulfil certain conditions - a *tribute*, most commonly in the form of the transfer of wealth, produce or slaves. God, as the *Great King*, accordingly initiated these kinds of major player/minor player treaties concerning His chosen people, but with the crucial difference that the motivation behind His covenants was always to use love, care, compassion and discipline to create a holy (sacred, sanctified, consecrated, blessed) and pure nation after His own heart. The covenants may be thought of as two basic types, *unconditional*, where God would do what He promised irrespective of the people's response and *conditional* where the fulfilment of His specific promises depended on their obedience.

Four of the generally recognised total of seven covenants are referred to as follows: The Abrahamic and The Davidic (both unconditional, and only briefly described), and The Mosaic and The New (conditional and unconditional respectively, and described in more detail).

The Abrahamic Covenant established the Hebrew race (subsequently Israel/Judah) as God's *chosen people* – a *special* relationship - and contained many unconditional promises relevant to Abraham himself, the future Israelite nation, and other nations worldwide. In brief, Abraham was to be the Father of a great nation, Israel, with many nations descending from him and causing his name to become great - as it is today among Jews, Christians and Muslims; Israel would possess all the Promised Land - partially fulfilled at present; and related spiritual blessings would ultimately extend to all Gentile nations - to be achieved by the Jewish Messiah, from the line or seed of Abraham, although the patriarch would presumably have had little specific insight. Even though full and final consummation still awaits, multitudinous related *first-fruits* have already been experienced worldwide during the past 2,000 years.

It must also be emphasised that while the context of belief has changed from age to age depending on progressive revelation, God's salvation is, and always has been, effected by human faith responses to His grace. For example, *"Abraham believed God, and it was credited to him as righteousness"* (Romans 4:3), a quotation linked to an original Scripture referring back to before Abraham's circumcision, and specifically included by the Apostle Paul to demonstrate Abraham's position as a figurehead of justification by faith.

The paramount significance and solemnity of this covenant between God and Abraham were to be marked by the latter's circumcision, a practice to be continued for all eight-day-old male babies as an outward *seal* or *sign* of the child's *Jewishness* (as is still the case today). The act of circumcision thus related to the baby boy being included in the covenant people and symbolically pointed to his coming of age (seemingly twenty years old in OT times) when he would be formally set apart and dedicated to God. This was based upon a commitment to *cut out* all things harmful to a holy relationship – that is the more important and difficult spiritual experience of consecration or 'circumcising the heart'. Circumcision has also been relevant to other nations throughout history, but not for similar covenantal reasons.

As an addendum to the above, it is now known that, due to the particular development of the blood-clotting agent, prothrombin, the safest time in a male's entire life to perform a circumcision is on the eighth day. Pretty good eh! Indeed, some modern physicians have concluded that to have come up with this knowledge, the ancient Hebrews would have needed to conduct thousands of circumcision experiments on each day of the newborn male babies' lives. But as Dr McMillen, author of *None Of These Diseases*, says, *"Why not accept the Bible's statement that God spoke to Abraham?"* [210] Infant circumcision is also likely to produce health benefits, particularly the avoidance of penile cancer.

The Davidic covenant between God and David again contained many unconditional promises, with the following representing a skeletal summary: David would have an eternal Dynasty or House, an eternal Kingdom and an eternal Throne, all ultimately fulfilled through an eternal Descendent, the Messiah Himself. Furthermore, the covenant clarified the human descent of the Messiah. Specifically, whereas it had been implicit within the Abrahamic Covenant that the Messiah would be a direct descendant of Abraham, the prophecy was now amplified to reveal that He would come from the Tribe of Judah, and, ultimately, from the House of David; all of which was true for Jesus.

The conditional Mosaic Covenant, as referred to in chapters five and six, and sealed/signed by the Seventh Day Sabbath (*Shabbat*), contained within it a total of 613 commandments (the Torah/Law) associated with

---

[210] I. McMillen, *None Of These Diseases*. Marshall, Morgan & Scott, 1984, pp.92-93.

every particular of life – moral, ceremonial (religious), and judicial (governance/civil) – all of which were relevant to the ancient Israelite community as a whole, but not to every individual. For instance, there were specific commandments for both men and women. Furthermore, as noted earlier, there was the burgeoning Oral Torah composed of multi-generational interpretations aimed at enabling the Torah to be put into practice at the everyday level as Jewish culture changed over time. By the time of Jesus, the religious leaders were attempting to elevate the importance of these oral teachings to the level of the Torah, something He vigorously opposed.

Part of the Law comprised the OT *sacrificial system*, four types of which related to livestock, doves and pigeons, and one to grain. The thought of animal sacrifice, which is the focus here, no doubt sounds primitive, cruel and incomprehensible to most citizens of today's Western societies, particularly given the increasing popularity of vegetarian and vegan diets. However, these acts were not as weird and irrelevant as they sound – and I'm keeping the associated descriptions as brief as possible – so please hang in there. In particular, the way that Jesus Christ's crucifixion and the OT sacrificial ceremonies dovetail together is very impressive, and clearly demonstrates that the reasons for, and necessity of, the former event were no afterthought. So if we don't at least get a basic handle on this subject, we inevitably limit our understanding of Christ's remarkable rescue mission. It's also probably beneficial, before providing outline details of these ceremonies, to highlight some of their radical differences from those of the surrounding contemporary pagan nations.

Most crucially, the sacrificing of children, or indeed any human being, was considered abhorrent and thus completely prohibited (obviously a *given* now, but these were primitive and very wild times). Following on from this, the Israelite people were taught that their obedience and behaviour rather than the sacrificial offerings themselves were the most important to God, whose very nature meant that any thought of Him needing animal flesh and blood for His own ends was completely and utterly unconscionable. Finally, every kind of sacrifice had a set purpose, representing and demonstrating God's grace by providing forgiveness following breaches of specific commandments.

A very strong emphasis on holiness, deemed to be symbolised by physical perfection, was central to all of the above, meaning that every animal sacrifice had to be perfect and without blemish. This perfection also extended to the method of killing, with an associated stipulation that no bones were to be broken during the process. In summary, all sacrificial offerings were to be undertaken in strict accordance with the relevant procedures, particularly as instructed within the books of Leviticus and Numbers. Additionally, as today, the slaughtered animals were sometimes cooked and eaten.

The presence of Leviticus, hardly a riveting read, within the Bible is actually rather reassuring. This is because it describes in detail the various procedures plus related reasons and purposes behind the sacrificial system, confirming it to be a well thought out and coherent whole, and certainly nothing that could be regarded as ad hoc or shoddy. Of these reasons/purposes, the following selection provides a general overview:

(I) The token, but still appreciable, costs to the people (whether the physically perfect animals for sacrifice were owned or purchased) due to an inability to keep the Law, revealed and clarified their true position in the grand scheme of things and, specifically, that they were sinners.

(ii) The Law took account of the sacredness of life, which was symbolised by the blood of human beings and animals. Hence its complete prohibition concerning the drinking or eating of blood (as commonly occurred during pagan rituals to appease their god or gods). Animal sacrifice under the Law represented substitutionary atonement – that is, the particular sin or sins of the person was/were confessed and symbolically transferred to the sacrificial animal during its slaughter under the supervision of the presiding priest.

Although this process did provide for the forgiveness of sin, it could not extend to full salvation/redemption – in particular, the substitutionary atonement was only able to *cover* the sins of the penitent, rather than having the capability of taking them away. This meant that people were only 'outwardly clean', with their consciences remaining relatively unaffected and hence essentially uncleansed. As a rather crude example of this, a concrete slab may be used to cover and temporarily make safe contaminated ground, but permanent 'cleansing' can only be effected by total removal of the contaminants. Repetition of the above priestly ceremony was also required upon the commitment of further sins.

(iii) Yearly provision was made for the sins of the Israelites to be atoned for en masse on the *Day of Atonement* or *Yom Kippur*. This was performed by the serving High Priest who, following a sacrificial offering for his own sin and that of his household, sacrificed one male goat (the body of which was burned outside the camp) representing substitutionary atonement, with another male goat (the *scapegoat* – sound familiar?) being sent away alive to symbolise the removal of sin and guilt.

Jesus Christ's perfect sacrificial offering on a cross at Golgotha, a location outside the city wall, satisfied both the payment for and removal of humankind's sin as represented by the two separate goats. This external position, as noted previously, symbolised His complete separation from God and all people, as was necessary for His sacrificial death to completely identify with human sin.

(iv) It follows from the above, particularly the emphasis on symbolism (something that points towards, rather than representing the real thing), that although the Law was very thorough and, in certain respects, effective, it was still only a temporary fix.

(v) The Law pointed to beyond itself, and specifically to the much greater and permanent New Covenant, which would be established by the Jewish Messiah (*Christ* in the Greek) and provide for the full salvation/redemption of innumerable multitudes.

Although, as before, much of this probably sounds foreign and unfamiliar to most of us modern Westerners, the selected points do, nevertheless, indicate the true significance of humankind's sin and how this causes real difficulties and barriers that need to be overcome in order to enjoy meaningful relationships with an awesome and perfect Creator God. Christians can sometimes also be guilty of having rather limited comprehension in this area, which would be improved by serious contemplation of the Mosaic Law and, in particular, the full extent of the very considerable measures necessary for the ancient believers to get right with God.

The Apostle Paul, in his letter to the Roman believers, also drew attention to the fact that the OT Israelites had generally not understood, or maybe refused to believe, that God's rescue plan was still based on grace, as evidenced by the *sacrificial system* within the Mosaic Covenant. [211] They were, therefore, to respond in faith to what they knew of Him, rather than religion by works. (Romans 9:31-32) In particular, it seems that some, or perhaps many, people felt that by mechanically following the rules and procedures laid down in the Law they were complying fully with God's requirements. In actuality, they may even have treated these actions with a degree of superstition or, possibly, *magic*; something that always 'worked' whatever their behaviour. However, unlike the demonic *gods* of other nations who delighted in rather than being offended by nominal and sometimes abominable forms of worship, the Israelites were dealing with the holiness of God Himself, who was definitely not pleased.

---

[211] Although the start of John's gospel contrasts the *Law* of Moses with the *grace* of Jesus Christ, it seems that most biblical commentators view these as overall or *blanket* terms rather than 100% black and white opposing definitions. In other words, while there was undoubtedly grace under Moses, the grace provided by Christ is monumental and essentially unbridled.

This is borne out by many passages within the OT, such as when He spoke through the prophet Amos a few decades before the continual wickedness of the northern ten tribes resulted in their conquest by Assyria, *"I hate, I despise your religious feasts; I cannot stand your assemblies. Even though you bring me burnt offerings and grain offerings, I will not accept them. Though you bring choice fellowship offerings, I will have no regard for them. Away with the noise of your songs! I will not listen to the music of your harps. But let justice roll on like a river, righteousness like a never-failing stream."* (Amos 5:21-24)

God was, therefore, warning the people that their religious rituals and practices meant absolutely nothing if there was no commensurate everyday behaviour (i.e., no circumcised heart). He intended that they should respond to and reflect His love and goodness, thereby being different to, and set apart from, the corrupt pagan surrounding nations, to whom their righteous and distinctive lives would be a shining beacon and moral/spiritual guide. He was therefore angry although not, of course, surprised that His chosen nation was not fulfilling His aspirations for them, and indeed were generally more influenced by the evil actions of their neighbours (practices such as child sacrifice, idolatry, divination and sorcery) than vice-versa. He thus continued to reprimand the Jews for the continual wickedness that would lead to their eventual downfall; on one occasion saying through the $7^{th}/6^{th}$ century BC prophet Jeremiah, *"'While you were doing all these things', declares the Lord, 'I spoke to you again and again, but you did not listen; I called you, but you did not answer'."* (Jeremiah 7:13)

God's remonstrations were thus to no avail. Little genuine repentance took place and the southern kingdom of Judah, as had previously happened to the northern kingdom of Israel, thus needed to learn the hard way by being taken captive. The prophet Ezekiel, speaking from within Babylon only a few decades later, confirmed the reasons behind Judah's woes by telling his fellow captives, *"Therefore this is what the Sovereign Lord says: 'You have been more unruly than the nations around you and have not followed my decrees or kept my laws. You have not even conformed to the standards of the nations around you'."* (Ezekiel 5:7)

It's therefore clear that even though there were intermittent periods of spiritual revival and usually at least some godly individuals knocking around who bucked the trend (typically the prophets), the overall performance of the ancient Israelites, who God referred to as a *"stiff-necked people"* (Deuteronomy 9:6b) and *"uncircumcised in heart,"* (Jeremiah 9:26b) could only be termed a failure.

Because of the inability and/or unwillingness of the Israelites to accomplish His purposes for them, God promised, again through Jeremiah and Ezekiel, that He would, in time, do something completely new concerning the whole spectrum of salvation.

'"This is the covenant that I will make with the house of Israel after that time', declares the Lord. 'I will put my law in their minds and write it on their hearts. I will be their God, and they will be my people.'" (Jeremiah 31:33)

And, *"I will give them an undivided heart and put a new spirit in them; I will remove from them their heart of stone and give them a heart of flesh."* (Ezekiel 11:19)

These then are clear references to the New Covenant although, as previously highlighted, it was actually promised before the beginning of time. In particular, it represents God going beyond the limited and ineffective attempts of individuals to circumcise their own hearts and live better lives, by offering to undertake the necessary *heart transplant* operations Himself.

It may not seem like it, but all of this stuff is pretty amazing and, maybe, even unique. Because what is going on here is, firstly, God interacting with His chosen nation by messages of appeal and warning, and then, secondly and unbelievably, allowing them to ignore and completely disregard His pronouncements, including the repeated offers of forgiveness and restoration if they would only repent and change their wicked ways. This stubbornness of the people thus illustrates that God's will is not always carried out in every particular; something that is seemingly a million miles away from many other worldviews with, as we have seen, Islam considering that every single act and occurrence on Earth results directly from the will of Allah and cannot be questioned.

Nevertheless, thirdly and most importantly, God is still sovereign and all-powerful, a being who can use both human rebellion and failure to achieve His ultimate purposes. This can be seen in the case of Judah, whose exile resulted in improved general conduct (e.g., no further idolatry) and a people more prepared for the arrival of the Messiah, who would Himself usher in God's predetermined and unstoppable New Covenant.

The main differences between the New Covenant and the old Mosaic Covenant can be summarised as follows: Firstly, the New Covenant is eternal because, unlike the required repetitive sacrificial duties and a seemingly never-ending succession of priests/High Priests, all of whom died, it is based on the consummate accomplishments of an *indestructible life* (Hebrews 7:16) - i.e., that of Jesus Christ. And in contrast to the physically perfect animal sacrifices, which were mere symbols foreshadowing what was to come, the total perfection of Christ's life and vicarious (*substitutionary*) death confirms Him as the long-awaited once and for all *Lamb of God* (see subsequently); thus permanently fulfilling all the relevant requirements of the Law and removing the need for any future sacrificial offerings. The necessary payment for the forgiveness *and* removal of the whole of humankind's sin is accordingly made in full, resulting in the internal cleansing of individual consciences compared to the largely external blessings conferred by the old covenant. Furthermore, Christ is a permanent High Priest of flawless character, having no need of personal repentance, with an intercessory priesthood encompassing both Jews and Gentiles.

All who call on His name in genuine repentance can, therefore, receive forgiveness and full salvation; becoming *"born again"* (John 3:3) and *"a new creation"* (2 Corinthians 5:17), with opportunities for more intimate and continuous relationships with God than had previously been possible. Finally, the entirety of the New Covenant, as an unconditional treaty, is based on God's promises rather than people's performance, with His Holy Spirit, given to all believers at conversion, imparting life and power rather than rules.

What then of the Mosaic Covenant and the integral Mosaic Law of 613 commandments is still relevant for us today? Although, as noted earlier, this treaty and legal content represented a temporary fix, this is still not an easy question to answer in its entirety. Perhaps the most appropriate Scriptures, as many have discovered, relate to Christ's teaching in *The Sermon on the Mount*, the fullest version of which can be found in Matthew's gospel, comprising three chapters and just a few pages. While various authors have, unsurprisingly, focussed on different aspects and related legitimate interpretations of this incredibly rich teaching, most would surely agree that it is one of a number of extraordinary examples concerning how Jesus can comprehensively explain profound matters using the most concise language imaginable. Indeed, Dr Martyn Lloyd-Jones, an acclaimed 20th century Welsh theologian, church leader and medical doctor, has produced a related work titled *Studies In The Sermon On The Mount* [212] which, at *only* 585 pages, is considered to be a *lightweight* spiritual classic.

My approach is to treat this teaching as primarily representing a transition from the Mosaic Covenant to the New Covenant and, because it provides a brief synopsis of the most pertinent points, to initially focus attention on the following passage,

"Do not think that I have come to abolish the Law or the Prophets; I have not come to abolish them but to fulfil them. I tell you the truth, until heaven and earth disappear, not the smallest letter, not the least stroke of a pen, will by any means disappear from the Law until everything is

---

[212] Martyn Lloyd-Jones, *Studies In The Sermon On The Mount.* William B. Eerdmans Publishing Company, 1976.

accomplished. Anyone who breaks one of the least of these commandments and teaches others to do the same will be called least in the kingdom of heaven, but whosoever practises and teaches these commands will be called great in the kingdom of heaven. For I tell you that unless your righteousness surpasses that of the Pharisees and teachers of the Law you will certainly not enter the kingdom of heaven." (Matthew 5:17-20)

The context of the sermon is that a large crowd has followed Jesus and His disciples onto a hillside in the general vicinity of the Sea of Galilee to hear Him speak. It additionally seems likely that many are somewhat confused, having directly witnessed or heard about Jesus' great miracles, but being told by their religious leaders, whom they revered and whose teaching they depended upon, that He was a charlatan and a fake. In particular, they would have heard these leaders accusing Jesus of peddling some new type of teaching, which opposed or at least lacked continuity with the OT/Tanakh.

In order to build a *basecamp* for the aforementioned transition, Jesus' strategy is, therefore, to put the record straight by drawing His audience's attention to the fact that His teachings are in complete harmony with the OT Scriptures and the Law in particular. Indeed, He confirms His elevated view of the still operative Mosaic Law by (seemingly) utilising hyperbole to emphasise the great divide between those who do and those who do not take seriously the related commands. Furthermore, He points out that the religious leaders are falling short by saying that, and this must have freaked out most of His listeners, unless they lived better lives than these men, they could wave bye-bye to any aspirations of heaven.

Christ explains that, rather than abolishing the OT Scriptures, He is, in actuality, fulfilling them. By this He means He is living out their true meaning according to the spirit; an attitude in sharp contrast with the practice of most of the religious leaders who perpetuated a hollow sham of external obedience by relying solely on the *letter of the Law*.

It's also very revealing that John's gospel records Jesus telling these leaders that much of the OT/Tanakh referred to Him, *"You diligently study the Scriptures because you think that by them you possess eternal life. These are the Scriptures that testify about me, yet you refuse to come to me to have life."* (John 5:39-40)

So what exactly did Jesus fulfil? In summary, He fulfilled the moral and ceremonial parts of the Law in every respect by living a perfect life and undergoing a perfect sacrificial death. Indeed, Dr Martyn Lloyd-Jones considers that this one vicarious act satisfied all the various types of OT sacrifice, as recorded in the books of Leviticus and Numbers; sacrifices that were thus rendered redundant. It is rather difficult to ascertain the precise context of the words, *"until heaven and earth disappear"*, but this phrase (or formula?) was also used by Christ on other occasions where the clear intention was to express the unchanging nature of God's Word.

Again, from Lloyd-Jones, *"Everything that is in the Law and the prophets culminates in Christ, and He is the fulfilment of them. It is the most stupendous claim He ever made."* [213] And from the Apostle Paul, *"Christ is the culmination of the law so that there may be righteousness for everyone who believes."* (Romans 10:4)

To provide further clarification of the relationship between the Mosaic Covenant and the New Covenant, it is helpful to widen the discussion to include a few factors relevant to the overall picture. Perhaps the first thing to emphasise is that the moral law, so beautifully lived out and brilliantly summarised by Christ (*"All the Law and the prophets hang on these two commandments."* - Matthew 22:40), represents God's essence of pure and unconditional love, and is thus, by association, unchanging and eternal. In other words, the moral law pre-dates and post-dates all circumstances and all covenants, for which it has always been the basis. It has invariably been wrong to murder, steal and abuse one's parents etc; moral values for all humanity, past, present and future, rather than being unique to the ancient Hebrews.

---

[213] Ibid, p.163.

The Law of Moses, while it incorporated the moral law, was not, therefore, its originator. Under the Mosaic Covenant, the moral law, in conjunction with the ceremonial and judicial, had two main purposes. The first of these was to educate and hopefully transform an originally naïve, uncoordinated and sometimes headstrong people, leading to the maturation and improvement of society over time. Secondly, and most importantly, the peoples' repeated unsuccessful attempts to keep the Law during a national *childhood* and *adolescence* of about 1,400 years undoubtedly brought home to them both God's holiness and perfection and their own unholiness and imperfection – again, progressive revelation. They, or at least the godlier among them, thus began to realise their need for a saviour, gradually becoming prepared for the New Covenant as instituted by Jesus Christ.

This process is well described in the Apostle Paul's letter to the Galatians, *"So the Law was put in charge to lead us to Christ that we might be justified by faith. Now that faith has come, we are no longer under the supervision of the Law."* (Galatians 3:24-25) And a simply amazing second passage, *"But when the set time had fully come, God sent His Son, born of a woman, born under the law, to redeem those under the law, that we might receive adoption to sonship. Because you are His sons, God sent the Spirit of His Son into our hearts, the Spirit who calls out, 'Abba, Father'. So you are no longer a slave* (to sin), *but God's child; and since you are His child, God has made you also an heir."* (Galatians 4:4-7)

Having already highlighted Christ's fulfillment of the moral and ceremonial laws, the destruction of Jerusalem and its Temple by the Romans in AD 70 (as He had prophesied) and the resultant diaspora served as the death knell for the judicial. Specifically, these events ended the ancient theocracy, thereby terminating, or one might say *fulfilling*, the judicial laws. The removal of the Temple, which ended the High Priesthood and the substitutionary animal sacrificial system of atonement, also seemingly confirmed that the OT ceremonial laws had ceased to have authority in relation to personal salvation.

So in answer to the original question, the Mosaic Law relevant to the ancient Israelites has been completely and permanently fulfilled, rendering the Mosaic Covenant powerless and obsolete.

What then has actually happened to the Mosaic Law? Is it entirely irrelevant? Well, not quite. In the first place, although the Mosaic Law is no longer a legal code requiring obedience to its various commandments and rules, it is still God's Word and, quoting the Apostle Paul, "useful for teaching, rebuking, correcting and training in righteousness." (2 Tim. 3:16)

Secondly, the fact that God's moral law is eternal and unchanging results in the relevant commandments and principles contained in the Mosaic Law being incorporated into the New Covenant. For example, nine of the ten OT commandments (perhaps not the 4th, the Sabbath, representing past ceremonial law) are repeated and involved in the judgement of those who have not availed themselves of the free forgiveness won for them by Christ.

The New Covenant's superiority over the Mosaic Covenant has already been described, with its central progression, for all those calling upon the Lord, relating to salvation, where sins are both forgiven and removed, individual consciences are cleansed, and relationships with God can become more intimate and continuous. This new covenantal relationship thus releases believers from being under God's moral judgments. Their salvation is not dependent on their obedience and morality (thank God!).

However, there is much more to the New Covenant than this; in particular, its content is commonly known as the *Law of the Messiah* or *Law of Christ*, so we must firstly get to the basis of these designations. Again, the Sermon on the Mount appears to be the best place to start, with its emphases on the spirit and real motives behind anger, adultery, public prayer, money etc. being confirmed and expanded upon in the NT letters. That said, it needs to be stressed that this *Law* is not to be treated as sets of rules and regulations to be complied with, but rather as attitudes and principles that should characterise Christian lives.

It seems to me that while most Western Christians, solidly grounded in the doctrine of God's grace, understand the first part of the latter sentence, significantly fewer, by their moral conduct and behaviour, have grasped the second.

The Sermon on the Mount moves us away from the letter of the law to the spirit behind it, something that can clearly be seen at its very beginning by the moral teaching contained within the *beatitudes*. These are mainly dealing with our inner selves rather than external actions, or alternatively, about *being* rather than *doing*; emphases that are clearly contrary to the way most of us in the West live our lives. Do we really, to quote just two of the beatitudes, hunger and thirst for righteousness or seek purity of heart? And then later on in this discourse, Christ tells us to love our enemies and pray for those who persecute us. Can He actually be serious? Because, at first sight, all of this appears to represent upside-down thinking.

Yes, Jesus is deadly serious and even says that we will be blessed (favoured, comforted, given inner peace) if we follow His teaching, indicating that it's perhaps human beings who are the upside-down ones. So, again, a question – Why should this be? I can think of two answers, although there must be more. Firstly, and I know we have been here before, the way we are made causes us to be happier when we have good attitudes and good relationships than when the reverse is true. But secondly, and this is the clincher, Christ by means of His Holy Spirit is going to help us. Of course He is! It would be madness to believe we could accomplish this type of living all on our own. It's, therefore, helpful to recall the previously described benefits of being yoked with Christ and the D. L. Moody quote, *"You might as well try to hear without ears or breathe without lungs, as to try to live a Christian life without the Spirit of God in your heart."* [214]

The Holy Spirit thus helps, encourages, and enables believers to live out the ethical and moral consequences of their faith so that His spiritual fruit is clearly evident - as previously, love, joy, peace, patience,

---

[214] D L. Moody, https://www.azquotes.com/quote/581700

kindness, goodness, faithfulness, gentleness and self-control. (Galatians 5:22-23a)

A desire to be more like Jesus Christ should, therefore, be right at the forefront of Christians' prayer lives. Non-believers, quite understandably, need to see something genuine; as I am sure they would if Western believers began to take the *Law* of Christ more seriously.

I wish I could say more about all of this, but decades of living much of the time as an *Adrenalin-filled Christian* have clearly held me back. One day I'm going to catch up!

Shortcomings with regard to the New Covenant do, nevertheless, still require repentance, with the huge difference now being the direct access to God through Jesus Christ as a perfect and permanent High Priest– that is forgiveness for sins can be received solely through personal prayer and genuine confession, with no need of sacrificial offerings and other religious procedures. These acts of necessary repentance are not, however, representing new justifications, but are rather renewed applications of an individual's previous *once-and-for-all* justification, so that intimacy with the Holy Spirit and the peace of God are maintained.

So now there is a new ball game whereby, instead of the motivation behind the Mosaic Covenant which could be expressed as, *"Do, in order to be favoured/blessed",* the New Covenant declares, *"You have been and are being favoured/blessed, therefore do."* This is wonderfully illustrated in the letter to the Hebrews where it says, *"Let us then approach the throne of grace with confidence, so that we may receive mercy and find grace to help us in our time of need."* (Hebrews 4:16)

How then did the Jewish people of the time, and particularly the leaders, cope with the loss of their Temple, their land, and their theocracy? Well, the fact that it became literally impossible for the Jewish community to fulfil all of the Law's commandments led to the importance of the Oral Torah being emphasised still further and written down in the *Mishnah* by the various leading rabbis (completed in about AD 200). This work, which comprises six tractates or volumes, elaborates upon the Torah by, for example, stating that the commandment for doing no work on the Sabbath is relevant to 39 prohibited tasks which it then lists. It does not, however, give any reasons for the particular selection which, along with many other rabbinic discussions and decisions on numerous aspects of the Mishnah, are provided in a massive document called the *Gemara* (63 tractates and probably completed in the 5th century). The Mishnah and the Gemara together form a comprehensive and extremely lengthy compilation (above 6,200 pages) named the *Babylonian Talmud*, completed in about AD 500 and subsequently edited for perhaps a further 200 years. Although a second Talmud was developed in Jerusalem, most scholars consider this to be inferior and less reliable than the Babylonian.

Furthermore, to provide guidelines concerning how the principal Talmud should be interpreted when addressing an absolute plethora of individual and society-based life circumstances, there are numerous associated legal codes, the most important being the *Mishneh Torah* (Maimonides, AD 1182) and the *Shulchan Aruch* (Yosef Karo, AD 1563). All the foregoing sources and more, such as an ancient interpretative work known as the *Midrash* and contemporary expert advice provided by *Responsa*, together with the Torah combine to form *Halacha*, meaning *Jewish Law* or, maybe more literally, *to go* or *to walk*. It is hardly surprising that many of today's Jewish scholars and rabbis insist that knowing and properly understanding Halacha requires a complete life's work.

Staying with modern Judaism, it seems that many denominational variations are principally due to different perceptions concerning the relevance and validity of Halacha, and particularly the divinity and immutability of the huge body of literature based ultimately on the Oral Torah. This results in the largest denominations of *Orthodox*, *Conservative*, and *Reform* becoming progressively more liberal and individualistic, thereby ranging from very strict adherence to either ignoring or re-interpreting various teachings to fit in with a person's perspective of life and the way they think it should be lived. As has already been highlighted, the main objective here is to review and compare biblical Judaism with Christianity, and as Orthodox Judaism is closest to the former, the ensuing discussion concentrates on this persuasion.

Orthodox Judaism, however, still differs from biblical Judaism in two very important respects. Firstly, as we have seen, many of the 613 commandments cannot now be obeyed, with the most popular view being that only 270, or less than 50%, are practicable. Secondly, Orthodox Jews consider that virtually all literature ultimately sourced from the Oral Torah, principally the Talmud, is divinely inspired by God and cannot be changed or modified. This mind-set thus appears to be similar to that of the religious leaders contemporary to Christ who seem to have believed that, at the very least, God gave Moses methodological instructions for the future derivation of the Oral Torah from the Torah, so that the former's *divine inspiration* would be ensured and maintained.

Before considering this opinion, it is worth giving thought to how today's Orthodox Jews view their practise of meticulously keeping endless laws, rules and regulations, which, to an outsider, seems more likely to damage rather than improve relationships with both God and other human beings. And yet *The World's Religions* says this, *"....orthodox Jews observe them (laws) to the finest detail. They take delight in obeying the will of God and find in these practices a meaning and significance which is not apparent to the casual observer"* [215] and, *"Pious Jews seek to love their God with their whole being and that love is expressed in practical obedience to the teaching of God in everyday life..."* [216] However this is viewed, Christians must surely be humbled by the sheer commitment and dedication to God demonstrated by these most zealous disciples of Judaism.

---

[215] *The World's Religions, A Lion Handbook*. Lion Publishing plc, 1994, p.273.
[216] Ibid.

Returning now to the task in hand, and particularly how Jesus Christ viewed the Oral Torah. As has already been noted, His attitude was one of dissension; something that is demonstrated by this run-in with the religious leaders, as recorded in Mark's gospel, *"The Pharisees and some of the teachers of the law who had come from Jerusalem gathered around Jesus and saw some of His disciples eating food with hands that were 'unclean', that is, unwashed. (The Pharisees and all the Jews do not eat unless they give their hands a ceremonial washing, holding to the tradition of the elders. When they come from the market-place they do not eat unless they wash. And they observe many other traditions, such as the washing of cups, pitchers and kettles). So the Pharisees and teachers of the law asked Jesus, 'Why don't your disciples live according to the tradition of the elders instead of eating their food with unclean hands?"* He replied, *'Isaiah was right when he prophesied about you hypocrites; as it is written: 'These people honour me with their lips, but their hearts are far from me. They worship me in vain; their teachings are but rules taught by men. You have let go of the commands of God and are holding on to the traditions of men."* (Mark 7:1-7)

So a very unequivocal response; an opinion that is borne out by at least some of the contents of the Talmud.

These are two examples described by Jim Bishop, both of which relate to the Sabbath, *"A Jew can walk two thousand cubits from the place where he lives. This is about thirty-five hundred feet. However, if he has the foresight to place two meals at a point of thirty-five hundred feet from his home, the place of the meal is considered part of his abode and he may walk another thirty-five hundred feet."* [217] And, *"If a man falls asleep on a journey and is overtaken by the Sabbath, he may move two thousand cubits in any direction. But the sages say: Only four cubits"'* [218]

Bishop also refers to how the religious leaders responsible for interpreting the Law split ecclesiastical hairs and then split them again, with one result being that the laws for cleaning dishes, pots and kitchen

---

[217] Jim Bishop, *The Day Christ Died*. Greenwich House. 1984, p.39.
[218] Ibid.

utensils became so complicated and extensive that they required a whole volume when written up in the Mishnah. Finally, he notes, *"Children from the age of five were taught the rules of the Sabbath before they were taught to add or subtract. There were admonitions against tying or untying a knot, putting out a lamp, sewing two consecutive stitches, writing two letters of the alphabet, lighting a fire and so forth"* [219] (all part of the previously mentioned 39 Sabbath prohibitions). Thus while the Talmud, apparently the most popular and consistently referenced literature in modern Judaism, is undoubtedly rich in historical resource material, there seem to be insurmountable difficulties in establishing claims of *wholesale* divine inspiration and authority.

How then do today's Jewish people seek forgiveness for their sins, given that the priestly sacrificial system as a facilitator to the means of God's grace is no more and most do not recognise Christ's ministry as representing grace's culminating and crowning hallmark? The answer to this, given throughout rabbinic literature and probably dating back to the earliest versions of the Midrash in the $2^{nd}/3^{rd}$ century, is that benevolent deeds, praying, and reading the Torah are more virtuous than animal sacrifice; with the first of these being assumed to replace the sacrificial system when the Temple is not in operation. As per the OT/Tanakh, regular personal repentance is considered central to God's forgiveness, with numerous guides to this act, which additionally has the object of ethical self-transformation, again being found in the rabbinic writings.

Judaism also places specific emphasis on the need for repentance during *The Ten Days of Repentance* (The Aseret Yemay Teshuvah) from the New Year (Rosh Hashanah) to the *Day of Atonement* (Yom Kippur). Besides repentance and crying out to G-D (a name considered too holy to be written or spoken in full), many also fast during this period - traditionally throughout Yom Kippur (25 hrs) when no food or water, including that required for cleaning teeth, is permitted! Fasting is also appropriate at other times of the year, and it seems that the importance a Jewish

---

[219] Ibid.

person places on all of the above depends largely on the type of Judaism followed plus, presumably, the spiritual guidance of the Senior Rabbi at his or her synagogue.[220]

There seems to be no fixed position in modern Judaism when it comes to life beyond the grave, something presumably related to the fact that this religion commonly appears to place more emphasis on life in the here and now than the afterworld. This is very different from the Christian faith, with the NT, which emphasises both, referring to eternal life on numerous occasions - as would be expected if Jesus Christ did indeed come from heaven.

This is an extract from a conversation He had with a guy called Nicodemus, one of the apparently few religious leaders who was open-minded and seeking, *"I have spoken to you of earthly things and you do not believe; how then will you believe if I speak of heavenly things? No-one has ever gone into heaven except the one who came from heaven – the Son of Man. Just as Moses lifted up the snake in the desert, so the Son of Man must be lifted up* (talking about His forthcoming crucifixion), *that everyone who believes in Him may have eternal life."* (John 3:12-15, parenthesis mine)

This is then followed by His *mission statement*, as referred to previously, *"For God so loved the world that He gave His one and only Son, that whoever believes in Him shall not perish but have eternal life."* (John 3:16)

Despite the foregoing, the immortality of the soul, the resurrection of the dead and the world to come all feature prominently in Jewish tradition, and one therefore assumes that these subjects must be considered from time to time. Even the strictest Jews, however, seem to have no certainty of eternal salvation and simply hope that their lives will ultimately be acceptable to God. This is because these hopes are

---

[220] Some Israeli citizens today are Jews in name only, with certain cities such as Tel Aviv being almost entirely secular in composition. This observation is no doubt relevant to some of the Jewish population within today's UK.

based on personal merit (human works), related to being a *good person* and carrying out good deeds or commands known as *Mitzvah*; as per those listed within the Torah, Talmud and legal codes etc., including observance of the Sabbath and Jewish Holy days/festivals.

It is, therefore, hardly surprising that many consider it to be sheer arrogance for Christians to confidently believe that they are going to heaven. However, we do so only on the back of Jesus Christ's achievements on our behalf – that is His vicarious fulfilment of the Law's demand for lifelong perfect righteousness and complete payment (*Tetelestai*) for humanity's multitudinous violations, plus His consequent assurances. Any other basis would be both arrogant and preposterous.

All that said, it's very important to acknowledge the incredible, and indeed *miraculous*, achievement of the Jewish race in keeping their religion alive through almost 1,900 years of enforced exile and unbelievable hardships – that is survival through Crusade, Inquisition, Pogrom and Holocaust. Whatever the future holds, we can be sure, from the repeated affirmations of Scripture, that the Jewish nation's ultimate destiny, which will include the fulfilment of all the exclusive inheritance and terrestrial promises contained in the OT/Tanakh, is going to be glorious.[221]

Not even an outline description of Judaism can be complete without reference to the Passover meal, and how this is inseparably linked with the Last Supper of Jesus Christ. Both are associated with deliverance, the first commemorating the freeing of the Israelites from their captivity in Egypt and the second, the freeing of all people (upon their petition) from the captivity of sin and death. This interrelation thus mirrors other parts of Scripture, whereby a lesser or *shadowy* event in the OT points to a similar but greater and clearer event in the NT.

Although its purpose remains the same, the Passover meal has nevertheless experienced certain changes over its almost 3,500 year

---

[221] Christ's ministry has resulted in every Christian believer and the true Christian Church receiving all the spiritual blessings of the New Covenant, but not the inheritance or terrestrial blessings promised only to Israel.

history, and even today there are variations concerning how it is celebrated. These celebrations are full of different elements such as blessings, prayer, narration, singing, eating and drinking, all of which are unhurried and contribute to an occasion always rich in experience and symbolism. This chapter is, of course, hardly the forum to discuss all of this in detail, and thus my aim is simply to draw out some of the more salient features, particularly as they relate to the Christian faith.

What then is the meaning of the word *Passover*? Well, basically, to *pass over*! Moses had been involved in an almighty struggle concerning his mission to get the Israelites out of Egypt, the repeated stubbornness of Pharaoh and his administrators causing God to subject the Egyptians to nine plagues of increasing severity. Even so, none of these had succeeded in achieving any more than limited, and soon rescinded, concessions for the Israelites. There was consequently to be a final and worst plague, whereby all first-born sons were to be killed - very drastic I know, but severe measures for brutal times - and the Egyptians could hardly say that they had not been warned.

To avoid this outcome, the Israelites (and quite possibly some Egyptian and other 'believers' who had heeded the previous warnings) were to take physically perfect male (Passover or *Paschal*) lambs, kill them without breaking any bones, and smear the blood on each family's doorframe; a symbol of protection, meaning that God would *pass over* their houses and no harm would come to any of the inhabitants, including first-born sons. Each lamb was then to be roasted and completely eaten on that night, together with unleavened bread and bitter herbs.

So that they never forgot this amazing deliverance, comprising approximately 600,000 men plus women, children and animals, out of Egypt, God commanded that the event be regularly and permanently celebrated by a meal comprising similar constituents to the above. The lamb would remind them that God had passed over their homes; the unleavened bread, which would continue to be eaten for the following 6 to 7 days, of His deliverance and its urgency (also indicated an absence of sin); and the bitter herbs, of the bitterness of their slavery under the Egyptians.

Of the many features linking the Passover Meal with the Last Supper, the most poignant is that Christ's crucifixion likely coincided with the sacrificing of the Paschal lambs. Indeed, given the small size of the ancient city of Jerusalem, these events may well have taken place within earshot of each other.

The drinking of four cups of wine, based on the *I will* promises God gave to Moses in Exodus 6:6-7, are understood to have always been part of the Passover meal and are taken in the following prescribed order:

- The Cup of Sanctification – *"I will bring you out from under the yoke of the Egyptians."*

- The Cup of Praise - *"I will free you from being their slaves."*

- The Cup of Redemption – *"I will redeem you and take you back as my rightful possession."*

- The Cup of Acceptance – *"I will take you as my own people, and I will be your God."*

All of these promises have their counterparts in, and can even be said to define, the Christian life – that is we are set apart to be a light of hope for God (sanctification); we have been set free from sin to serve the living God (praise); we have been redeemed by the blood of the Lamb (redemption); we have been accepted by God through the saving work of His son (acceptance).

It is a particularly touching feature that in many contemporary Passover meals drops of red wine are allowed to carefully fall from the cups to express the Jewish people's sadness over the sufferings that the ten plagues caused to the ancient Egyptians.

Luke's gospel, in describing the Last Supper, records the following episode, *"And He* (Jesus) *took bread* (*matzah* - unleavened bread), *gave thanks and broke it, and gave it to them* (his disciples), *saying, 'This is my body given for you; do this in remembrance of me'* (until He comes again). *In the same way, after the supper He took the cup, saying, 'This cup is the new covenant in my blood, which is poured out for you.'"* (Luke 22:19-20, parentheses mine)

It seems probable that this cup was the third, and thus associated with redemption. However, of much greater significance in the overall scheme of things were the truly shocking claims that the unleavened bread represented Jesus' destroyed physical body (smashed almost to obliteration, but involving no broken bones) and the cup of wine, His shed blood - both of which were to shortly usher in the New Covenant.

So Christ is here deliberately identifying Himself as the true Passover/Paschal lamb, given up for the sins of the world and the actual being to whom all the innumerable sacrificed lambs pointed, *"he was led like a lamb to the slaughter"* (Isaiah 53:7 prophecy) and *"For Christ, our Passover lamb, has been sacrificed."* (1 Corinthians 5:7b)

Furthermore, the requirement that the 'perfect' sacrificial lambs were to be killed without breaking any bones is again consistent with the crucifixion of Jesus Christ, the ultimate perfect sacrificial lamb. As previously described, although the legs of the thieves on either side of Christ were indeed broken, the fact that He had already died rendered this operation unnecessary.

Today's Passover meals are ceremonial ritual services and dinners celebrated in (mainly) Jewish homes for the first night or first two nights of Passover. However, two of the items on the customary *Seder Plate* did not form part of the ancient Passover celebrations. The first of these, called *zeroa*, is a roasted lamb shank bone (no edible meat), included as a reminder of the Paschal lamb sacrifices made during the period of the Temple. The second addition is known as the *afikomen*, a Greek word that scholars often take to mean *that which comes after*, although there are other slightly different interpretations such as *the coming one*.

In many of today's Jewish celebrations, three pieces of matzah (wafer-like in appearance and taste) are placed in a special bag, known as the *matzah tosh* and containing three compartments. The piece from the middle compartment is then removed and broken in two, with one portion being returned to the bag and the other, which becomes the afikomen, being wrapped in a cloth and hidden for others, normally children, to find. There is usually joy when the afikomen is found, with the successful child sometimes being given a small reward. The afikomen, split into small pieces according to the numbers present, is then eaten for *dessert* (consistent with the *that which comes after* interpretation).

Although the afikomen has been a part of Passover celebrations going back many centuries within Jewish communities, there seems to be no related meaningful symbolism - the most common theory perhaps being that the prospect of the afikomen search keeps the children awake throughout the service. There is, however, what appears to be a perfectly good symbolic explanation provided by Christianity: The middle wafer represents Jesus Christ's position within the *Father, Son, and Holy Spirit* Trinity; the fact that the afikomen is unleavened bread represents the leaven-free perfect life of Christ; the fact that it is a broken piece represents His broken body on the cross; the fact that it is wrapped in a cloth and hidden represents Christ's burial, His dead body also being wrapped up; finally, the fact that it is found and brought out into the light represents Christ's resurrection.

That, therefore, completes these brief investigations into Eastern spirituality, Islam, and Judaism; something I have never done before, and which leaves me with two specific words buzzing around my head – shock and surreal. Dealing first with shock; although I have known for decades that Jesus Christ belongs in a different category to religions and worldviews, I had previously not fully appreciated the truly immense intervening gulf.

This exists because, firstly, Christ is not some religious teacher or guru reaching out for divine enlightenment, but God Himself, reaching in with voluntary and deliberate self-disclosure and revelation. Secondly, He is not some impersonal ordering structure behind the universe with which we must align ourselves by doing such and such so that we can become such and such, but rather a person – the *God-man*, totally committed to qualifying us for heaven and eternal life. Finally, although His objective is always that our lives become more and more like His, He is not some rule book simply telling us to get on with it. On the contrary, He is the agape-loving Son of God who, through His Holy Spirit, can transform and empower us in a reciprocal arrangement as we live through Him and He lives through us.

Alternatively, with a bit more scholarly weight behind it, the American philosopher and theologian, Kenneth Samples, says this, *"Of all the world's religions, only Christianity proclaims that God became embodied as a human being. Of all the founders of the great religious traditions, only Jesus Christ claims to be God. Only the historic Christian Faith proclaims that to encounter Jesus Christ is to directly and personally encounter God Himself. Indeed, at the very heart of historic Christianity is a truly astounding - one might say 'dangerous' - truth claim. This central article of the Christian faith is the incarnation: 'God became man in Jesus of Nazareth.' This truth is a distinctive feature of the Christian Faith, for it is unique to Christianity to discover a God who not only takes the initiative in becoming flesh but also does so in order to redeem sinful human beings."* [222] Just notice the proactivity of God!

Also from Samples, *"Jesus' credentials as the divine Messiah are indeed formidable – matchless personal character, incalculable influence upon history, fulfilment of prophecy, power to perform miracles, extraordinary wisdom, bodily resurrection and so forth. Alternatives that deny His true deity offer no adequate explanation for these credentials."* [223]

A final summary quotation from Erwin W. Lutzer, a Canadian-born Christian pastor, teacher and author, *"The divinity of Christ sharply divides Christianity from all of the other religions of the world. This is the*

---

[222] Kenneth Samples, *7 Truths That Changed the World: Discovering Christianity's Most Dangerous Ideas.* Grand Rapids, MI, 2012, p.61.
[223] Kenneth Samples, *Without a Doubt: Answering the 20 Toughest Faith Questions.* Grand Rapids, MI, 2004, p.118.

great divide, the unbridgeable chasm, a gulf that extends from here to eternity." [224]

It is, of course, recognised that some religions, such as Islam, find it offensive and even blasphemous for the image of the invisible God to be born in the same way as every other human child - a truly humiliating descent to the level where all of humanity, with its many frailties and weaknesses, abides. I believe that previous discussions have already, either directly or indirectly, covered this aspect, and so will simply reply with yet another quote from C.S. Lewis, *"The Son of God became a man to enable men to become sons of God."* [225]

Before leaving this subject, a slight digression appears warranted. This concerns the fact that genuine Christian faith and Jesus Christ in particular could not be described as 'religious' in any conventional sense of this word. For example, in a culture that lived by its multitudinous religious laws and rules, Jesus, as we have seen, was interested only in the prevailing underlying spirit, which He wonderfully summarised and exemplified as unconditional love for both God and our fellow human beings.

He also wasn't big on religious dietary codes, emphasising that it was not what went into the mouth but rather the words that came out of it that were important. (Mark 7: 19-23)

And, as might be expected, it's not possible to say that Christ was big on religious buildings.[226] In seemingly the only reference to this in Scripture,

---

[224] Erwin W. Lutzer, *Christ Among Other Gods*. Chicago IL: Moody Press, 1994, p.103.

[225] C.S. Lewis, *Mere Christianity*. Fontana, 1977. Goodreads. https://www.goodreads.com/quotes/754464-the-son-of-god-became-a-man-to-enable-men

[226] Christ did not say that having religious buildings was actually wrong. Many of the amazing cathedrals and other outstanding related structures, with their incredible artwork and sculptures, would undoubtedly have been built to the glory of God and are thus clearly praiseworthy. It, therefore, seems to be a question of relative importance and, perhaps most significantly given our human nature, avoiding the possibility that the focus of men and women could be transferred away from the uncreated God onto created artefacts.

His disciples, all of whom appeared to be completely gob-smacked, are recorded as drawing His attention to the amazing Jerusalem Temple. His reply, which probably wouldn't have gone down too well in Westminster Abbey, was simply, *"Do you see all these things? I tell you the truth, not one stone here will be left on another; every one will be thrown down."* (Matthew 24:2)

This prophecy, as noted on previous occasions, refers to the destruction of the Temple by the Romans in AD 70; Josephus, consistent with comparatively recent archaeological finds, recording that some stones were up to 11m long by 3.5m high by 5.5m wide – approx. 500 English tons each! So rather than talking about religious buildings, Jesus Christ's clear emphases were, firstly, on Himself as the New Temple and, secondly, the interrelated kingdom of God, exemplified by the presence of His power and authority - His *reign* - experienced primarily within and through human beings.

Above all else, He wasn't big on Himself, having no need of ornamental robes or similar, and saying that true greatness derived from servanthood - in Matthew's gospel, as referred to previously, *"...just as the Son of Man did not come to be served, but to serve, and to give His life as a ransom for many."* (Matthew 20:28) Finally, as a resurrected being, Christ could hardly be big on shrines.

So why is all of this so surreal? Well, on the one hand, there is an amazing triune, infinite, and agape-loving God who not only wishes to help us with this life but, incredibly, has also done everything necessary for us to experience a fulfilled and wonderful eternal life; while on the other, there are the citizens of UK 2020 who, in the main, don't want to know anything about it. Surely the biblical affirmation that those who follow Christ will, upon death, receive a rich welcome into His eternal kingdom has got to be way up on winning the lottery!

The fact is that most people in the UK, and presumably other Western societies, seem to begin from a position of cynicism, even sometimes placing an individual who's found God in the same bracket as a person who's been taken in by some ridiculous scam and completely crashed their life– it's really quite nuts. However, many Christians, including me, have held similar views at one time or another and I've little doubt that if I hadn't (eventually) responded to God's overtures, I would have remained one of the worst antagonists. And this recognition doesn't necessarily have to result in a dilution of the gospel message, but should instead lead to expressed passions being matched by equal measures of humility.

I have already discussed several potential and probable reasons behind much of this general apathy and animosity (in the West), and have no wish to talk it all to death by repeating them. Suffice it to say just two things. Firstly, God, because He is love, is continually speaking to those who do not yet know Him, the distinctive internal *voice* of His Holy Spirit penetrating right down into their inner souls. My hope for them is that they will respond positively to this voice. Then, as per this quote from Billy Graham, *"The Holy Spirit illuminates the minds of people, makes us yearn for God, and takes spiritual truth and makes it understandable to us."* [227]

Secondly, and this particularly applies to Christians - we must not take for granted the incredible blessings and benefits won for humanity by Jesus Christ, but rather come to God with a sense of urgency as we pray for Him to change the spiritual atmosphere of the UK and Western society in general. He has certainly done this before and is indeed doing it right now in various countries around the world.

I suppose this next question, which almost everybody asks, cannot be put off any longer. "What happens to those people who do not come to Christ asking forgiveness for their sins and making Him the Lord of their lives?" I guess the easiest answer is to say "I simply don't know for certain." The thing is that, although Christians have been commissioned to tell everyone the great news of Christ's gospel and are well aware of various accompanying severe warnings if it is ignored, we have definitely

---

[227] Billy Graham, *Daily Devotion*. 27-09-20. https://billygraham.org/devotion/the-holy-spirit/

not been given the role of ticket-masters concerning who will and won't be in heaven. For one thing, who knows the exact condition of a person's heart and what happens between them and God at the point of death?

Perhaps the most helpful practice when it comes to dealing with questions such as this is to check whether an attempted answer is not only unworthy of God, whose perfect nature we see unveiled in Jesus Christ, but is also unworthy of your average, far from perfect, human being. If it's the latter, then something is being misunderstood. God's judgments must always be consistent with His perfect character and are therefore, as noted previously, based on what people know rather than on what they don't. This is evident throughout Scripture, as demonstrated by the following couple of examples:

From the OT prophet, Ezekiel, *"Yet O house of Israel, you say, 'The way of the Lord is not just'. But I will judge each of you according to his own ways'."* (Ezekiel 33:20)

And from Jesus' Sermon on Mount, *"Do not judge, or you too will be judged. For in the same way as you judge others, you will be judged, and with the measure you use, it will be measured to you."* (Matthew 7:1-2) Can any of us claim that we're in the clear when it comes to not judging and looking down at others, both in thought and word? We may even be guilty of judging other people judging other people!

Staying with the perfect, absolutely fair, and completely unbiased character of God, let's firstly consider the eternal destinies of OT 'heroes' such as Abraham and Moses, both of whom surely had little, if any, specific knowledge concerning the far greater scope and capability of the New Covenant compared with the covenants under which they lived. Thus, taking it as read that it all turned out well for these guys, we are inevitably left with the realisation that the full significance of the ministry of Jesus Christ must be, and must always have been, utterly monumental, extending way beyond the confines of the NT and both forwards and backwards in our experience of time; including, amongst other major accomplishments, the underwriting of the preceding OT sacrificial system. It is, of course, difficult to know exactly how God views this entity, although my take on this is that while He undoubtedly operates within a precise time-frame when dealing with human beings, time itself is ultimately within Him.

In any event, as the New Covenant was promised before the beginning of time, it seems reasonable to assume that the cross of Christ has always been the bridge spanning the chasm between God and humankind – a solution originating solely from His side. And so just as it's possible to drive across a bridge at night without realising the existence of this structure and a great chasm below, it also appears feasible for Abraham, Moses and other OT Israelites to have benefitted from the cross of Christ, the efficacy of which should never be underestimated, without knowing of its presence.

Can we then go even further and propose that the cross of Christ does, and has, benefit(ted) people who have no knowledge of its existence and indeed may also be/have been unaware of the Bible itself? My guess, and it is only a guess, is that the answer is 'yes', particularly when individuals are wholeheartedly seeking God in accordance with the knowledge available to them – that is, as previously, the visible creation and their consciences, piqued by His universal inner voice.

Things appear to become slightly clearer when we move on to those who hear but then reject the message of Christ. This is because it seems reasonable to assume that the people belonging to this group will possess, or at least have had the opportunity to possess, a rudimentary grasp of the principal gospel truths. However, it's surely not possible to go beyond this very preliminary observation, with Christians, and perhaps particularly their leaders, needing to tread very carefully given the type of people on the receiving end of Christ's severest criticisms.

More specifically, although Jesus Christ quite regularly warned of 'hell', most of these utterances were addressed to the Jewish religious leaders; men who probably knew the OT/Tanakh inside out and were certain of their own *holiness/goodness* before both God and others. Many of these guys were accordingly described by Jesus as proud, judgmental [228] and hypocritical, individuals whom He likened to whitewashed tombs – looking beautiful on the outside, but full of dead and rotting bodies on the inside. Indeed, their punishment, unless they repented, would be more severe than others with less understanding.

So what is hell? Well, we're not told a whole lot about it, but it's clear that it represents something awful that God desperately desires to protect us all from – hence the extremity of Jesus' rescue mission. The most well-known description is called ECT (eternal, conscious torment), and indeed many Christians around the world believe that this is the only legitimate explanation. Others, however, such as Forster and Marsdon in their masterful two-volume work, *God's Strategy in Human History*, [229] consider that 'annihilation', 'obliteration' or 'to perish' are equally valid interpretations when it comes to scholarly exegesis. They subsequently go on to argue that eternal punishment will not be 'punishment that goes on forever', but *punishment that has eternal consequences*, and draw attention to the fact that the idea of hell being eternal torment was not well known until it was taught by Augustine of Hippo in the 4th/5th century AD. This view then completely dominated the medieval period, being vividly portrayed by Dante's *Inferno*.

Along with Forster and Marsdon, and other biblical scholars such as John Stott and John Wenham, I cannot personally accept that infinite punishment for finite sins is worthy of the character of God as revealed in Scripture. So, for me, annihilation is the most likely outcome for those who die *outside of Christ*. He who gives life in the first place clearly has the authority for its removal. But given a choice, do any of us really want this!? As discussed before, eternity is built into our spiritual DNA, with the thought of death followed by total and utter oblivion being both

---

[228] '*Judgmentalism*' carries with it the sense of being better than, and looking down upon, someone else. To refrain from 'judging' a person's character when, say, an important legitimate decision needs to be made would, of course, be naïve.

[229] Roger Forster & Paul Marston, *God's Strategy in Human History, Vols. 1& 2*. PUSH Publishing, 2013.

foreign and quite terrifying to most; something that we seem to intuitively realise represents a horrendous and unnecessary departure from our intended ultimate destiny.

I think we can reasonably conclude that the whole subject of hell is hardly straightforward, especially when we add into the mix the fact that some will be judged more severely than others and that there will also be judgments concerning whole nations. What can be said though is that hell will undoubtedly represent a future without God, whose judgments will be completely just and impartial. And maybe therein lies the clue to our destiny. C. S. Lewis once wrote, *"There are only two kinds of people in the end: those who say to God, 'Thy will be done', and those to whom God says, in the end, 'Thy will be done'. All that are in hell, choose it...."* [230]

Or to quote his predecessor, the Scottish minister and author, George MacDonald (1824-1905), *"the one principle of hell is - I am my own."*[231] So whatever hell is in actuality, it undoubtedly represents a monumental and unspeakable loss, because every good and positive thing we experience in our present life here on Earth has its ultimate source in the riches of God. The thought of choosing ourselves over Him is overwhelmingly terrifying; we simply must put our trust in Jesus Christ.

In closing, what about the fact that some people consider it to be unreasonable that entrance into God's heaven depends entirely on His grace, and that it would be more fair-minded to base all judgments on the quality of our individual lives so that we could *pay our own way* (that is *salvation by works*)? This, however, assumes that we are all *good* and not that far off from being acceptable as we stand; something I have made considerable efforts to demonstrate is simply not the case (the *light bulbs picture* in chapter five may be particularly relevant).

---

[230] C.S. Lewis, *The Complete C. S. Lewis Signature Classics.* Harper, San Francisco, 2002, p.340.
[231] George MacDonald, *C. S. Lewis Anthology*, 2012. https://www.goodreads.com/.../1164554-the-one- principle-of-hell-is-i-am-my-own

Furthermore, on this basis, our present lives on Earth could well turn out to be an endless series of trying to do good stuff, in conjunction with repeated examination and introspection, as we desperately attempted to achieve some mythical pass mark. This would evidently not be a good approach for naturally competitive people like me, who would forever be comparing themselves with their perceptions of how others were doing. All our efforts might, therefore, easily result in *external shows* and the same ugly traits exhibited by many of the religious leaders of Jesus' time – no internal work, no God-assisted sanctification. As noted earlier, our future destinies are *about our own wills and related decisions rather than having to achieve certain standards, transformations or enlightenments* – thank God!

Finally, we are again not told much about the nature of heaven. However, just for starters, it seems clear that this will be a place where our inbuilt and most intense longings, which frequently come up short when faced with the realities of this present world, will be completely and wonderfully fulfilled.

APPENDIX

Accuracy of the Biblical Record – Further Appraisal

I can still remember, during the early months of my civil engineering degree course, getting so fatigued and cheesed off from countless pages of hand-written structural analysis that, instead of producing the *crowning glory* detailing drawing, I photocopied a typical illustration from a textbook and sellotaped it in (none of your namby-pamby scanners and word-processors back then). Needless to say, it was not well received - I seem to recall the red-inked comment, *Is this it?* And the reason for sharing this specific and sensitive experience?

The thing is that biblical appraisal is such a vast subject that it requires the *sellotaping in* of various scholarly tomes to do it justice – hardly practicable, and even hardlier (my word) likely to be read. It is, therefore, necessary to undertake the difficult task of restricting this appendix to fairly brief discussions concerning those points that might generally be considered as the most important and relevant. As such, the chosen contents extend and build upon the information contained in the first part of chapter four.

When it comes to the Bible (and other ancient literature), the most important measure concerning authenticity and accuracy is known as the *Bibliographical Test*; relating to the age of the earliest extant (surviving) manuscript (MS), the total number of extant manuscripts (MSS – ranging from fragments of text up to virtually complete documents), and the approximate dating of the original writings (*autographs*). This information can also be supplemented and corroborated by various secondary sources such as archaeological finds, historical writings relating to Josephus, Tacitus and others, and rabbinic discussions as recorded in the Talmud.

Indeed Josephus, whose very considerable works can barely be touched on in a book of this nature, is regarded as one of the great historians of ancient times with Josh & Sean McDowell, in their 2017 updated edition of *Evidence That Demands A Verdict,* stating, *"He makes many statements that verify, either generally or in specific detail, the historical nature of both the Old and New Testaments of the Bible."* [232] Similarly, Tacitus is regarded as a great historian and certainly the greatest from Rome.

Archaeology in NT terms relates to Palestine and the governing Roman Empire, with the Ancient Near East (ANE) being relevant to the OT. ANE archaeology has a wide and generalised application, which can be broken down into the following broad and loosely defined sub-divisions: Egyptology (Egypt and parts of modern-day Sudan), Assyriology (Mesopotamia – Fertile Crescent encompassing the Tigris and Euphrates rivers in Western Asia), and Levantine (Palestine or Syro-Palestine).

As might be expected from the fact that almost all would have been written on a perishable material called papyrus (source of the English word, paper), there are no extant autographs for any biblical texts or indeed for those relating to ancient literature in general, such as Roma–Greek classical authors. There are, nevertheless, certain available *tools* for estimating the dates of autographs, some of those particularly relevant to the NT being as follows:

- ❖ The inclusion or omission of certain events contained within the available written copies of the specific document under consideration, and the nature of the associated descriptions. For example, the letter to the Hebrews makes regular references to the Jerusalem Temple and its normal functions, which presumably places it before the destruction of this building by the Romans in AD 70.

---

[232] Josh McDowell & Sean McDowell, *Evidence That Demands A Verdict.* Authentic Media Ltd., 2017, p.84.

- ❖ Language nuances or similar, plus male names and their frequency in copies of the autograph, compared with those within the general society of a given culture and period.
- ❖ The witness of the letters of the early church fathers – for instance, Irenaeus writing in the 2nd century AD, revealed that *"Matthew composed his gospel 'while Peter and Paul were preaching the Gospel and founding the church in Rome',"* [233] seemingly dating it to the early or mid-60s (although it could have been a little later).
- ❖ Existing and ongoing archaeological finds.

The following dates, based on the above and other accepted methods, are considered to represent reasonable estimates for a selected 19 autographs of the 27 NT books:

TABLE 2: APPROXIMATE DATES OF NEW TESTAMENT BOOKS (Autographs)	
Matthew	Early AD 60s to 80
Mark	Late AD 50s to late 60s
Luke	AD 65 to 85
John	AD 80 to 100
The Acts	AD 65 to 85
Paul's Letters (13No.)	AD 50s
Hebrews	pre-AD 70

All these autographs are very early and would undoubtedly have been known about, along with the *Oral Tradition* (subsequently described in connection with the OT), and in general circulation during the lifetimes of many of the eyewitnesses to the ministry of Jesus Christ (traditionally AD 30 to 33, although some scholars place it some four years earlier). This dissemination would additionally have reached those opposed to Christ's mission, who could have disputed anything that they considered to be incorrect. These very limited time intervals are, therefore, much too short for the development of legendary material.

---

[233] Irenaeus, *Against Heresies, III. I.I.* (2nd century AD). Cited by Josh McDowell & Sean McDowell, *Evidence That Demands A Verdict.* Authentic Media Ltd., 2017, p.43.

As a confirmatory example of this, it is now 54 years since England's one and only World Cup victory. I was coming up to my 13th birthday, and can still remember so much stuff - the disappointing 0-0 opening match draw against Uruguay; Bobby Charlton's two goals in the next match with Mexico; Argentina's captain, Rattin, being sent off in the quarter-final; Lev Yashin, the greatest goalkeeper in the world at the time, making a schoolboy error in the   semi-final against West Germany; even the name of a little North Korean player (*Pak do ik*) who scored the goal that put Italy out at the group stage; and of course the final itself plus countless other memories. Try telling me or my mates (BC nearly died from stress) that England didn't win the World Cup in 1966! I wonder, can any of us live long enough to see them do it again?

The following three tables, all adapted from the 2017 edition of *Evidence That Demands A Verdict*, summarise much of the principal data pertinent to the bibliographical test, thus enabling direct comparisons to be made between the NT writings and other ancient literature.

TABLE 3: CHRISTIAN NT MANUSCRIPTS (MSS)		
Language	Earliest MS	Number of MSS
Greek (original language)	AD 130 (or slightly earlier)	**5,856**
Armenian	AD 862	**2,000+**
Coptic	Late 3rd Century AD	975
Gothic	5th or 6th Century AD	6
Ethiopian	6th Century AD	600+
Old Latin Latin Vulgate	4th Century AD 4th Century AD	110 10,000+
Syriac	Late 4th/Early 5th Century AD	350+
Georgian	5th Century AD	89
Slavic	10th Century AD	4,000+
Total Non-Greek Manuscripts		**18,130+**

Note 1: The numerous copies in various languages demonstrate that, from the beginning, Christianity has always had a *missionary existence*.

Note 2: Categorisation of ancient documents is a comparatively recent discipline, and has not yet even nearly covered all those biblical manuscripts discovered so far. Because of this, figures are continually changing.

Note 3: The National Geographic magazine (December 2018 Edition) [234] confirms the present number of Greek manuscripts (5,500+) and records that about 125 date back to the 2nd or 3rd centuries AD, with the majority of the remainder ranging between the 9th and 16th centuries. The earliest copies of virtually complete NT manuscripts are the Codex Vaticanus (AD 300 to 325) and the Codex Sinaiticus (AD 330 to 360); 'Codex' (plural 'codices') meaning book-form, as opposed to the earlier rolled up scrolls.

---

[234] National Geographic, *National Geographic Magazine*. December 2018 Edition, p.74.

TABLE 4: MANUSCRIPTS (MSS) OF SELECTED MAJOR CLASSICAL WORKS			
Work	Date of Autograph (approx.)	Earliest MS	Number of MSS
Caesar's Gallic Wars	58 to 52 BC	9th Century AD	251
Tacitus's Annals – 1st half	AD 110 to 120	AD 850	36
Herodotus – 'The Histories'	440 BC	150 to 50 BC	106
Homer's Iliad	8th Century BC	415 BC	1900+
Plato's Tetralogies	375 BC	9th Century AD (apart from a few 2nd/3rd Century BC frags.)	238
Pliny the Elder's Natural History	AD 50 to 79	5th Century AD (1No. fragment)	200+
Total Manuscripts			**2731+**

Note 1: In addition to the above, the most reliable information concerning Alexander the Great (356 to 323BC) is considered to come from the Greek historian, Arrian, writing some 400 years later; although he may have had access to subsequently lost original sources.

Note 2: As per the NT, further categorisation of manuscripts is continuing.

TABLE 5 - NT SCRIPTURE CITATIONS FROM SELECTED EARLY CHURCH FATHERS						
Writer	Gospels	Acts	Apostle Paul's letters	General letters	Revelation	Totals
Justin Martyr	268	10	43	6	3 (266 allusions)	330
Irenaeus	1,038	194	499	23	65	1,819
Clement (Alex.)	1,107	44	1,127	207	11	2,496
Origen	9,231	349	7,778	399	165	17,922
Tertullian	3,822	502	2,609	120	205	7,258
Hippolytus	734	42	387	27	188	1,378
Eusebius	3,268	211	1592	88	27	5,186
Grand Totals	19,468	1,352	14,035	870	664	36,389

Note: All these 'patristic' quotations relate to the period ending at approximately AD 325, and it is generally agreed that if all NT texts were destroyed, they would be sufficient on their own to enable a virtually complete reconstruction.

Although the information contained in these tables may well seem to be as 'dry as dust' to some, they nevertheless clearly demonstrate the very significant supremacy of the NT documents over ancient classical works. NT scholar J. Harold Greenlee says the following, *"Since scholars accept as generally trustworthy the writings of the ancient classics even though the earliest MSS were written so long after the original writings* and the number of extant MSS is in many instances so small, it is clear that the reliability of the text of the N.T. is likewise assured." [235]

This opinion is backed up by Bible scholar Dr W. Edward Glenny, *"No one questions the authenticity of the historical books of antiquity because we do not possess the original copies. Yet we have far fewer manuscripts of these works than we possess of the NT."* [236]

And from Daniel Baird Wallace, a professor of New Testament studies, *"If we have doubts about what the autographic NT said, those doubts would have to be multiplied a hundredfold for the average classical author."* [237]

This final quotation is from F.F. Bruce, a renowned former Professor of Biblical Criticism and Exegesis at the University of Manchester, *"The evidence for our New Testament writings is ever so much greater than the evidence for many writings of classical authors, the authenticity of which no one dreams of questioning. And if the New Testament were a question of secular writings their authenticity would generally be regarded as beyond any doubt."* [238]

F.F. Bruce thus considers the supernatural content of the NT to be the main reason for some scholars giving preference to the comparatively sparse bibliographical evidence associated with the ancient classical writings. And whereas all those named in Table 4 are, to say the least, long-since dead, Jesus Christ is not. Sadly, the perception of so many, whether recognised or not, is that Christ represents some kind of threat to their wellbeing whereas, in truth, He offers exactly what all our innermost souls desire and crave the most.

---

[235] J. Harold Greenlee, *Introduction To New Testament Textual Criticism*. Grand Rapids, MI: Eerdmans, 1977, p.16.

[236] W. Edward Glenny, The Preservation of Scripture, in the Bible Version Debate. Minneapolis: Central Baptist Theological Seminary, 1977, p.96.

[237] Daniel Baird Wallace, *Revisiting the Corruption of the New Testament*. Grand Rapids, MI: Kregel, 2011, p.29.

[238] F.F. Bruce, *The New Testament Documents: Are They Reliable?* Inter-Varsity Fellowship, 1949, p.15.

The McDowells' comment on the bibliographical test as follows, *"For any particular work or collection of works, the greater the number and the earlier the dating of the manuscripts, the easier it is to reconstruct a text closer to the original and identify errors or discrepancies in subsequent copies. The importance of the sheer number of manuscripts and early patristic quotations of Scripture cannot be overstated."* [239] It is, therefore, hardly surprising that, as referred to previously, the accuracy of the NT is generally considered to be approximately 99 to 99.5%.

This is a fairly typical example, from the *NIV Study Bible,* of the rare required caveats for the 0.5 to 1% inaccurate or uncertain texts. *"Serious doubt exists as to whether the last 12 verses (Ch. 16: 9-20) belong to the Gospel of Mark. They are absent from important early manuscripts and display certain peculiarities of vocabulary, style and theological content that are unlike the rest of Mark. His Gospel probably ended at 16:8, or its original ending has been lost"* - In summary, they're on it!

The information obtained from archaeological discoveries to date, as touched on in chapter four, is also very strong with approximately forty major finds that corroborate the NT record.

The transmission of the OT Scriptures has been a rather more complicated affair, with many different contributory strands. So that these may be best appraised, the chosen approach is to describe the most relevant strands utilising three distinct and consecutive periods - working in reverse sequence. The first of these extends from the 1st century AD to the present time, with the Masoretic Text being deemed to be the most important, followed by the Septuagint, Dead Sea Scrolls and Samaritan Pentateuch. At the outset, it should be recognised that the copying of Scripture by ancient scribes seems to have almost always been accompanied by reverence, or even awe, for the text and an absolute obsession for accuracy.

---

[239] Josh McDowell & Sean McDowell, *Evidence That Demands A Verdict.* Authentic Media Ltd., 2017, pp. 46-47.

Quoting from the McDowells', *"Various rabbinic rules regarding transmission procedures such as the selection of writing materials, preparation of leather, error correction, transcribing of divine names, storage and reading of scrolls, and measurements of sheets, columns and margins all point to the reverence with which rabbinic scribes approached the biblical text. This reverence for Scripture was so highly regarded that it even precluded other aspects of the scribes' religious life."* [240]

In addition to this, there were usually very stringent *external tests*, such as the counting of all the newly written letters, words and paragraphs, with the document becoming invalid if two letters touched each other. The middle letter, word and paragraph of the entire new document were subsequently checked to ensure an exact copy of the original manuscript (the *Vorlage*).

The Masoretic Text (MT), from which most English translations of the OT are principally derived, is considered to date from about the 8th century AD until the end of the 11th century, with the earliest extant copies being written in the $9^{th}/10^{th}$ centuries. It is, however, understood that there were *pre-Masoretic* or *proto-Masoretic* texts going back to the 1st century AD although, regrettably, no associated manuscripts have been found to date. Virtually all the Masoretic text is written in Hebrew, the only exceptions being the books of Daniel, Ezra and Jeremiah, which contain portions of Aramaic, a similar Semitic language prominent in the Assyrian and Babylonian empires.

The McDowells' state the following - *"The tradition of the MT is significant for the following reasons: (1) it provided the only textual witness to the Old Testament for more than 1,000 years (ninth century AD to 1947); (2) its internal consistency clearly attests to the care, precision, and systematic rigour which the Masoretic scribes copied the manuscripts.... (3) the MT tradition allows the textual critic to reasonably posit a prior tradition going back as early as AD 70: and (4) it provides the primary textual witness by which all other textual witnesses are*

---

[240] Ibid. p.97

measured....However, regardless of the stability of the MT, there was still one question that loomed for biblical scholars at the beginning of the twentieth century. The late classical biblical scholar Sir Frederick Kenyon surmised, 'The great, indeed all-important, question which now meets us is this – Does this Hebrew text, which we call Masoretic, and which we have shown to descend from a text drawn up about AD 100, faithfully represent the Hebrew text as originally written by the authors of the Old Testament books?'"[241]

So are there any other MSS going back to significantly before the $9^{th}/10^{th}$ centuries AD when the earliest surviving Masoretic manuscripts were written? Yes, there are – for instance, the previously noted *Codex Vaticanus* (AD 300 to 325) and the *Codex Sinaiticus* (AD 330 to 360), containing virtually all and over 50% of the OT respectively, plus additional books, some of which are included in the Roman Catholic Apocrypha. However, both of these OT manuscripts, which Sir Frederick Kenyon would have known about, are copies of the *Septuagint* (LXX), a Greek translation originating in the 3rd century BC and, as such, a language foreign to the Hebrew-Aramaic source text. More specifically, in addition to the usual debates over accuracy, there has been historical uncertainty concerning the necessary reconstructions back into this original source text, and consequently the subsequent translations into other languages such as English. Questions have particularly been raised concerning the overall fidelity of the resultant texts and whether the precise meanings of certain words or phrases have been accurately conveyed. This brings us to the Dead Sea Scrolls (DSS).

The first DSS were discovered in 1946/7 by Bedouin shepherds in a cave close to an ancient site known as Qumran, located approximately one mile to the West of the Dead Sea and about thirteen miles to the east of Jerusalem. Subsequent comprehensive archaeological investigations of eleven caves revealed fragments (estimated totals of up to 50,000!) corresponding to more than one thousand scrolls, written predominantly in Hebrew with a significant minority relating to Aramaic

---

[241] Ibid. p.102

and Greek. Of these reconstituted scrolls, three hundred have now been classified as OT manuscripts. Much smaller numbers of manuscripts were also discovered at other sites close to the Dead Sea, in particular, Wadi Murabba'at, Nahal Hever, and Masada.

The writing of all the above scrolls has been dated to between approximately 250 BC and AD 130 when, according to most scholars, this area was inhabited by a strict Jewish sect called the Essenes. The scrolls' preservation over so many centuries is considered to be the result of the hot and dry climate of the Judean Desert, plus the fact that only 8 -13% relate to papyri with at least 85% being written on parchment, a more robust material made from domestic animal skins.

The DSS have resulted in a plethora of associated books covering a range of perspectives, with the following very brief comments touching on a few particularly important features. The first of these concerns the *pride and joy* of biblical theologians, the 'Great Isaiah Scroll'. This was found in Cave 1 at Qumran, with the National Geographic magazine (December 2018 Edition) stating the following, *"Scholars were thrilled to find that among them (the biblical manuscripts) was a nearly complete copy of the Book of Isaiah from the Hebrew Bible. Its content was virtually identical to another copy of Isaiah dated almost a thousand years later."* [242]

This faithful transmission, including within it the extremely important messianic prophecies of Isaiah 53, thus again points to the extreme care and precision with which the Masoretic (and indeed pre-Masoretic) text is understood to have been copied. Further corroboration of copying accuracy over this period is provided by Dr Paul D. Wegner, a professor of Old Testament Studies from Iowa, who writes, *"All the manuscripts found at Wadi Murabba'at are very similar to the MT....and help to confirm that during the first century AD the MT had indeed become unified...All the biblical texts (found at Nahal Hever). . . .are dated to about AD 130 and their translations are virtually identical to the MT.... The Masada manuscripts are written in 'Hebrew square script'* (also

---

[242] National Geographic, *National Geographic Magazine*. December 2018 Edition, p.69.

known as 'Aramaic-Hebrew square script', wherein the Hebrew language is written utilising the Aramaic alphabet) *and are virtually identical to the MT (in wording as well as the divisions of the lines), except for slight differences in the Ezekiel text."* [243]

One further advantage of the DSS is intertextuality. For instance, in addition to supporting the stability of the MT, the DSS aid our appreciation of this text by revealing more about the contexts relevant to its forerunner, the pre-Masoretic text.

How then does the Septuagint (LXX) relate to all of this? This is a quotation from Emanuel Tov, Professor Emeritus of the Hebrew University of Jerusalem, *"The understanding and use of the LXX as a tool in biblical criticism were significantly advanced in the middle of the present century (20th) by the finds of Hebrew scrolls at Qumran. It was then recognised that many of the Hebrew readings (variants) tentatively reconstructed from the LXX did indeed exist as readings in Hebrew scrolls from Qumran...These agreements between the Hebrew scrolls from Qumran and the Jewish-Greek translation of the LXX....enhanced the credibility of the LXX, although there inevitably continued to be a great deal of argument over matters of detail. The LXX has definitely been recognised by most biblical scholars as a tool that provides important information for the textual criticism of the Bible."* [244]

In other words, despite a variety of omissions, insertions and amendments discovered in both the Codex Vaticanus and the Codex Sinaiticus, there is still sufficient core information to advance the solidity of the OT Scriptures. Furthermore, some insertions and amendments may well represent clarification and overall improvement.

Finally, the Samaritan Pentateuch (SP). Quoting the McDowells', *"The Samaritan Pentateuch is a version of the Hebrew Torah (the first five*

---

[243] Paul D. Wegner, *A Student's Guide to Textual Criticism of the Bible.* InterVarsity Press, 2004, pp.150-151, 153, 155.
[244] Emanuel Tov, *The Text-Critical Use of the Septuagint in Biblical Research.* Winona Lake, IN: Eisenbrauns, 2015, pp. 33-35.

books of the Old Testament) that is written in a special version of an early Hebrew script..." [245] More specifically, it appears that the extant manuscripts (Middle Ages) have been ultimately derived from an ancient script closely related to Paleo-Hebrew (subsequently defined). Although there are differing opinions regarding the value of the SP, most would agree that, at the very least, it provides helpful insights into the earlier forms of the Hebrew Pentateuch.

Having described the four main OT textual traditions, what can be said about their overall correlation? Difficult to provide a *one answer covers all* because some comparisons are clearly closer than others. Nevertheless, it seems clear that, despite the many readings or variants, the vast majority simply come down to differences in spelling and grammatical constructions. Indeed, if *one single word is misspelt in, say, one thousand different manuscripts, this is considered to equate to one thousand variants; a* general triviality that is consistent with my own findings.

For instance, perusal of a comprehensive table by Joel Kalvesmaki (scholar and computer languages specialist) comparing the Masoretic (KJV) and Septuagint (Brenton) scripts, at more than 200 places where the NT quotes the OT,[246] revealed various, generally unimportant, differences in phraseology and specific words (*formal equivalence*) plus close convergence when it came to the thoughts and meanings underlying and explaining the main messages (*dynamic equivalence*).

In case some further clarification of formal and dynamic equivalence is required, let's consider the phrase, *it's raining cats and dogs*. Formal/literal translation into French results in, *il pleut chats et chiens* (according to my 1969 Grade 6 GCE O-level). However, these words have no corresponding meaning in French, which is best conveyed utilising dynamic equivalence to change the original phrase for translation into, *it's raining very heavily*.

---

[245] Josh McDowell & Sean McDowell, *Evidence That Demands A Verdict*. Authentic Media Ltd., 2017, p.106.
[246] https://kalvesmaki.com/LXX/NTChart.htm

Notwithstanding the fact that most differences are probably best described as *inconsequential*, the whole subject of variants is taken very seriously by scholars who normally consider them under two groups, *Unintentional Scribal Errors* and *Scribal Changes* (redaction - editing). Concerning the first group, the McDowells' list four main categories as follows: the confusion of similar-looking letters; the substitution of words that sound familiar, such as 'there' or 'their'; the omission of a letter or word; and the doubling of a letter or word. They conclude, *"For the most part, these mistakes are easily identified by the text critic and, therefore, do very little to obfuscate* (obscure) *the determination of a most plausible reading of the text."* [247] This task can also, on occasions, be facilitated by the repetition and clarification of so-called problem texts elsewhere in the document under consideration.

Moving on to the second group, the McDowells' make reference to a classification from Paul D. Wegner, [248] which comprises six different categories as follows:

- *Spelling and grammar changes* due to the need to accommodate contemporary language – e.g., the 1611 King James Version (KJV) of the Bible is probably a difficult read for most of us.
- *Harmonisation*, such as when a particular town or city has had its name changed from the original.
- *Euphemistic changes*, such as when a word or phrase that originally represented a modest rebuke subsequently corresponds to something much worse.
- *Theological changes*, such as when modifications in language cause an initially positive-sounding attribute of God to subsequently come across as rather derogatory.

---

[247] Josh McDowell & Sean McDowell, *Evidence That Demands A Verdict*. Authentic Media Ltd., 2017, p.116.
[248] Paul D. Wegner, *A Student's Guide to Textual Criticism of the Bible*. InterVarsity Press, 2004, pp.50-55.

- *Additions and Glosses* relating to, say, explanatory notes inserted next to the text to add short supplementary information.
- *Other changes*, needed to perhaps explain rare words or words used in an uncharacteristic manner etc.

To ascertain the most plausible reading out of several variants, the McDowells' suggest that, after collecting all available relevant evidence, the following process, again formulated by Paul D. Wegner,[249] is undertaken:

- Determine the reading that would most likely give rise to the other readings.
- Carefully evaluate the weight of the manuscript evidence.
- Determine if the reading is a secondary reading or a gloss (a commentary or annotation appearing alongside Scripture text).
- Determine which reading is most appropriate in its context.

All of this and much more has been performed ad infinitum by the various scholars/ theologians down through the ages, with the reliability and authenticity of the (complete) biblical text being summarised by the McDowells' as follows:

"Despite the fact that there have been intentional modifications to the text in order to provide clarity and relevance to the community contemporary with the scribe, modern readers need not be concerned that these changes compromise the reliability or accuracy of the Bible we

---

[249] Ibid. p.125.

have today. In many cases the changes are obvious and scholars can identify the original reading with a high degree of confidence." [250]

The cumulative effect of the four traditions is thus very strong and gives no suggestion that the OT Scriptures within main Bible translations today are appreciably different from those contemporary to Jesus Christ and the NT authors; all of whom considered them to represent the inspired Word of God. Indeed, Jesus often confirmed their ultimate authority with the Apostle Paul declaring that *"All Scripture is God-breathed."* (2 Timothy 3:16)

The second period for consideration is the 1st millennium BC. The history of this earlier age is inevitably based on less knowledge than that relating to the past 2,000 years, with no OT manuscripts of any substance surviving beyond the DSS at the end of this millennium. That said, there is no reason to suggest that scribal activity during this period was any less thorough and precise than that already described, with the nature and approximate timeline of the main scripts being well established. These are summarised in the following table:

---

[250] Josh McDowell & Sean McDowell, *Evidence That Demands A Verdict*. Authentic Media Ltd., 2017, p.117.

TABLE 6: WRITTEN LANGUAGES RELEVANT TO BIBLICAL HISTORY IN THE 1st MILLENNIUM BC

Period	Title	Remarks
5th Century BC to 1st Century AD	Aramaic-Hebrew square script	Manuscript copies thought to have been produced by the *Soferim*, a group of scribes quite possibly of priestly descent, and likely to be skilled in both the copying and knowledge of Scriptural texts. These scribes or 'teachers of the Law' could also be called 'rabbis', the generic 'teacher' definition covering all three names until formalisation in approximately AD 100 (sourced from the Mishnah rabbinic writings). This script, in which the Hebrew language was written utilising the Aramaic alphabet, originated during the Jews' captivity in Babylon, and gradually took over from Paleo-Hebrew.
11th Century BC to 5th Century BC	Paleo-Hebrew Script	Writing utilised an alphabet of 22 consonantal letters, less pictorial and thus more developed than those of Hieroglyphic Hebrew – See Table 7.

Switching disciplines; although the Ancient Near East (ANE) archaeological finds are, unsurprisingly, less than those bearing witness to the NT Scriptures, they can still provide a significant secondary source of knowledge by corroborating and giving added insight into recorded OT events and their contexts. It may also be expected, for what is a comparatively young discipline, that further discoveries will resolve a number of present-day conundrums. Indeed, the vast majority of archaeological sites, some 30,000 of which have been identified in Israel, are still to be excavated, either in whole or part.

ANE archaeology as a serious enterprise only dates back to the very end of the eighteenth century when a great surge in interest was triggered by the discovery in Egypt of the *Rosetta Stone*. John Currid, a Professor in Old Testament studies, describes this remarkable find in his book, *Doing Archaeology in the Land of the Bible*,

"The most significant find of the Napoleonic excursion was the Rosetta Stone (1799). It proved to be invaluable because it was the key to

unlocking ancient Egyptian hieroglyphics, a picture script unutilised for over fourteen hundred years. Dating to the time of King Ptolemy V (204-180 B.C.), the Rosetta Stone is inscribed in three scripts: demotic (an ancient Egyptian script), Greek, and hieroglyphs. The Greek proved to be a translation of the ancient Egyptian language on the stone.

The linguistic study of the Rosetta Stone by the English physician Thomas Young (1819) and the Frenchman Jean-Francois Champollion (1822) 'marked the beginning of the scientific reading of hieroglyphs and the first step toward formulation of a system of ancient Egyptian grammar, the basis of modern Egyptology' [Andrews, Rosetta Stone, 1996, pp. 619-20]. Thus the first true archaeological find in the Near East was one of the greatest and most critical discoveries in the history of the discipline!" [251]

Modern Egyptology has significantly impacted the chronologies of other ANE countries, with the following list comprising some of the most relevant archaeological discoveries from all three sub-divisions - Egypt, Assyria/Mesopotamia and the Levant:

I) The relief on the Bubastite Portal of the main temple (to Amon, an ancient Egyptian deity) at Karnak, close to the modern city of Luxor. The relief recounts the invasion of the Pharaoh Shishak into Judah/Israel in the 10th century BC when Rehoboam, son of Solomon, was king of Judah, and corresponds very closely with the biblical accounts. (1 Kings 14:25-26 & 2 Chron. 12: 2-4)

ii) Annals of the Assyrian king, Sargon II (reigned 722 – 705 BC), discovered in Mesopotamia and describing his conquests within the northern ten tribes, exiling many thousands of upper-class citizens whom he subsequently replaced with foreigners. These records provide valuable background information to the biblical account.

---

[251] John Currid, *Doing Archaeology in the Land of the Bible: A Basic Guide.* Grand Rapids, MI: Baker, 1999, pp.18-20.

iii) The Siloam inscription in Paleo-Hebrew on Hezekiah's Tunnel, a water channel carved beneath Jerusalem to prepare for an impending siege by the Assyrians, led by King Sennacherib, in about 701 BC. The inscription describes how the tunnel was excavated by two teams who met in the middle (unlike 'Crossrail', there are no reports of time delays or overspends!). Complements the biblical account in 2 Kings 20:20.

iv) The discovery in Jerusalem of the Hezekiah Bulla, a small clay seal inscribed in Paleo-Hebrew with the words 'Belonging to Hezekiah (son of) Ahaz king of Judah' – reigned from approximately 715 to 686 BC.

v) A six-chambered gate (and other structures) discovered in large archaeological digs in the city of Hazor, Northern Israel, and apparently relating to the kingship of Solomon in the 10th century BC.

vi) Silver Scroll Amulets found near to the old city of Jerusalem, which are dated to the 7th century BC and inscribed in Paleo-Hebrew. The markings, however, constitute the Aaronic Blessing given during the much earlier Mosaic period - *"The Lord bless you and keep you; The Lord make His face shine upon you and be gracious to you; The Lord turn His face towards you and give you peace."* (Numbers 6:24-26)

These selected finds, all dated to the first half of this millennium, correlate well with the contemporary biblical history of Israel/Judah and thus, along with other relevant archaeological discoveries and the previously noted fulfilled prophecies, provide further confidence in the accuracy of the OT and its transmission.

Finally, what has been the history of Scriptures written prior to the 1st millennium BC? This is hardly an easy question because, as for other ancient records, everything becomes more opaque and less well defined the deeper one delves into biblical history. Nevertheless, even though there are no existing manuscripts and only a few archaeological finds, much can still be known about this period, starting with the estimated timeline of the likely methods of communication.

TABLE 7 – RELEVANT COMMUNICATIVE METHODS PRIOR TO 1st MILLENNIUM BC		
Period	Title	Remarks
19th Century to 11th Century BC (earlier date is the subject of current debate).	Hieroglyphic Hebrew	Writing based on an alphabet of 22 letters representing consonantal sounds, understood to have been principally derived from Egyptian hieroglyphs.
Pre -19th Century BC	Oral Hebrew (subsequently discussed)	Cuneiform or Sumerian cuneiform existed as early as the latter part of the 4th millennium BC and was distinguished by wedge-shaped marks made by blunt instruments on clay tablets. Tens of thousands of these tablets have now been found, including 19 at the Hazor site, one of which dates to the 18th/17th centuries BC. Cuneiform could represent a variety of fairly primitive languages, but would not have been sufficiently developed to accommodate the more complex OT writings.

In terms of scope, it is considered sufficient to limit this study to the Pentateuch – Genesis, Exodus, Leviticus, Numbers and Deuteronomy, the autographs of which have traditionally been held to date from the middle of the 2nd millennium BC.

There are different views concerning the origin of the Pentateuch and the relevant autographs, with at least three possible sources acting either individually or in some combination with each other. Of these, the best known is the view that most of the contents of the Pentateuch were either imparted directly from God to Moses or were important events occurring during Moses' life, both of which God commanded to be recorded in writing.

This standpoint is certainly consistent with the biblical record and its many confirmatory citations. The following verses accordingly represent a very brief selection:

"Then the Lord said to Moses, 'Write this on a scroll as something to be remembered and make sure that Joshua hears it'," (Exodus 17:14)

"Moses then wrote down everything the Lord had said." (Exodus 24:4)

"Then the Lord said to Moses, 'Write down these words, for in accordance with these words I have made a covenant with you and with Israel'." (Exodus 34:27)

"At the Lord's command, Moses recorded the stages in their journey." (Numbers 33:2)

And in Leviticus (almost entirely Law-based), the phrase, *The Lord said to Moses...* is repeated on many occasions, with this particular book concluding as follows, *"These are the commands the Lord gave Moses on Mount Sinai for the Israelites."* (Leviticus 27:34)

This proactivity of God when it comes to the origin of Scripture is again found in the NT where, for example, Christ says to His disciples, *"All this I have spoken while still with you. But the counsellor, the Holy Spirit, whom the Father will send in my name, will teach you all things and will remind you of everything I have said to you."* (John 14:25-26)

The second possible contributor to the composition of the Pentateuch is known as The Oral Tradition, a designation that almost certainly raises immediate suspicions for most of us living in today's Western societies. However, this was not the case in ancient times, where *orality* was often preferred and took precedence over *textuality*. For instance, Greco-Roman orators had great abilities to recite prodigious amounts of information, with Craig S. Keener, an American professor of New Testament, stating, *"Difficult as it may seem to most readers today, the* elder Seneca testifies that in his younger days he could repeat 2,000 names in exactly the sequence in which he heard them, or recite up to 200 verses given to him, in reverse. Even if his recollections of youthful prowess are exaggerated, they testify to an emphasis on memory that far exceeds standards and expectations today." [252]

Keener also adds, "In the circles of trained storytellers and sages, memories may preserve information accurately from one generation to the next. Indeed, oral traditioning might invite less redaction than written sources would. Folklorists have shown that some communities transmit traditions faithfully, with minimal modifications; storytellers create and vary within the constraints of communal tradition. Some suggest that writers were far more likely to introduce substantial changes." [253]

The third possible contributor is some kind of pre-existing written record; meaning that Moses would have been involved in the compilation as well as the authorship of the Pentateuch.

The oral tradition and/or a pre-existing written record could indeed have been involved in the formation of the Pentateuch, particularly concerning the history of the Patriarchs such as Abraham, Isaac and Jacob. It may accordingly be of relevance that a number of the Israelites undoubtedly retained at least some knowledge of God and His purposes during their long exile in pagan Egypt. For instance, the midwives at the time of Moses' birth are recorded as refusing a sovereign edict to kill all male babies because they feared God more than Pharaoh. That's *get your head chopped off time* – where did a faith as robust as that come from?

Moving on from the formation of the Pentateuch Scriptures to their subsequent transmission, there is good reason to believe that accuracy and integrity would have been maintained over time with assiduous

---

[252] Craig S. Keener, *The Gospel of John: A Commentary*. Grand Rapids, MI: Baker Publishing Group, 2000, p.57.
[253] Ibid.

copying techniques again probably being centre stage. To pick just one relevant quotation, *"So Moses wrote down this law and gave it to the priests, the sons of Levi, who carried the ark of the covenant of the Lord, and to all the elders of Israel."* (Deuteronomy 31:9) In other words; the *most important* people.

This is, therefore, wholly consistent with the view that right from the get-go the Scriptures were held in the highest possible esteem, the ancient priestly scribes having a reverence for the text and an overriding obsession for accuracy. Although a number of these scribes would undoubtedly have engaged in at least some degree of redaction (the recording of Moses' death comes to mind), this is something that, as previously noted, can usually be reliably identified by scholars and translators.

Having considered how the Pentateuch's contents have arrived in today's OT/Tanakh, what can be said about their correlation with contemporary ex-biblical sources? What is the present state of play?

Relevant archaeological discoveries before the 1st millennium BC are, as noted above, few in number, with associated dating also being subject to controversy. When we add in the increasingly secular influence that Western society has had on the archaeological profession during approximately the past 70 years and the previous errors resulting from misdirected attempts to correlate almost all finds with the biblical record, it's perhaps understandable that many contemporary archaeologists believe that much of the OT can be regarded as fictional. Indeed, some hold to the opinion that a large proportion of the Pentateuch originates directly from the ANE records of neighbouring countries, as indicated by certain similarities between the Torah and the much earlier Babylonian *Code of Hammurabi*, and have even gone so far as to claim downright plagiarism.

These similarities, however, also extend to even older law codes and simply indicate that all the ANE nations had to address societal problems such as murder, kidnapping, adultery and theft. Furthermore, and most importantly, the Law of Moses went far beyond the legal, with its moral principles and judgments being based on the perfectly righteous character of God. This meant that it considered the cause of crime rather than simply its effects, with the associated emphases on personal and national holiness hopefully resulting in an elevated view of both God and human beings. This concentration on the spiritual and associated behaviour thus distinguished the Mosaic Law from the penal codes of other nations, including the Babylonian, who seemingly gave little attention to these matters.

To continue, while acknowledging the parallels between ANE writings and the Pentateuch, John Currid and others maintain that, from the Hebrew side, this relationship is often polemical – that is the Hebrew author is denouncing the ANE literature and even ridiculing its writers. So in this sense, to achieve the polemic style, he could be said to be *copying* or *borrowing*.

This polemical approach is best seen by comparing the Genesis record with ANE literature concerning the nature of creation and the Creator/*gods*. The contrast is described by Currid as follows, *"...in regard to the very nature of the creator, all societies of the ancient Near East, save the Hebrews, were polytheists. The gods themselves were immanent, that is, personified in various powers and elements of the universe. These gods were not omnipotent but were restricted in power to the capacity of the natural elements they personified. In addition, the temperament of the gods often reflected human nature – so that the deities frequently acted in a depraved, perverted manner. To the contrary, the God of the Hebrews is presented as transcendent, that is, set apart from the cosmos. He works within the universe, but He is not part of it. The universe is God's creation, but it is not God. The God of Israel, moreover, does not act humanly by reflecting the flaws of human nature. Mankind is created in His image and not the other way around. He is pure, just, righteous, and true. Yahweh is holy and wholly other."* [254]

---

[254] John D. Currid, *Against The Gods: The Polemical Theology Of The Old Testament.* Crossway, 2013, p.40.

And in a subsequent passage, Currid adds, "*The creation account of Genesis, in contrast, presents God as all-powerful, incomparable, and sovereign. He owes nothing to the agency of another. In addition, creation did not occur as the result of a contest or a struggle between gods, as it did in the Mesopotamian myths.*" [255]

And while on the subject of ANE *gods*, the sun god, *Re*, worshipped by the ancient Egyptians, is perhaps worthy of a special mention. *Re* is said to have come into being through a specific act of self-generation and is described as driving out (that is giving birth to) other gods from within his own body using methods such as sneezing, spitting, and masturbation. It certainly seems that these Egyptians went for it big time when it came to their gods because they are also known for worshipping prize bulls who they thought were supernatural beings with magical powers. These animals were glorified in both life and death, with archaeological digs at *Saqqara* revealing twenty four massive solid granite coffins, each weighing about ninety tons, buried in vast, deep underground cemeteries and originally containing huge mummified bulls (one remained for examination).

It is obvious that there are fundamental differences between the Hebrew Creator God/His creation and other corresponding accounts. Unlike the ANE and the previously mentioned Greek/Roman *gods*, all with their mythical stories, the totally unique and highly elevated character of the Hebrew narrative is entirely consistent with a divinely inspired origin. It is, therefore, not surprising that, in what was then (December 1968) the most-watched TV broadcast of all time, the crew of Apollo 8 read the first ten words of Genesis while orbiting the moon. This majestic passage of Scripture, which has been quoted previously, states, "*In the beginning, God created the heavens and the earth....*" (Genesis 1:1)

He is the only one who is utterly transcendent and *wholly other* when compared to the created universe and all its contents from giant stars

---

[255] Ibid. p.41.

and ultramassive black holes to human beings to the tiniest sub-atomic particles.

To return to the somewhat controversial archaeological arena and the rarity of finds prior to the 1st millennium BC, there is one very significant artefact which bucks the trend. This is the *Merneptah Stele,* a monument named after a pharaoh who reigned in Egypt between approximately 1213 and 1203 BC. Among the various inscriptions (ancient Egyptian hieroglyphs) detailing victories over forces in Libya and Canaan, the monument includes a phrase which most scholars translate as Israel is laid waste. Although this is probably a propaganda-related overstatement, it nevertheless indicates that the Israelites were present as a nation within the Promised Land by at least the end of the 13th century BC. This stela is the earliest textual reference to Israel.

A Test OF Time [256] by the English Egyptologist, David Rohl, an academic with no specific religious affiliations, is one of the more adventurous and *non-conformist* archaeological books to be published over the past few decades. While I am in no position to comment on the book's main objective to radically revise the conventional Egyptian Chronology and hence those of Israel and other nearby countries, I am intrigued by the fact that Rohl's extensive research recognises the factual genre present within much of the OT; as evidenced by the book's subtitle, *The Bible - From Myth To History.*

This is a view robustly supported by Steven Collins, an American professor of archaeology, who, in connection with some positive 21st century archaeological developments, concludes, *"It is hard to understand how any scholar – regardless of 'pet' theories about textual origins – could toss the Bible out of the repertoire of archaeological tools. Seriously? – eliminate an ancient text full of geographical and historical clues from the archaeological process?"* [257]

---

[256] David Rohl, *A Test Of Time: The Bible – From Myth To History.* Century,1995.
[257] Steven Collins, *Has Archaeology Gone Overboard in Throwing Out the Bible?* https://asorblog.org/2013/10/10/has-archaeology-gone-overboard-in-throwing-out-the-bible/

The present position can probably be best summarised as 'polarised' with a second quotation from Steven Collins being particularly apt, *"Has archaeology gone too far in throwing out the Bible? Yes! But have some scholars gone too far in throwing out archaeology? Yes!"* [258]

It may reasonably be concluded from the foregoing that the evidence for the reliable transmission of the NT Scriptures is simply overwhelming and indeed far superior to that underpinning the ancient classical works, whose authenticity is taken for granted by most historians. Although there is less direct evidence relating to the OT Scriptures, as might be expected given their greater age, the cumulative effect of the various available sources is still very impressive, and more than sufficient to account for overall accurate transmission. Of particular significance, as noted earlier, is the fact that there appear to have been no fundamental changes in these Scriptures over the past 2,000 years – that is since the time of Jesus Christ and the NT writers, who undoubtedly considered them to represent the inspired Word of God.

That said, there are known to be many other theological writings, such as the *Pseudepigrapha* of the NT and the OT Apocrypha (included in Roman Catholic Bibles) – how do we know that these aren't also God-inspired and authoritative? And if so, why have they been left out of most modern versions of the Bible?

The thirty nine OT and twenty seven NT books of the Bible are included simply because they satisfy the related two *canons* or standards of Scripture. Starting with the NT, the McDowells' comment as follows, *"The church did not create the canon; it did not determine which books would be called Scripture, the inspired Word of God. Instead, the church recognised, or discovered, which books had been inspired from their inception."* [259]

---

[258] Ibid.
[259] Josh McDowell & Sean McDowell, *Evidence That Demands A Verdict*. Authentic Media Ltd., 2017, pp.25-26.

In other words, it would be like holding a meeting today to agree on a definitive list of the great classical composers such as Mozart, Beethoven, Handel etc. What could this achieve, apart from perhaps producing a neat alphabetical or chronological record? We already know that these men, and of course many others, were great composers and not simply average street buskers.

There were various compliance requirements for the inclusion of books within the NT canon, with the following five selections representing some of the most important:

(I) The book had to be written by either the apostles themselves or approved under their authority.

(ii) The book had to be authentic; the early church fathers had the attitude of "If in doubt, throw it out." The language, therefore, had to represent typical 1st century Koine Greek, and the nature of the recorded events needed to be consistent with that cultural period – that is no anachronisms. The normal style also had to be prosaic as opposed to *flowery language* and be free from *fantastic elements* and sayings. Some may take exception here to the inclusion of *Revelation* at the end of the NT, although it should be emphasised that this book seemingly passes the other four tests.

(iii) The book had to have been accepted (received, collected, approved, read and used) by the early church. In other words, there had to be continuity between the canonical writings and early church tradition, something that could not be claimed for Gnosticism (see below).

(iv) The book had to come with some 'fire' - that is the life-transforming power of God.

>   (v) The book should be free from historical and geographical inaccuracies, as per the whole NT, but most evident in Luke's gospel and the Acts of the apostles.

Literature is described as *pseudepigraphical* where a writer attempts to obtain credibility by falsely claiming authorship under the name of an already famous person. So a number of the *gospels* falling within this category are attributed to persons such as Thomas, Peter, Philip and even Judas (surely this last name should arouse our suspicions). The book *The Da Vinci Code* by Dan Brown refers to this group of literature, and rather surprisingly, given that Brown acknowledges his writing to be a work of fiction, somehow managed to arouse a certain amount of religious ire upon publication.

NT pseudepigraphical writings, generally originating in the 2nd to 4th centuries, are particularly associated with Gnosticism, which centres on knowledge and, expressly, *secret* or *special* knowledge. The main credo of this Gnosticism relates to a matter-spirit dualism, where matter is evil and spirit is good. This led, in the Gnostics' eyes, to the belief that Jesus only *appeared* to be human and thus had no physical body – a belief known as *Docetism* and briefly referred to in connection with Islam. Gnostic thoughts and teachings in this context may also reflect a strong trend towards asceticism.

A number of the Gnostics attempted to use their 'gospels' to influence orthodox Christianity but were thwarted by the early church fathers, who argued that they merely represented invented new ideas; and thus held fast to the gospel proclaimed from apostolic times.

These leaders no doubt knew that the pseudepigraphical writings are later than, and commonly show dependence upon, the canonical NT autographs. They are also often flowery and unordered in style, and do indeed contain *fantastic elements*.

For instance, the *gospel* of Thomas is essentially a collection of sayings, some true and others false, attributed to Jesus with no narrative and thus no chronological order – that is, unlike Luke's writings in particular, there is nothing to suggest the work of a thorough and reliable historian. Furthermore, the writing has all the overtures of Gnosticism, with its *fanciful* contents including this brief discussion, *"Simon Peter said to them: 'Let Mary go away from us, for women are not worthy of life'. Jesus said, 'Look, I will draw her in so as to make her male, so that she too may become a living male spirit, similar to you', (But I say to you): 'Every woman who makes herself male will enter the kingdom of heaven'."* (Saying 114)

And the gospel of Peter includes giant angels, whose heads reach up to heaven, accompanying Jesus, whose head reaches beyond heaven, away from the burial tomb together with a cross that talks! The spurious nature of these pseudapigraphical writings accordingly means that they fail all five of the selected compliance requirements for the inclusion of books within the NT canon. In particular, they bear no resemblance to the careful, diligent, eyewitness quality of the four canonical gospels, and thus excluded themselves from being taken seriously at an early stage. There were no conspiracies to suppress them by the Church, the various governing political bodies, or anybody else – inevitably irrelevant because these writings simply *weren't up to it.*

When it comes to the OT Canon, it is particularly telling that, although Jesus Christ and the NT writers quote the OT/Tanakh approximately 300 times, they make absolutely no reference to the Apocrypha. Indeed, Jerome, the 4th/5th century AD scholar, provided stout resistance to translating the Apocrypha, producing only a partial Latin version. This literature was therefore only brought into the *Latin Vulgate*, the forerunner of the Roman Catholic Bible, after his death.

Finally, *Ungers Bible Dictionary*, while accepting that the apocryphal books do have some historical worth, provides four reasons for excluding them from the OT canon:

- They abound in historical and geographical inaccuracies and anachronisms.

- They teach doctrines that are false and foster practices that are at variance with inspired Scripture.

- They resort to literature types and display an artificiality of subject matter and styling out of keeping with inspired Scripture.

- They lack the distinctive elements that give genuine Scripture its divine character, such as prophetic power and poetic and religious feeling.

In summary, it seems self-evident that only the twenty seven NT and thirty nine OT books of today's main Bible translations are God-inspired, authoritative and trustworthy.

However, even if it's accepted that the Bible records are reliable and trustworthy, as has been one of the main objectives throughout, what is to stop its readers from 'cockeyed interpretations', thereby coming up with all sorts of weird and wonderful stuff? Isn't that how cults and extreme sects start? Well, as touched on earlier, the answer seems to be quite straightforward – the Bible should be read like any other book, and not subjected to pulling bits out from all over the place to justify a person's preferred opinions. Nevertheless, it doesn't hurt to have a few basic guidelines, with the seven listed below, the majority of which are common to much everyday literature, hopefully being of some assistance:

Genre – We undoubtedly take this into account without even thinking most of the time. For instance, we automatically distinguish between, say, a main article and an advertisement in a newspaper. This process thus usually works well in differentiating between literal and non-literal sections of the Bible – e.g., the gospels have an overriding factual reporting genre and should thus be taken literally, whereas the passionately romantic and clearly non-literal Song of Songs (attributed to King Solomon), contains portions such as: *"How beautiful your sandaled feet, O prince's daughter! Your graceful legs are like jewels, the* *work of an artist's hands. Your navel is a rounded goblet that never lacks blended wine. Your waist is a mound of wheat encircled by lilies. Your breasts are like two fawns, like twin fawns of a gazelle. Your neck is like an ivory tower."* (Song of Songs 7:1-4a)

So rather than the intended beauty and intimacy, any attempt to interpret all the various elements in a strictly literal fashion would inevitably conjure up a most grotesque and undesirable creature.

Co-text – When considering a specific passage, account should be taken of the verses immediately preceding and following. Pretty obvious, but not always undertaken.

Context – This is very important, and may even have reversed the Jehovah Witnesses' tragic ban on blood transfusions if they'd only realised and accepted that all references relate to the forbidden eating or drinking of blood (in particular, when it was involved in idol worship). Although it is true that Scripture always considers blood to be sacred with phrases such as *the life of every creature is in the blood (Leviticus 17:14a)*, applying this to transfusions is much too far a stretch and, indeed, is also at variance with the revealed character of God as a loving Father. And while on the subject, it's also important to realise that, because God is Spirit with no biological disposition, this male designation has nothing to do with gender – for example, He lavishly gives both motherly and fatherly love to all His creation.

The context, as far as I can make out, is that the title of *Father* rather than *Mother* is preferred in order to avoid Creator God being confused with the spurious and imaginary *Mother Nature* or *Mother Earth* goddess, present in various forms within pagan religions dating back many millennia. Even today, it's not uncommon to hear weather reporters and sports commentators saying something like, "Mother Nature's been kind to us today"; leading to many people unconsciously buying into this myth.

Audience – It is important to consider what the various writings would have meant to, and their resultant impact upon, the original readers or hearers. This is because, although the teachings of Christianity can rightly be regarded as universal and for all generations, a greater and more rounded understanding can often be gained by, for instance, knowing how the initial recipients might have understood certain words and phrases.

Reasons for the inclusion of a specific passage – For instance, Psalm 22 (a *Messianic psalm*), which is traditionally thought to have been written by an initially deeply depressed King David, and then, perhaps surprisingly, expands out to prophesy many of the details relating to Christ's crucifixion. As touched on previously, this is an example of a lesser or 'shadowy' event in the OT pointing to a similar but greater and clearer event in the NT.

Consistency with other parts of Scripture linked to the same topic – All the main themes of the Bible are invariably repeated many times by different authors. For instance, Scripture constantly emphasises God's love for us and His unceasing and endless faithfulness. It's also very important, particularly when dealing with complex and sensitive issues, to consult a range of relevant Scriptural references so that balanced and sensible opinions can be proffered.

Life within Scripture – As already described and explained, Scripture became *alive* as the words simply jumped out at me from its pages almost immediately after I converted to Christ. This experience was incredibly exciting and, as per the downhearted followers on the Emmaus Road, is best explained by a *burning inside*. I take this to be an example of my spiritual DNA firing up on all cylinders, something I still get from time to time.

It should, of course, be emphasised that the adoption of these guidelines does not automatically make everything in the Bible crystal clear. Some parts require a lot of thought and maybe re-reading several times (plus, on occasions, a bit of research), and even then their meaning might not be altogether apparent. Ultimately though, the Bible message is spiritually rather than intellectually discerned, as is evident from both my own and innumerable other conversions to Christ.

Thankfully, this spiritual insight does not require the learning of another language, as per certain schools of thought within Islam, but, as highlighted throughout, is obtained instead by repentance and offering our lives back to God through Jesus Christ.

>Do this, and you will never be the same again.

www.ingramcontent.com/pod-product-compliance
Lightning Source LLC
Chambersburg PA
CBHW070459120526
44590CB00013B/694